BAKING
EASY & ELEGANT

HPBooks®

Sweeten your pleasure in good food with these exceptional baking recipes. From bewitching pastries and cookies to artistically decorated gâteaux, we give you a wide selection of tested and proven baked goods.

Enjoy the tantalizing taste and aroma of home-baked cookies, cakes, tarts, flans, coffeecakes, pastries and more. Save time with recipes from the convenience section by using prepared mixes and frozen doughs to make pizza, yeast breads, coffeecakes, cookies and luscious cakes and pastries. Whether you prefer plain or fancy baking, this book has recipes you've been waiting for.

Contents

Cookies

8-35

Creative Cakes

36-77

Tarts & Flans

78-95

Quick Breads & Coffeecakes
96-107

Cherry-Raisin Coffeecake, page 102.

Yeast Baking
108-127

Savory Artichoke Pizza, page 110.

Pastries
128-155

Marzipan & Raisin Pastry, page 130.

Convenience Baking

156-189

Royal Apple Cake, page 174.

Confections

190-197

Marzipan Sweets, page 195.

Holiday & Special Occasion Baking

198-229

Amaretto-Chocolate Gâteau, page 202.

Basic Information
230-235

Index
236-240

Apple Dumpling, page 141.

ANOTHER BEST-SELLING VOLUME FROM HPBooks®

Publisher: Rick Bailey
Editorial Director: Retha M. Davis
Editor: Carroll P. Latham
Art Director: Don Burton
Book Assembly: Leslie Sinclair
Typography: Cindy Coatsworth, Michelle Claridge
Recipe testing by International Cookbook Services: Barbara Bloch, President; Rita Barrett, Director of Testing; Nancy Strata, Bridget Sweeney, Recipe Testers.

Published by HPBooks, Inc.
P.O. Box 5367, Tucson, AZ 85703   602/888-2150
ISBN 0-89586-335-9
Library of Congress Catalog Card Number 84-81774
©1984 HPBooks, Inc. Printed in Germany
Cover Photo: Cherry-Raisin Coffeecake, page 102

First published under the title *Das beste Dr. Oetker Backbuch*
©1982 by Ceres-Verlag Rudolf-August Oetker KG, Bielefeld

Cookies

Brown & White Cookies

1/2 cup butter or margarine, room temperature
3/4 cup sugar
1 egg yolk
1/4 cup milk
1 teaspoon rum extract
2 cups all-purpose flour
1 teaspoon baking powder
1/4 teaspoon baking soda
1 oz. semisweet chocolate, melted
Sugar

In a medium bowl, beat butter or margarine, sugar, egg yolk, milk and rum extract until creamy. Blend flour, baking powder and baking soda; gradually stir into sugar mixture. Divide dough in half. Stir chocolate into 1/2 of dough until thoroughly blended. Shape each half into a 1-1/2-inch-thick log. Roll logs in sugar. Cover; refrigerate 6 hours or overnight. Preheat oven to 350F (175C). Grease baking sheets. Using a sharp knife, cut refrigerated logs into 1/4-inch slices. Dip 1 side of each slice in sugar. Place slices, sugar-side up and 1 inch apart, on greased baking sheets. Bake 10 to 12 minutes or until firm. Remove from baking sheets; cool on wire racks. Makes about 60 cookies.

Brown & White Cookies

Choco-Orange Cookies

2/3 cup butter or margarine, room temperature
1 cup sugar
2 eggs
1 teaspoon orange extract
2-1/4 cups all-purpose flour
1 teaspoon baking powder
1/4 teaspoon baking soda
1-1/2 tablespoons grated orange peel
4 oz. semisweet chocolate, finely chopped

In a medium bowl, beat butter or margarine, sugar, eggs and orange extract until creamy. Blend flour, baking powder, baking soda and orange peel; gradually stir into sugar mixture. Stir in chocolate. Shape dough into a 2-inch-wide, 1-1/2-inch-thick rectangle. Cover; refrigerate 6 hours or overnight. Preheat oven to 350F (175C). Grease baking sheets. Cut refrigerated dough into 1/4-inch slices. Place slices, 1 inch apart, on greased baking sheets. Bake 12 to 14 minutes. Remove from baking sheets; cool on wire racks. Makes about 60 cookies.

On previous pages: Medieval Castle, pages 34-35.

Choco-Applesauce Bars

2 oz. unsweetened chocolate
1/2 cup butter or margarine
1 cup packed light-brown sugar
1/4 teaspoon ground cloves
1/4 teaspoon ground nutmeg
1/4 teaspoon ground cinnamon
1/4 teaspoon ground allspice
2 eggs, beaten
1 teaspoon vanilla extract
3/4 cup applesauce
1 cup all-purpose flour
1/2 teaspoon baking powder
1/4 teaspoon baking soda
1/4 teaspoon salt
1/2 cup chopped walnuts or pecans

Preheat oven to 350F (175C). Grease a 13'' x 9'' baking pan; set aside. Melt chocolate and butter or margarine in a small saucepan over low heat. Set aside to cool. In a medium bowl, blend brown sugar, cloves, nutmeg, cinnamon and allspice. Stir in eggs and vanilla. Stir in cooled chocolate mixture and applesauce. Blend flour, baking powder, baking soda and salt; gradually fold into applesauce mixture. Stir in nuts. Pour into greased pan. Bake 25 minutes. Cool in pan on a wire rack. Cut into 36 bars.

Maple-Crunch Bars

1-1/2 cups all-purpose flour
1/2 cup granulated sugar
1 teaspoon baking powder
1/2 cup butter or margarine, chilled
1/4 cup packed dark-brown sugar
2 eggs, beaten
3/4 cup maple syrup
3/4 cup chopped walnuts or pecans
1/2 cup chopped golden raisins

Preheat oven to 350F (175C). Grease a 13'' x 9'' baking pan; set aside. In a medium bowl, blend 1-1/4 cups flour, granulated sugar and baking powder. Use a pastry blender or 2 knives to cut in butter or margarine until mixture resembles coarse crumbs. Press dough into greased baking pan. Bake 10 minutes. Cool in pan on a wire rack 10 minutes. In same bowl, blend remaining 1/4 cup flour and brown sugar. Beat in eggs and maple syrup. Stir in nuts and raisins. Pour over cooled crust. Return to oven; bake 25 to 30 minutes or until top is set. Cool in pan on a wire rack. Cut into 36 bars.

Vanilla Zig-Zags

1/2 cup butter or margarine, room temperature
2/3 cup sugar
1 egg
2 teaspoons vanilla extract
2 cups sifted all-purpose flour
1/2 teaspoon baking soda

Chocolate Glaze:
2 oz. semisweet chocolate
1 tablespoon butter or margarine

Preheat oven to 350F (175C). Grease baking sheets; set aside. In a medium bowl, beat butter or margarine, sugar, egg and vanilla until creamy. Blend flour and baking soda; gradually stir into sugar mixture. On a lightly floured surface, roll out dough until 1/4 inch thick. Flour a 3-inch fluted cookie cutter; use to cut dough. Place cut dough, 1-1/2 inches apart, on greased baking sheets. Bake 10 to 12 minutes or until edges are golden. Remove from baking sheets; cool on wire racks.
To make chocolate glaze, melt chocolate and butter or margarine in a small saucepan over low heat. Cool to room temperature. Drizzle over cookies in a zig-zag pattern. Let stand until chocolate sets. Makes about 30 cookies.

Vanilla Zig-Zags

Chocolate-Nut Sandwiches

Peanut-Butter Cookies

1/2 cup butter or margarine, room temperature
1/2 cup packed dark-brown sugar
1/2 cup granulated sugar
2 eggs
1 teaspoon vanilla extract
1/2 cup chunk-style peanut butter
1-1/2 cups all-purpose flour
1/2 teaspoon baking powder
1/2 teaspoon baking soda
1/2 cup coarsely chopped salted peanuts

In a medium bowl, beat butter or margarine, brown sugar, granulated sugar, eggs and vanilla until creamy. Stir in peanut butter until blended. Blend flour, baking powder and baking soda; fold into sugar mixture. Stir in peanuts. Cover; refrigerate at least 1 hour. Preheat oven to 350F (175C). Grease baking sheets. Shape refrigerated dough into walnut-size balls. Place balls, 2 inches apart, on greased baking sheets. Flatten each ball with tines of a fork. Bake 8 to 10 minutes. Remove from baking sheets; cool on wire racks. Makes about 60 cookies.

Butter Buttons

1 cup butter, room temperature
1 cup powdered sugar
2 teaspoons vanilla extract
1 egg white
2-1/2 cups cake flour

Preheat oven to 350F (175C). In a medium bowl, beat butter, powdered sugar, vanilla and egg white until creamy. Gradually stir in cake flour. Cover dough; refrigerate 1 hour. Shape refrigerated dough into 1/2- to 3/4-inch balls. Place balls, 2 inches apart, on ungreased baking sheets. Press tops with tines of a fork. Bake 12 to 14 minutes or until golden. Remove from baking sheets; cool on wire racks. Makes about 40 cookies.

Chocolate-Nut Sandwiches

1 cup butter or margarine, room temperature
1 cup powdered sugar, sifted
1 teaspoon vanilla extract
3 egg yolks
1-3/4 cups sifted all-purpose flour
3 tablespoons unsweetened cocoa powder
1 teaspoon baking powder
1 teaspoon ground cinnamon
3/4 cup ground hazelnuts, almonds or walnuts

Chocolate Filling & Glaze:
5 oz. semisweet chocolate
2 tablespoons butter or margarine

Preheat oven to 350F (175C). Grease baking sheets; set aside. In a medium bowl, beat butter or margarine, powdered sugar, vanilla and egg yolks until creamy. Blend flour, cocoa powder, baking powder and cinnamon; gradually stir into sugar mixture. Stir in nuts. Spoon dough into a pastry bag fitted with a serrated-ribbon tip. Pipe 1-3/4- to 2-inch strips, 1 inch apart, on greased baking sheets. Bake 10 to 12 minutes or until firm. Remove from baking sheets; cool on wire racks.

To make chocolate filling and glaze, combine chocolate and butter or margarine in a small saucepan over medium heat. Stir until melted. Spread chocolate mixture over bottoms of 1/2 of cookies. Sandwich with remaining cookies, placing bottoms together. Dip both ends of cookies into chocolate mixture; place on foil until chocolate is set. Makes about 60 cookies.

Butter Buttons; Chocolate Crescents

Rosettes & Bear Claws

1 cup butter, room temperature
1 cup sugar
1 teaspoon vanilla extract
1 egg
3 cups cake flour
1/2 cup finely ground almonds
8 red candied cherries, quartered
2 tablespoons apricot jam
3 oz. semisweet chocolate, melted

Preheat oven to 350F (175C). Grease baking sheets; set aside. In a large bowl, beat butter, sugar, vanilla and egg until creamy. Gradually stir in cake flour. Stir in almonds. Spoon dough into a pastry bag fitted with a serrated-ribbon tip. Pipe 30 rosettes, turning tube as dough is piped out, and 60 bear claws, 2 inches apart, on greased baking sheets. Or, press through a cookie press fitted with a serrated-ribbon plate. Place a candied cherry piece in center of each rosette. Bake 12 to 14 minutes or until golden. Let stand on baking sheets 2 minutes. Remove from baking sheets; cool on wire racks. Spread bottoms of 15 claws with apricot jam and bottoms of another 15 claws with melted chocolate. Sandwich with remaining 30 claws, placing bottoms together. Dip ends of claws into chocolate; place on wire racks until chocolate sets. Makes 60 cookies.

Rosettes & Bear Claws

Chocolate Crescents

1 cup butter, room temperature
1-1/2 cups sifted powdered sugar
1 egg
1 egg yolk
2 teaspoons vanilla extract
2 cups all-purpose flour
1/4 cup unsweetened cocoa powder, sifted
5 tablespoons apricot jam

Chocolate Glaze:
2 oz. semisweet chocolate
1 tablespoon butter or margarine

Preheat oven to 350F (175C). Grease baking sheets; set aside. In a large bowl, beat butter, sugar, vanilla and egg until creamy. Gradually stir in cake flour. Stir in almonds. Spoon dough into a pastry bag fitted with a serrated-ribbon tip. Pipe 30 rosettes, turning tube as dough is piped out, and 60 bear claws, 2 inches apart, on greased baking sheets. Or, press through a cookie press fitted with a serrated-ribbon plate. Place a candied cherry piece in center of each rosette. Bake 12 to 14 minutes or until golden. Let stand on baking sheets 2 minutes. Remove from baking sheets; cool on wire racks. Spread bottoms of 15 claws with apricot jam and bottoms of another 15 claws with melted chocolate. Sandwich with remaining 30 claws, placing bottoms together. Dip ends of claws into chocolate; place on wire racks until chocolate sets. Makes 60 cookies.

Fancy Florentines

1/2 cup coarsely chopped red candied cherries
1/2 cup sliced or slivered almonds
1/2 cup chopped hazelnuts or walnuts
1/2 cup sugar
1/4 cup chopped candied orange peel
1/2 cup all-purpose flour
1/4 cup butter or margarine, melted
1/4 cup whipping cream
4 oz. semisweet chocolate

Preheat oven to 350F (175C). Grease baking sheets; set aside. In a medium bowl, combine cherries, almonds, hazelnuts or walnuts, sugar and orange peel. Sprinkle with flour; toss to coat. Stir in butter or margarine and cream. Shape into small balls using 1 rounded teaspoon of fruit-nut mixture in each ball. Place balls, 3 inches apart, on greased baking sheets. Grease bottom of a water glass. Flatten balls with greased glass. Bake 8 to 10 minutes or until edges are golden brown. Let stand on baking sheets on wire racks 1 minute. Carefully remove baked cookies from baking sheets; cool on wire racks. Melt and cool chocolate. Spread melted chocolate on bottom of cooled cookies. Place cookies, chocolate-side up, on racks; let stand until chocolate sets. Makes about 24 cookies.

Almond Crescents

Butter Rings

Almond Crescents

1 (7-oz.) pkg. marzipan or Marzipan, page 232
2 egg whites
1/2 cup sugar
3 tablespoons all-purpose flour
1/4 cup sliced almonds
2 oz. semisweet chocolate
1 tablespoon butter or margarine

Preheat oven to 350F (175C). Grease and flour baking sheets. Crumble marzipan into a medium bowl. Add egg whites; beat until creamy. Gradually beat in sugar and flour. Spoon mixture into a pastry bag fitted with a medium plain tip. Pipe dough in half-moons, 1 inch apart, on prepared baking sheets. Sprinkle with almonds. Bake 10 to 12 minutes or until edges are golden. Let stand on baking sheets 3 minutes. Remove from baking sheets; cool on wire racks. Melt chocolate and butter or margarine in a small saucepan over low heat. Dip ends of cooled cookies in melted-chocolate mixture. Place on racks until chocolate sets. Makes about 30 cookies.

Butter Rings

1 cup butter, room temperature
1 cup sugar
2 teaspoons vanilla extract
1 egg
3 egg yolks
3-1/4 cups cake flour
Red and green candied cherries, if desired, cut in thin strips

Preheat oven to 350F (175C). In a medium bowl, beat butter, sugar, vanilla, egg and egg yolks until creamy. Gradually stir in cake flour. Spoon dough into a pastry bag fitted with a small star tip. Pipe 2-inch rings, 1 inch apart, on ungreased baking sheets. Or, pack dough into a cookie press fitted with a star plate. Hold press in a horizontal position; shape rings on ungreased baking sheets, moving cookie press in a circle. Press pieces of red and green cherries onto cookies to decorate, if desired. Bake 10 to 12 minutes or until golden. Remove from baking sheets; cool on wire racks. Makes about 60 cookies.

Lemon Tea Wafers

3/4 cup butter or margarine, room temperature
1 cup sugar
1 egg
1 egg yolk
2 teaspoons grated lemon peel
3 tablespoons lemon juice
2-1/2 cups sifted all-purpose flour
1 teaspoon baking powder
1/4 teaspoon salt
Sugar

Preheat oven to 375F (190C). Grease baking sheets; set aside. In a medium bowl, beat butter or margarine, sugar, egg, egg yolk and lemon peel until creamy. Stir in lemon juice. Blend flour, baking powder and salt; gradually stir into sugar mixture. Shape dough into 1-inch balls. Place balls, 1-1/2 inches apart, on greased baking sheets. Grease bottom of a juice glass; dip in sugar. Use to flatten balls until 1/4 inch thick. Bake 12 to 15 minutes or until edges are lightly browned. Remove from baking sheets; cool on wire racks. Makes about 42 cookies.

Vanilla-Shortcake Rings

Vanilla-Shortcake Rings

3/4 cup butter, room temperature
1/2 cup powdered sugar, sifted
1/3 cup dairy sour cream
2 cups all-purpose flour
Milk
1/3 cup chopped blanched almonds

In a medium bowl, beat butter and powdered sugar until creamy. Stir in sour cream. Gradually stir in flour. Shape dough into a flat ball. Cover; refrigerate 3 hours. Preheat oven to 400F (205C). On a lightly floured surface, roll out refrigerated dough until 1/2 inch thick. Flour a 2-1/2-inch doughnut cutter; use to cut dough. Place dough rings, 1 inch apart, on ungreased baking sheets. Press doughnut centers together; roll and cut. Brush tops of cookies with milk; sprinkle with almonds. Bake 12 to 15 minutes or until golden. Remove from baking sheets; cool on wire racks. Makes about 18 cookies.

Coconut Cookies

1 cup butter or margarine, room temperature
1/2 cup sugar
2 eggs
1-1/2 teaspoons almond extract
2 cups all-purpose flour
1/2 teaspoon baking powder
2 cups shredded or flaked coconut

In a medium bowl, beat butter or margarine and sugar until creamy. Beat in eggs and almond extract. Blend flour and baking powder; gradually stir into sugar mixture. Stir in coconut. Shape dough into a flat ball. Cover; refrigerate 1 hour. Preheat oven to 350F (175C). On a lightly floured surface, roll out refrigerated dough until 1/4 inch thick. Flour a 2-inch fluted cookie cutter; use to cut dough. Place cut dough, 1 inch apart, on ungreased baking sheets. Bake 12 to 15 minutes or until edges are golden. Remove from baking sheets; cool on wire racks. Makes about 60 cookies.

Spritz Cookies

Spritz Cookies

1-3/4 cups butter
1-1/2 cups sugar
4 egg yolks
2 teaspoons vanilla extract
1 tablespoon grated lemon peel or orange peel
4 cups all-purpose flour
1-1/2 teaspoons baking powder

Chocolate Icing:
1 cup powdered sugar, sifted
2 tablespoons unsweetened cocoa powder
3 tablespoons butter or margarine, melted
1 to 2 tablespoons hot water

Preheat oven to 350F (175C). In a large bowl, beat butter, sugar, egg yolks, vanilla and lemon peel or orange peel until creamy. Blend flour and baking powder; stir into sugar mixture, 1 cup at a time, beating well after each addition. Pack dough into a cookie press; press out in wreaths, bars, fingers, scrolls or rosettes, 1 inch apart, on ungreased baking sheets. Bake 12 to 15 minutes or until golden. Remove from baking sheets; cool on wire racks.

To make chocolate icing, in a small bowl, blend powdered sugar and cocoa powder. Add butter or margarine and water; stir until smooth. Spoon icing into a pastry bag fitted with a small, plain, writing tip. Pipe icing over cookies. Makes about 72 cookies.

Raisin-Citron Cookies

Raisin-Citron Cookies

1/2 cup butter or margarine, room temperature
3/4 cup plus 1 teaspoon sugar
1 whole egg
1 egg, separated
1/2 teaspoon lemon extract
2 cups all-purpose flour
1-1/2 teaspoons baking powder
1 tablespoon milk
1/3 cup raisins
1/4 cup chopped almonds
3 tablespoons chopped citron

Preheat oven to 375F (190C). Grease baking sheets; set aside. In a medium bowl, beat butter or margarine and 3/4 cup sugar until creamy. Beat in whole egg, egg yolk and lemon extract. Blend flour and baking powder; stir flour mixture and milk into sugar mixture. Shape dough into walnut-size balls. In a small bowl, combine raisins, almonds and citron. Blend egg white with 1 teaspoon sugar; brush over tops of dough balls. Dip balls in raisin mixture; arrange 1-1/2 inches apart, on greased baking sheets. Bake 15 minutes or until golden. Remove from baking sheets; cool on wire racks. Makes about 24 cookies.

Crumb-Topped Cookies

Cookies:
1 cup butter or margarine, room temperature
1/2 cup sugar
2 cups all-purpose flour
1/3 cup ground almonds

Crumb Topping:
2 cups all-purpose flour
1/2 cup sugar
1 teaspoon ground cinnamon
1/4 teaspoon ground nutmeg
3/4 cup butter or margarine, chilled
About 36 maraschino cherries, halved

To make cookies, in a medium bowl, beat butter or margarine and sugar until creamy. Blend flour and almonds; gradually stir into sugar mixture. Shape dough into a flat ball; cover and refrigerate 1 hour. Preheat oven to 350F (175C). On a lightly floured surface, roll out refrigerated dough until 1/8 inch thick. Flour a 2-inch fluted cookie cutter; use to cut dough. Place cut dough, 1 inch apart, on ungreased baking sheets.
To make topping, in a medium bowl, blend flour, sugar, cinnamon and nutmeg. Use a pastry cutter or 2 knives to cut in butter or margarine until mixture resembles coarse crumbs. Spoon 1 teaspoon crumb topping on top of each cookie; top each with a cherry half. Bake 15 minutes or until edges are golden. Remove from baking sheets; cool on wire racks. Makes about 72 cookies.

Crumb-Topped Cookies

Almond Wafers

1 cup butter or margarine, room temperature
1/2 cup granulated sugar
1/2 cup packed light-brown sugar
2 eggs
1 teaspoon almond extract
2-1/2 cups all-purpose flour
1-1/2 teaspoons baking powder
1/2 teaspoon salt
1 cup sliced almonds, coarsely chopped

In a medium bowl, beat butter or margarine, granulated sugar, brown sugar, eggs and almond extract until creamy. Blend flour, baking powder and salt; gradually stir into sugar mixture. Stir in almonds until distributed. Divide dough in half. Shape each portion into a 1-3/4-inch-thick log. Cover; refrigerate 3 hours. Preheat oven to 350F (175C). Cut refrigerated logs into 1/4-inch slices. Place slices, 1 inch apart, on ungreased baking sheets. Bake 12 to 15 minutes or until edges are golden. Remove from baking sheets; cool on wire racks. Makes about 96 cookies.

Almond Wafers

Jam Cookies

1/2 cup butter, room temperature
1/2 cup granulated sugar
1 egg
1 egg yolk
1 teaspoon vanilla extract
2-1/4 cups all-purpose flour
2 teaspoons baking powder
1/2 teaspoon salt
Strawberry or raspberry jam
Powdered sugar

In a medium bowl, beat butter and granulated sugar until creamy. Beat in egg, egg yolk and vanilla. Blend flour, baking powder and salt; gradually stir into sugar mixture. Shape dough into a flat ball. Cover; refrigerate 1 hour. Preheat oven to 350F (175C). On a lightly floured surface, roll out refrigerated dough until 1/8 inch thick. Flour a 3-inch fluted cookie cutter; use to cut dough. Place cut dough, 1 inch apart, on ungreased baking sheets. Cut 3 (3/4-inch) holes in center of 1/2 of cookies. Bake 8 to 10 minutes or until edges are golden. Remove from baking sheets; cool on wire racks. Spread jam over bottom of cookies without holes. Sprinkle remaining cookies with powdered sugar, place over jam-covered cookies, sugar-side up. Makes about 18 cookies.

Jam Cookies

Terraces

Terraces

3/4 cup butter or margarine, room temperature
1 cup granulated sugar
1 egg
2 tablespoons milk
2 teaspoons vanilla extract
2-1/2 cups all-purpose flour
1-1/2 teaspoons baking powder
Strawberry preserves
Powdered sugar
Candied cherries, halved

In a medium bowl, beat butter or margarine and granulated sugar until creamy. Beat in egg, milk and vanilla. Blend flour and baking powder; gradually stir into sugar mixture. Shape dough into a flat ball. Cover; refrigerate 1 hour. Preheat oven to 350F (175C). On a lightly floured surface, roll out refrigerated dough until 1/4 inch thick. Flour 2-1/2-inch, 2-inch and 1-3/4-inch fluted cookie cutters. Cut out 36 cookies with each cookie cutter. Place cut dough, 1 inch apart, on ungreased baking sheets. Bake 8 to 10 minutes or until golden. Remove from baking sheets; cool on wire racks. Spread a little preserves on centers of 2-1/2- and 2-inch cookies. Stack cookies with largest on bottom and smallest on top to make terraces. Sprinkle with powdered sugar; decorate with candied cherries. Makes 36 cookies.

Viennese Hearts

1 cup butter or margarine, room temperature
1-1/2 cups sifted powdered sugar
2 egg yolks
2 teaspoons vanilla extract
2-1/2 cups all-purpose flour
1 tablespoon grated lemon peel
1/4 teaspoon salt

Apricot Filling & Glaze:
5 tablespoons apricot jam
1 tablespoon apricot-flavored brandy or water

In a medium bowl, beat butter or margarine, powdered sugar, egg yolks and vanilla until creamy. Blend flour, lemon peel and salt; stir into sugar mixture. Cover; refrigerate 2 hours. Preheat oven to 350F (175C). On a lightly floured surface, roll out refrigerated dough until 1/8 inch thick. Flour a 2-inch heart-shaped cookie cutter; use to cut out dough. Place cut dough, 1 inch apart, on ungreased baking sheets. Bake 8 to 10 minutes or until edges are golden. Let stand 2 minutes. Remove from baking sheets; cool on wire racks.
To make filling and glaze, press jam through a sieve into a small saucepan. Place over low heat. Stir constantly until jam melts. Cool to room temperature; stir in brandy or water. Spread apricot mixture over bottoms of 1/2 of cookies. Sandwich with remaining cookies, placing bottoms together. Brush remaining apricot mixture over tops and sides of cookies. Place on wire racks until glaze sets. Makes about 48 cookies.

Viennese Hearts

Orange Sandwich Cookies

3/4 cup butter or margarine, room temperature
1/2 cup sugar
1 egg
1 teaspoon orange extract
2-1/2 cups all-purpose flour
1/2 teaspoon salt

Orange Icing:
1-3/4 cups powdered sugar
2 to 2-1/2 tablespoons orange juice
About 1/2 cup chopped candied orange peel

Orange Sandwich Cookies

In a medium bowl, beat butter or margarine and sugar until creamy. Beat in egg and orange extract. Blend flour and salt; gradually stir into sugar mixture. Shape dough into a flat ball. Cover; refrigerate 1 hour. Preheat oven to 350F (175C). Grease baking sheets; set aside. On a lightly floured surface, roll out refrigerated dough until 1/8 inch thick. Flour a 2-inch fluted cookie cutter; use to cut dough. Arrange cut dough, 1 inch apart, on greased baking sheets. Bake 10 to 12 minutes or until golden. Remove from baking sheets; cool on wire racks.
To make orange icing, in a small bowl, blend powdered sugar and orange juice until smooth. Spread a thin layer of icing over bottoms of 1/2 of cookies. Sandwich with remaining cookies, placing bottoms together. Spread icing over tops of cookies. Decorate with candied orange peel. Place on wire racks until icing sets. Makes about 36 cookies.

Raspberry Thumbprints

3/4 cup butter or margarine, room temperature
1 cup sugar
1 teaspoon vanilla extract
3 egg yolks
2 cups all-purpose flour
1/2 teaspoon baking soda
1/4 teaspoon salt
1 egg white, slightly beaten
1/3 cup finely chopped blanched almonds
3 tablespoons raspberry jam

In a medium bowl, beat butter or margarine and sugar until creamy. Beat in vanilla and egg yolks. Blend flour, baking soda and salt; stir into sugar mixture. Cover; refrigerate dough at least 2 hours. Preheat oven to 350F (175C). Shape refrigerated dough into slightly flat walnut-size balls. Dip bottom halves of balls into egg white, then into almonds. Place balls, nut-side up and 2 inches apart, on ungreased baking sheets. Press your thumb or end of a wooden spoon into centers of dough balls, making depressions. Spoon raspberry jam into depressions. Bake 10 to 12 minutes or until golden. Let stand on baking sheets 5 minutes. Remove from baking sheets; cool on wire racks. Makes 30 to 36 cookies.

Dainty Toadstools

1 cup butter or margarine, room temperature
1 (3-oz.) pkg. cream cheese, room temperature
1 cup granulated sugar
1 egg, separated
1 teaspoon vanilla extract
2-1/2 cups sifted cake flour
Milk
Whole blanched almonds, split lengthwise
Red candied cherries, halved
Green candied cherries, cut in thin strips
1 cup powdered sugar, sifted
Dash cream of tartar

In a medium bowl, beat butter or margarine, cream cheese and granulated sugar until creamy. Beat in egg yolk and vanilla. Gradually stir in cake flour. Shape dough into a flat ball. Cover; refrigerate 1 hour. Preheat oven to 350F (175C). On a lightly floured surface, roll out refrigerated dough until 1/4 inch thick. Flour a 2-inch fluted cookie cutter; use to cut dough. Place cut dough, 1 inch apart, on ungreased baking sheets. Brush tops with milk. Make toadstools on top of cookies, using split almonds for stems. Place a red-cherry half above each almond. Place green-cherry strips on each side of almonds for leaves. Bake 10 to 12 minutes or until edges are golden. Remove from baking sheets; cool on wire racks. Beat egg white until stiff but not dry. Beat in powdered sugar and cream of tartar. Spoon into a pastry bag fitted with a small writing tip. Pipe dots onto red candied cherries to decorate. Or, use a wooden pick to place dots of icing on cherries. Makes about 72 cookies.

Oatmeal-Orange Cookies

1/2 cup butter or margarine, room temperature
1 cup packed light-brown sugar
1 egg
1-1/2 teaspoons grated orange peel
1 cup all-purpose flour
1/2 teaspoon baking soda
1/4 teaspoon salt
3 tablespoons orange juice
1 cup rolled oats
1/2 cup chopped pitted dates
1/2 cup chopped walnuts or pecans

Preheat oven to 375F (190C). Grease baking sheets; set aside. In a medium bowl, beat butter or margarine, brown sugar, egg and orange peel until creamy. Blend flour, baking soda and salt; gradually stir into sugar mixture alternately with orange juice. Stir in oats, dates and nuts. Drop by rounded teaspoons, 1-1/2 inches apart, on greased baking sheets. Bake 15 to 18 minutes or until edges are browned. Remove from baking sheets; cool on wire racks. Makes about 60 cookies.

Dainty Toadstools

Chocolate Rocky Roads

1/3 cup butter or margarine, room temperature
1/2 cup sugar
1-1/2 teaspoons rum extract
1-1/4 cups all-purpose flour
1 teaspoon baking powder
2 tablespoons milk

Rocky Road Filling:
1/2 cup butter or margarine, melted
1/2 cup powdered sugar
2 tablespoons unsweetened cocoa powder
1 egg
1/2 cup shredded or flaked coconut
1/2 cup chopped walnuts or almonds
1-1/2 cups miniature marshmallows

Chocolate Coating:
6 oz. semisweet chocolate
2 tablespoons butter or margarine
1 tablespoon half and half

In a medium bowl, beat butter or margarine, sugar and rum extract until creamy. Blend flour and baking powder; stir flour mixture into sugar mixture alternately with milk. Shape dough into a flat ball. Cover; refrigerate 2 hours. Preheat oven to 350F (175C). Grease baking sheets. On a lightly floured surface, roll out refrigerated dough until 1/4 inch thick. Flour a 2-inch fluted cookie cutter; use to cut dough. Place cut dough, 1 inch apart, on greased baking sheets. Bake 8 to 10 minutes or until golden. Remove from baking sheets; cool on wire racks.
To make rocky road filling, in a medium bowl, combine all ingredients. Place 1 heaping teaspoon of filling on each cooled cookie.
To make chocolate coating, melt chocolate and butter or margarine in a small saucepan over low heat. Remove from heat; stir in half and half. Dip filled cookies into chocolate, covering completely. Place on foil until chocolate is set. Makes about 24 cookies.

Sweetheart Cookies; Chocolate Rocky Roads

Sweetheart Cookies

1/3 cup butter or margarine, room temperature
1/2 cup sugar
1 teaspoon vanilla extract
1 egg
1 egg yolk
1-1/4 cups all-purpose flour
1/2 teaspoon baking soda
1/4 cup ground almonds
Colored sprinkles

Lemon Icing:
1-1/4 cups powdered sugar, sifted
1 egg white
1 teaspoon lemon extract
3 to 4 teaspoons hot water

In a medium bowl, beat butter or margarine, sugar, vanilla, egg and egg yolk until creamy. Blend flour, baking soda and almonds; gradually stir into sugar mixture. Shape dough into a flat ball. Cover; refrigerate 2 hours. Preheat oven to 350F (175C). Grease baking sheets; set aside. On a lightly floured surface, roll out refrigerated dough until 1/8 inch thick. Flour a 2-inch heart-shaped cookie cutter; use to cut dough. Place cut dough, 1 inch apart, on greased baking sheets. Bake 10 to 12 minutes or until edges are golden. Remove from baking sheets; cool on wire racks.
To make icing, in a small bowl, combine all ingredients. Spread over cookies; decorate with sprinkles. Makes about 36 cookies.

Confetti Cookies

1/2 cup butter or margarine, room temperature
3/4 cup sugar
1 egg
1-1/2 teaspoons vanilla extract
2 cups all-purpose flour
1/2 teaspoon salt
1 teaspoon baking powder
1/2 cup finely chopped candied fruit

In a medium bowl, beat butter or margarine, sugar, egg and vanilla until creamy. Blend flour, salt and baking powder; gradually stir into sugar mixture. Stir in candied fruit. Shape dough into a 2-inch-thick log. Cover; refrigerate 3 hours. Preheat oven to 375F (190C). Cut refrigerated dough into 1/8-inch slices. Place slices, 1 inch apart, on ungreased baking sheets. Bake 10 to 12 minutes. Remove from baking sheets; cool on wire racks. Makes about 48 cookies.

Ginger Cookies

Ginger Cookies

1/2 cup butter or margarine, room temperature
1/2 cup packed light-brown sugar
1/2 cup honey
1 egg
2-1/2 cups all-purpose flour
3/4 teaspoon baking soda
2 teaspoons ground ginger
1/2 teaspoon ground cinnamon
1/4 teaspoon ground cloves
2 tablespoons orange juice
1 cup blanched hazelnuts or almonds

In a medium bowl, beat butter or margarine and brown sugar until creamy. Beat in honey and egg. Blend flour, baking soda, ginger, cinnamon and cloves; stir into sugar mixture alternately with orange juice. Shape dough into a flat ball. Cover; refrigerate 3 hours. Preheat oven to 350F (175C). Grease baking sheets. On a lightly floured surface, roll out refrigerated dough until 1/8 inch thick. Cut dough into 2-1/2" x 1" rectangles. Place rectangles, 1 inch apart, on greased baking sheets. Decorate each cookie with 1, 2 or 3 hazelnuts or almonds. Bake 10 to 12 minutes or until browned. Remove from baking sheets; cool on wire racks. Makes about 48 cookies.

Chocolate-Cherry Squares

1/2 cup chopped candied cherries
1/2 cup all-purpose flour
1-1/2 cups rolled oats
1/2 cup butter or margarine
1/2 cup packed light-brown sugar
2 tablespoons light corn syrup
8 oz. semisweet chocolate

Preheat oven to 375F (190C). Grease an 11" x 7" baking pan. Place cherries in a medium bowl. Sprinkle with flour; toss to coat. Add rolled oats; toss to distribute. In large saucepan, combine butter or margarine, brown sugar and corn syrup. Stir constantly over low heat until melted. Remove from heat; stir in cherry mixture. Press mixture into greased pan. Bake 20 minutes. While still warm, cut into 1-inch squares. Cool in pan on a wire rack. Melt chocolate in a small saucepan over low heat. Dip one side of each square into melted chocolate; place on foil until chocolate sets. Makes 77 squares.

Strawberry-Jam Bars

2/3 cup butter or margarine, room temperature
2/3 cup sugar
2 eggs, separated
1-1/2 cups all-purpose flour
2 egg whites
1/2 cup chopped pecans
1 cup strawberry jam

Preheat oven to 350F (175C). In a medium bowl, beat butter or margarine and 1/3 cup sugar until creamy. Beat in egg yolks, 1 at a time. Fold in flour, 1/4 cup at a time. Press into an ungreased 13'' x 9'' baking pan. Bake 15 minutes. In a medium bowl, beat 4 egg whites until stiff but not dry. Gradually beat in remaining 1/3 cup sugar until stiff peaks form. Fold in nuts. Spread strawberry jam over baked crust; top with egg-white mixture, covering completely. Bake 10 to 12 minutes or until top is lightly browned. Cool in pan on a wire rack. Cut into 32 bars.

Sugar Eyes

3/4 cup butter or margarine, room temperature
1/2 cup granulated sugar
1-1/2 teaspoons vanilla extract
2 cups all-purpose flour
2 teaspoons baking powder
1 egg, slightly beaten
1/3 cup crystal sugar or crushed sugar cubes
8 to 10 red or green candied cherries, quartered

Preheat oven to 350F (175C). In a medium bowl, beat butter or margarine, granulated sugar and vanilla until creamy. Blend flour and baking powder; gradually stir into creamed mixture. Shape dough into walnut-size balls; flatten slightly. Dip one side of balls in beaten egg, then in crystal sugar or crushed sugar cubes. Place sugar-side up, 1-1/2 inches apart, on ungreased baking sheets. Decorate each cookie with a piece of candied cherry. Bake 15 to 18 minutes or until edges are golden. Remove from baking sheets; cool on wire racks. Makes about 30 cookies.

Filled Pecan Sandies

Sugar Eyes

Filled Pecan Sandies

1 cup butter or margarine, room temperature
3/4 cup granulated sugar
1/4 cup packed light-brown sugar
1 egg yolk
1 teaspoon vanilla extract
3 cups all-purpose flour
3/4 cup ground pecans
Strawberry or raspberry jam

In a medium bowl, beat butter or margarine, granulated sugar, brown sugar, egg yolk and vanilla until creamy. Blend flour and pecans; gradually stir into sugar mixture. Shape dough into a flat ball. Cover; refrigerate 1 hour. Preheat oven to 350F (175C). Grease baking sheets. On a lightly floured surface, roll out refrigerated dough until 1/4 inch thick. Flour a 2-inch fluted cookie cutter; use to cut dough. Place cut dough, 1 inch apart, on greased baking sheets. Bake 12 to 14 minutes or until golden. Remove from baking sheets; cool on wire racks. Press jam through a sieve. Spread jam on bottoms of 1/2 of cookies. Sandwich with remaining cookies, placing bottoms together. Makes about 42 cookies.

onto vanilla dough. Peel off top waxed paper. Trim edges of dough. Starting at a long side, roll dough jelly-roll fashion, peeling off bottom waxed paper as you roll. Cover rolled dough; refrigerate 3 hours or until firm. Preheat oven to 350F (175C). Grease baking sheets. Using a sharp knife, cut refrigerated dough into 1/4-inch slices. Place slices, 1 inch apart, on greased baking sheets. Bake 12 to 15 minutes or until edges are lightly browned. Remove from baking sheets; cool on wire racks. Makes about 48 cookies.

Checkerboards: Sprinkle a rolling pin and a large sheet of waxed paper with powdered sugar. Divide each piece of dough in half. On sugar-coated waxed paper, roll out both chocolate pieces and 1 piece of vanilla dough to 1/4-inch-thick squares. Cover; refrigerate 1 hour. Lightly brush top of each refrigerated square with egg white. Cut each square into 1/4-inch-wide strips. Lifting strips from waxed paper, arrange 3 dough strips side by side, alternating colors, with sides touching. Top with 3 more strips, placing chocolate on vanilla and vanilla on chocolate. Top with a third layer of 3 strips, alternating colors; set aside. Repeat with remaining half pieces of dough; trim edges. Roll out remaining vanilla dough to a thin rectangle as wide as checkerboard is long. Brush with beaten egg white. Place 1 set of stacked strips on rolled-out vanilla dough. Carefully wrap checkerboard with vanilla dough, leaving 2 ends open. Repeat with remaining checkerboards and vanilla dough. Cover; refrigerate 3 hours or until firm. Bake as for pinwheels.

Wheels: Divide each chocolate and vanilla dough into 3 equal pieces. Shape chocolate dough into 3 (1-1/4-inch-thick) logs. Roll out each piece of vanilla dough until 1/8 inch thick. Wrap each log in vanilla dough. Cover; refrigerate 3 hours or until firm. Cut each log into 1/4-inch slices. On greased baking sheets, arrange slices in groups of 3 with edges touching and with groups 2 inches apart. Bake as for Pinwheels.

Pinwheels, Checkerboards & Wheels

3/4 cup butter or margarine, room temperature
2/3 cup granulated sugar
1 egg
1 teaspoon vanilla or almond extract
2 tablespoons milk
2 cups all-purpose flour
1 teaspoon baking powder
1 oz. semisweet chocolate, melted
Powdered sugar, sifted
1 egg white, slightly beaten, for Checkerboards

In a medium bowl, beat butter or margarine, granulated sugar, egg and vanilla or almond extract until creamy. Beat in milk. Blend flour and baking powder; gradually stir into sugar mixture. Divide dough in half. Stir chocolate into half of dough; blend well.

Pinwheels: Sprinkle a rolling pin and a large sheet of waxed paper with powdered sugar. Roll out vanilla dough on sugar-coated waxed paper to a 12" x 8" rectangle. Repeat with chocolate dough. Invert chocolate dough

Pinwheels, Checkerboards & Wheels

Nut Triangles

2/3 cup butter or margarine, room temperature
1 cup sugar
1 egg
1 teaspoon vanilla extract
1-1/4 cups all-purpose flour
1/2 teaspoon baking powder
2 to 3 tablespoons apricot jam
3/4 cup finely chopped hazelnuts, almonds,
    walnuts or pecans
2 tablespoons water
2 oz. semisweet chocolate, melted

Preheat oven to 350F (175C). Grease a 13'' x 9'' baking pan; set aside. In a medium bowl, beat 1/3 cup butter or margarine, 1/2 cup sugar, egg and vanilla until creamy. Blend flour and baking powder; stir into sugar mixture all at once. Spread or pat dough evenly into greased pan. Spread jam over top. In a small saucepan, melt remaining 1/3 cup butter or margarine. Stir in remaining 1/2 cup sugar and water; stir in nuts. Spread nut mixture evenly over dough. Bake 25 to 30 minutes or until top is golden brown. Cool in pan on a wire rack 10 to 15 minutes. While still warm, cut into 24 bars, 2-1/2'' x 2-1/8''. Cut each bar diagonally to make triangles. Remove from pan; cool on wire racks. Dip 2 points of each triangle in melted chocolate. Let stand on wire racks until chocolate sets. Makes 48 cookies.

Variation
Coconut Triangles: Substitute 1-1/2 to 2 cups flaked or shredded coconut for nuts.

Spicy Fruit Cookies

2 cups all-purpose flour
1 teaspoon baking powder
1/2 teaspoon salt
1/2 teaspoon ground cloves
1/2 teaspoon ground cardamom
1/2 teaspoon ground cinnamon
1/2 cup butter or margarine, room temperature
3/4 cup sugar
2 eggs
1 teaspoon vanilla extract
1/2 cup chopped almonds, hazelnuts, walnuts or pecans
3 tablespoons chopped candied lemon peel
3 tablespoons chopped candied orange peel

Lemon or Orange Glaze:
1-1/4 cups powdered sugar, sifted
1 to 2 tablespoons lemon juice or orange juice

Preheat oven to 350F (175C). Grease baking sheets; set aside. In a medium bowl, blend flour, baking powder, salt, cloves, cardamom and cinnamon; set aside. In a large bowl, beat butter or margarine and sugar until creamy. Beat in eggs and vanilla. Stir in flour mixture. Stir in nuts and candied peels. Drop by rounded teaspoons, 1 inch apart, on greased baking sheets. Bake 14 to 16 minutes or until edges are browned. Remove from baking sheets; cool on wire racks.
To make glaze, in a small bowl, blend powdered sugar and lemon juice or orange juice until smooth; spoon over cookies. Let stand until icing sets. Makes about 36 cookies.

Nut Triangles

Molasses Crisps

2/3 cup butter or margarine, room temperature
1 cup packed dark-brown sugar
1/2 cup molasses
4 cups sifted all-purpose flour
1-1/2 teaspoons baking soda
2 teaspoons ground cinnamon
1 teaspoon ground ginger
3 tablespoons milk
6 tablespoons water
2 tablespoons powdered sugar
Blanched almond halves

In a medium bowl, beat butter or margarine and brown sugar until creamy. Stir in molasses. Blend flour, baking soda, cinnamon and ginger; stir into sugar mixture alternately with milk. Divide dough in half; shape each half into a flat ball. Cover; refrigerate at least 1 hour. In a small saucepan, combine water and powdered sugar; bring to a boil. Boil 3 to 5 minutes or until syrupy; set aside. Preheat oven to 350F (175C). Grease baking sheets; set aside. On a lightly floured surface, roll out each refrigerated ball until 1/8 inch thick. Flour a round 3-inch cookie cutter; use to cut dough. Place dough circles, 1 inch apart, on greased baking sheets. Brush sugar syrup over tops of dough circles; decorate with almonds. Bake 10 minutes. Let stand on baking sheets 2 minutes. Remove from baking sheets; cool on wire racks. Makes about 42 cookies.

Marzipan-Orange Sticks

1/2 (7-oz.) pkg. marzipan or 1/2 recipe Marzipan, page 232, crumbled
2/3 cup butter or margarine, room temperature
1 cup sifted powdered sugar
1 egg
1 teaspoon orange extract
2 tablespoons grated orange peel
2 cups sifted all-purpose flour

Chocolate Icing:
1 cup powdered sugar, sifted
2 tablespoons unsweetened cocoa powder
2 tablespoons butter or margarine, melted
2 to 2-1/2 tablespoons hot water

Preheat oven to 350F (175C). In a medium bowl, combine marzipan, butter or margarine, powdered sugar, egg, orange extract and orange peel. Beat until creamy. Gradually stir in flour. Pack dough into a cookie press fitted with a 1/2-inch star tip. Press dough into 2-inch-long strips, 1 inch apart, on ungreased baking sheets. Bake 10 to 12 minutes or until edges are golden. Let stand on baking sheets 1 minute. Remove from baking sheets; cool on wire racks.
To make chocolate icing, in a small bowl, blend powdered sugar and cocoa powder. Stir in butter or margarine and water until smooth. Dip top of each cookie into icing; place on wire racks until icing sets. Makes about 60 cookies.

Chocolate-Ginger Bars

Chewy Brownies

2 oz. unsweetened chocolate
1/3 cup butter or margarine
2 eggs
1 cup sugar
1 tablespoon dark corn syrup
1 teaspoon vanilla extract
3/4 cup all-purpose flour
1/2 teaspoon baking powder
1/2 teaspoon salt
1/2 cup coarsely chopped walnuts, pecans or almonds

Preheat oven to 350F (175C). Grease a 9-inch-square baking pan; set aside. Melt chocolate and butter or margarine in a medium saucepan over low heat. Remove from heat; beat in eggs, 1 at a time, until blended. Stir in sugar, corn syrup and vanilla. Blend flour, baking powder and salt; stir into chocolate mixture. Stir in nuts; spread in greased pan. Bake 30 to 35 minutes. Cool in pan on a wire rack. Cut into 16 bars.

Chocolate-Ginger Bars

1/2 cup butter or margarine, room temperature
1 cup packed light-brown sugar
3 eggs
1 teaspoon vanilla extract
2 cups all-purpose flour
1 tablespoon ground ginger
1 teaspoon baking powder
6 oz. semisweet chocolate, finely chopped, or 1 cup miniature semisweet chocolate pieces (6 oz.)
1 cup raisins

Chocolate Glaze:
5 oz. semisweet chocolate, coarsely chopped
2 tablespoons butter or margarine
1 tablespoon milk
1 tablespoon light corn syrup
Red and green candied cherries, if desired, halved

Preheat oven to 350F (175C). Grease a 15'' x 10'' jelly-roll pan. In a medium bowl, beat butter or margarine, brown sugar, eggs and vanilla until creamy. Blend flour, ginger and baking powder; stir into sugar mixture. Stir in chocolate and raisins. Spread mixture in greased pan; smooth top. Bake 25 to 30 minutes or until a wooden pick inserted in center comes out clean. Cool in pan on a wire rack.
To make chocolate glaze, melt chocolate and butter or margarine in a small saucepan over low heat. Cool to room temperature. Stir in milk and corn syrup. Spread glaze over top of cookies; let stand until set. Cut into bars. Decorate with cherry halves, if desired. Makes about 50 cookies.

Spicy-Pumpkin Drops

3/4 cup butter or margarine, room temperature
1/2 cup granulated sugar
1/2 cup packed light-brown sugar
2 eggs
1 cup cooked or canned pumpkin
2 cups all-purpose flour
1/2 teaspoon baking powder
1/2 teaspoon baking soda
1 teaspoon ground cinnamon
1/2 teaspoon ground nutmeg
1/4 teaspoon ground cloves
1 cup raisins

Preheat oven to 375F (190C). Grease baking sheets; set aside. In a medium bowl, beat butter or margarine, granulated sugar and brown sugar until creamy. Beat in eggs and pumpkin. Blend flour, baking powder, baking soda, cinnamon, nutmeg and cloves; stir into sugar mixture. Stir in raisins. Drop by rounded teaspoons, 1-1/2 inches apart, on greased baking sheets. Bake 12 to 15 minutes or until lightly browned. Remove from baking sheets; cool on wire racks. Makes about 60 cookies.

Crispy Crunchies

1/3 cup butter or margarine
1/2 cup packed light-brown sugar
1/4 cup light corn syrup
2 cups toasted rice cereal
1 cup rolled oats
1/4 cup chopped almonds, walnuts or pecans

Preheat oven to 350F (175C). Grease an 8-inch-square baking pan. Melt butter or margarine, brown sugar and corn syrup in a large saucepan over low heat, stirring constantly. Remove from heat; stir in rice cereal, rolled oats and nuts. Spread in greased pan. Bake 20 minutes; cool 10 minutes in pan on a wire rack. Cut into 2-inch squares while still warm. Cool completely. Before removing squares from pan, re-cut, if necessary. Makes 16 squares.

Coconut-Rum Drops

1/4 cup butter or margarine, room temperature
1/2 cup sugar
1 egg
1 teaspoon rum extract
1 cup all-purpose flour
1-1/2 teaspoons baking powder
1 tablespoon milk
1-1/2 cups flaked or shredded coconut

Preheat oven to 350F (175C). Grease baking sheets; set aside. In a medium bowl, beat butter or margarine and sugar until creamy. Beat in egg and rum extract. Blend flour and baking powder; stir into sugar mixture alternately with milk. Stir in coconut. Drop by rounded teaspoons, 1-1/2 inches apart, on greased baking sheets. Bake 12 to 15 minutes or until golden. Remove from baking sheets; cool on wire racks. Makes about 30 cookies.

Coconut-Rum Drops

Banana-Walnut Cookies

2/3 cup butter or margarine, room temperature
1 cup sugar
2 eggs
2 large ripe bananas, mashed
1/2 cup coarsely chopped walnuts
1 teaspoon vanilla extract
2-1/4 cups all-purpose flour
2 teaspoons baking powder
1/4 teaspoon baking soda
1 teaspoon ground cinnamon
1/2 teaspoon ground nutmeg

Preheat oven to 400F (205C). In a medium bowl, beat butter or margarine, sugar and eggs until creamy. Stir in bananas, nuts and vanilla. Blend flour, baking powder, baking soda, cinnamon and nutmeg; stir into sugar mixture. Drop by rounded teaspoons, 1-1/2 inches apart, on ungreased baking sheets. Bake 12 to 14 minutes or until lightly browned around edges. Remove from baking sheets; cool on wire racks. Makes about 48 cookies.

Raisin-Walnut Cookies

1/2 cup butter or margarine, room temperature
1/2 cup granulated sugar
1/2 cup packed light-brown sugar
2 eggs
1 teaspoon vanilla extract
2 cups all-purpose flour
1 teaspoon baking soda
1 teaspoon ground cinnamon
1/4 teaspoon ground allspice
1 cup raisins
1/2 cup coarsely chopped walnuts

Preheat oven to 375F (190C). Grease baking sheets; set aside. In a medium bowl, beat butter or margarine, sugars, eggs and vanilla until creamy. Blend flour, baking soda, cinnamon and allspice; stir into sugar mixture. Stir in raisins and walnuts. Drop by rounded teaspoons, 1-1/2 inches apart, on greased baking sheets. Bake 12 minutes or until golden. Remove from baking sheets; cool on wire racks. Makes about 36 cookies.

Fudge Drops

8 oz. semisweet chocolate
1 tablespoon butter or margarine
2 eggs
3/4 cup sugar
1/2 teaspoon vanilla extract
1/4 cup all-purpose flour
1/4 teaspoon baking powder
1/8 teaspoon salt
3/4 cup finely chopped walnuts, pecans or almonds

Preheat oven to 350F (175C). Grease baking sheets; set aside. Melt chocolate and butter or margarine in a small saucepan over low heat. Set aside to cool. In a medium bowl, beat eggs. Beat in sugar until creamy. Stir in cooled chocolate mixture and vanilla. Blend flour, baking powder and salt; stir into chocolate mixture. Stir in nuts. Drop by teaspoons, 2 inches apart, on greased baking sheets. Bake 8 to 10 minutes. Let stand on baking sheets 2 minutes. Remove from baking sheets; cool on wire racks. Makes about 36 cookies.

Nutty Meringues

Nutty Meringues

3 egg whites
3/4 cup powdered sugar
1 teaspoon vanilla extract
4 oz. semisweet chocolate, grated
1-1/4 cups finely chopped almonds, pecans or walnuts

Preheat oven to 300F (150C). Line baking sheets with foil. In a medium bowl, beat egg whites until stiff but not dry. Gradually beat in sugar, 2 tablespoons at a time. Fold in vanilla, chocolate and nuts. Drop by tablespoons, 2 inches apart, on foil-lined baking sheets. Bake 30 to 35 minutes or until golden brown. Cool on baking sheets. Remove from foil; store in a container with a tight-fitting lid. Makes about 30 cookies.

Coconut-Meringue Rings

1 cup butter or margarine, room temperature
3/4 cup granulated sugar
1 teaspoon vanilla extract
3 eggs, separated
2 cups sifted all-purpose flour
1/2 teaspoon baking soda
1/2 cup powdered sugar, sifted
1 tablespoon grated lemon peel
2 cups flaked or shredded coconut

Preheat oven to 350F (175C). Grease baking sheets; set aside. In a medium bowl, beat butter or margarine, granulated sugar, vanilla and egg yolks until creamy. Blend flour and baking soda; gradually stir into sugar mixture. Spoon dough into a pastry bag fitted with a medium writing tip. Pipe 2-inch rings, 1-1/2 inches apart, on greased baking sheets. Beat egg whites until stiff but not dry. Beat in powdered sugar, 2 tablespoons at a time. Beat until stiff peaks form. Fold in lemon peel and coconut. Spoon coconut mixture into center of each cookie, filling centers completely. Bake 10 to 12 minutes or until edges are golden. Cool on baking sheets 2 to 3 minutes. Remove from baking sheets; cool on wire racks. Makes about 42 cookies.

Coconut Macaroons

4 egg whites
1 cup powdered sugar, sifted
1/2 teaspoon ground cinnamon
1/2 teaspoon almond extract
2 cups shredded or flaked coconut

Preheat oven to 300F (150C). Line baking sheets with foil. In a medium bowl, beat egg whites until stiff but not dry. Gradually beat in powdered sugar and cinnamon. Beat until stiff, glossy peaks form. Fold in almond extract and coconut. Drop by heaping teaspoons, 1-1/2 inches apart, on foil-lined baking sheets. Or, pipe through a pastry bag. Bake 20 to 25 minutes or until lightly browned. Cool on baking sheets. Remove cooled macaroons from foil; store in a container with a tight-fitting lid. Makes about 36 cookies.

Almond Macaroons

2 egg whites
2/3 cup sugar
1/4 teaspoon ground cinnamon
1/2 teaspoon almond extract
1/2 cup ground almonds
1/2 cup finely chopped almonds

Preheat oven to 250F (120C). Line baking sheets with foil. In a medium bowl, beat egg whites until stiff but not dry. Gradually beat in sugar and cinnamon. Beat until stiff, glossy peaks form. Beat in almond extract. Combine ground almonds and chopped almonds; fold into egg-white mixture. Drop by rounded teaspoons, 1-1/2 inches apart, on foil-lined baking sheets. Bake 30 to 35 minutes or until golden. Cool on baking sheets. Remove cooled macaroons from foil; store in a container with a tight-fitting lid. Makes about 15 cookies.

Coconut Macaroons

Sour-Cream Pretzels

Sour-Cream Pretzels

1 cup butter or margarine, room temperature
1 cup powdered sugar, sifted
1 egg
1/2 cup dairy sour cream
3 cups sifted all-purpose flour
1/2 teaspoon baking soda
1/4 cup finely chopped blanched almonds
1/4 cup granulated sugar
1 egg beaten with 1 tablespoon water for glaze

In a medium bowl, beat butter or margarine, powdered sugar, egg and sour cream until creamy. Blend flour and baking soda; gradually stir into sugar mixture. Shape dough into a flat ball. Cover; refrigerate 2 hours. Preheat oven to 400F (205C). Grease baking sheets; set aside. On a lightly floured surface, roll out 1/2 of dough until 1/2 inch thick. Cut dough into 8" x 1/2" strips. Roll strips between your hands to make ropes. Twist each rope into a pretzel. Place pretzel-shaped dough, 1-1/2 inches apart, on greased baking sheets. Repeat with remaining dough. In a small bowl, combine chopped almonds and granulated sugar. Brush each pretzel lightly with egg glaze; sprinkle with almond-sugar mixture. Bake 12 to 15 minutes or until golden brown. Remove from baking sheets; cool on wire racks. Makes about 30 cookies.

Raisin-Nut Bars

1/2 cup butter or margarine
1 cup sugar
2 cups all-purpose flour
1 teaspoon baking powder
1/2 teaspoon salt
1 cup chopped raisins
2 eggs, beaten

Nut Topping:
1 tablespoon butter or margarine
1 tablespoon lemon juice
1 teaspoon grated lemon peel
1 tablespoon boiling water
2 cups powdered sugar, sifted
1/2 cup slivered almonds or chopped walnuts

Preheat oven to 350F (175C). Grease a 13" x 9" baking pan; set aside. Melt butter or margarine in a small saucepan over low heat. Stir in sugar; set aside to cool. In a medium bowl, blend flour, baking powder and salt. Stir in raisins. Stir in cooled sugar mixture and eggs. Spread in greased pan. Bake 20 minutes. Cool in pan on a wire rack. **To make nut topping,** melt butter or margarine in a medium saucepan over low heat. Stir in lemon juice, lemon peel and water. Gradually beat in powdered sugar. Pour over cooled crust; smooth surface. Sprinkle with nuts. Allow to set. Cut into 18 bars.

Fig-Pecan Bars

1 cup coarsely chopped dried figs
2 tablespoons granulated sugar
1/2 cup orange juice
3/4 cup coarsely chopped pecans
1/2 cup butter or margarine, room temperature
1/2 cup packed dark-brown sugar
1-1/2 cups quick-cooking rolled oats
3/4 cup all-purpose flour
1 teaspoon baking powder

Preheat oven to 350F (175C). Grease an 8-inch-square baking pan; set aside. In a medium saucepan, combine figs, granulated sugar and orange juice. Stirring constantly, cook over medium heat until thickened. Stir in 1/4 cup pecans; set aside to cool. In a medium bowl, beat butter or margarine and brown sugar until creamy; stir in oats. Blend flour, baking powder and remaining 1/2 cup nuts. Stir into oat mixture. Reserve 1-1/2 cups oat mixture. Press remaining oat mixture into greased baking pan. Spread fig-nut mixture over top; cover with reserved oat mixture. Bake 30 minutes. Cool in pan on a wire rack. Cut into 12 bars.

Honey-Lemon Cookies

Honey-Lemon Cookies

1/2 cup honey
1/2 cup granulated sugar
1/4 cup butter or margarine, room temperature
2 tablespoons water
2-1/2 cups all-purpose flour
1-1/2 teaspoons baking powder
1 teaspoon ground cinnamon
1/4 cup chopped almonds or walnuts
1/4 cup chopped candied lemon peel
1 egg, beaten
1 teaspoon lemon extract
Milk
Crystal sugar or crushed sugar cubes

In a medium saucepan, combine honey, granulated sugar, butter or margarine and water. Stirring constantly, cook over low heat until butter or margarine melts and sugar dissolves. Cool to room temperature. In a large bowl, blend flour, baking powder, cinnamon, nuts and lemon peel; set aside. Stir egg and lemon extract into cooled honey mixture. Stir honey mixture into flour mixture; refrigerate 2 hours. Preheat oven to 350F (175C). Grease baking sheets. Shape refrigerated dough into slightly flattened 1-inch balls. Brush balls with milk; dip half of each ball into crystal sugar or crushed sugar cubes. Place coated balls, sugar-side up, 1 inch apart, on greased baking sheets. Bake 12 to 14 minutes or until cookies are firm. Remove from baking sheets; cool on wire racks. Makes about 42 cookies.

Frosted Fir Trees

To complete, build fir trees by placing large star cookies on a flat surface. Place a dab of icing in center of each star; cover icing with small round cookies. Place a dab of icing on each small cookie. Cover with next largest star cookies; press down lightly. Continue with remaining stars and round cookies, ending with smallest star cookies. Drizzle icing over trees, letting it drip down sides. Cover a cardboard with foil. Arrange trees on foil-covered cardboard. To make a winter scene, add small pine cones, if desired. Makes 6 fir trees.

Frosted Fir Trees

1/3 cup honey
1/4 cup packed dark-brown sugar
2 tablespoons butter or margarine
1 egg, slightly beaten
1 teaspoon vanilla extract
1-3/4 cups all-purpose flour
1/4 cup unsweetened cocoa powder
2 teaspoons baking powder
1/2 teaspoon baking soda
1/2 teaspoon salt
2 teaspoons ground cinnamon
1/2 teaspoon ground nutmeg

Snow Icing:
2 cups powdered sugar, sifted
1 egg white
1 to 2 teaspoons water

To make dough, in a small saucepan, combine honey, brown sugar and butter or margarine. Stir over low heat until butter or margarine melts and sugar dissolves. Pour into a large bowl; let stand until cool. Stir in egg and vanilla. Blend flour, cocoa powder, baking powder, baking soda, salt, cinnamon and nutmeg. Stir into honey mixture; shape into a flat ball. Wrap dough in plastic wrap or waxed paper; refrigerate 1 hour. Preheat oven to 350F (175C). Grease baking sheets; set aside.
To make trees, on a lightly floured surface, roll out dough until 1/4 inch thick. Using a 6-piece star cookie-cutter set, cut out 6 stars in each size. Gather dough scraps; reroll. Using a nickel as a guide, cut out 30 small circles. Using a wide spatula, lift stars; place stars, 1 inch apart, on greased baking sheets. Bake stars and circles 10 to 13 minutes or until cookies are firm when touched. Remove from baking sheets; cool on wire racks.
To make icing, in a small bowl, combine powdered sugar and egg white. Mixture will be stiff. Add 1 teaspoon water; beat until smooth and spreadable. Add more water, if necessary.

Medieval Castle
Photo on pages 8-9.

1 cup butter or margarine, room temperature
1/2 cup sugar
1 egg
1/3 cup honey
2-3/4 cups all-purpose flour
1 teaspoon baking powder
2 teaspoons ground cinnamon
1/2 teaspoon ground ginger
1/4 teaspoon ground cloves
1 egg white blended with 1 tablespoon water for glaze
Ground cinnamon

In a large bowl, beat butter or margarine, sugar, egg and honey until blended. Blend flour, baking powder, 2 teaspoons cinnamon, ginger and cloves. Stir into sugar mixture. Wrap dough in plastic wrap or waxed paper; refrigerate 2 hours. Preheat oven to 350F (175C). Grease a 20" x 18" baking pan or large baking sheet; set aside. On a lightly floured surface, roll out dough until 1/2 inch thick. Cut dough, using diagram at right. Using a wide flat spatula, lift dough pieces onto center of greased baking pan or sheet, so pieces barely touch. Pat seams together making 1 large cookie. Use some of remaining dough to make small balls, long thin strips, windows, arches and towers, as shown. Brush underside of each piece with egg-white glaze; attach to castle. Cut 3 or 4 free-form bushes from remaining dough; place in corners of baking pan. Lightly sprinkle cinnamon over castle and bushes. Bake 20 minutes or until edges are lightly browned. Cool in baking pan or on baking sheet on a wire rack. Carefully slide a thin piece of cardboard under castle; remove castle and cardboard from pan. Makes 1 castle.

Medieval Castle

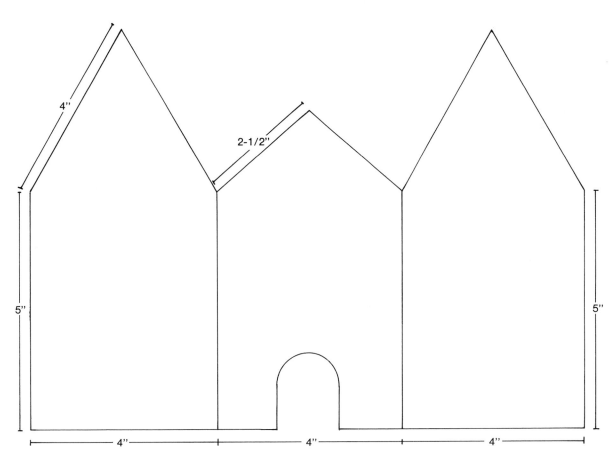

4"

2-1/2"

5"

5"

4"

4"

4"

Enlarge castle as desired.

Creative Cakes

Porcupine Cake

Chocolate Cake:
1/2 cup butter or margarine, room temperature
3/4 cup sugar
3 eggs
1 teaspoon vanilla extract
3/4 cup all-purpose flour
1/4 cup unsweetened cocoa powder
1 teaspoon baking powder
2 tablespoons milk
1/3 cup ground almonds

Chocolate Glaze:
5 oz. semisweet chocolate
4 teaspoons vegetable shortening
About 1 cup slivered almonds

To make cake, preheat oven to 325F (165C). Grease a 12" x 4" round-bottom loaf pan; set aside. In a medium bowl, beat butter or margarine and sugar until creamy. Add eggs and vanilla; beat until blended. Blend flour, cocoa powder and baking powder. Stir into sugar mixture alternately with milk. Fold in ground almonds. Pour batter into prepared pan; smooth top. Bake 40 to 45 minutes or until a wooden pick inserted in center comes out clean. Cool in pan on a wire rack 10 minutes. Remove from pan; cool on wire rack. Place cooled cake, top-side down, on a platter or cake plate.

To make glaze, in a small heavy saucepan, combine chocolate and shortening. Stir over low heat until melted and smooth. Spread glaze over cake; let stand until set. Stud cake with slivered almonds. Makes 1 cake.

Porcupine Cake

Peach Upside-Down Cake

Topping:
1/4 cup butter or margarine
1/2 cup packed light-brown sugar
1 (16-oz.) can sliced peaches, drained

Cake:
1/3 cup butter or margarine, room temperature
1 cup packed light-brown sugar
2 eggs
1-1/2 cups cake flour
1-1/2 teaspoons baking powder
1/2 teaspoon salt
1/2 teaspoon ground cloves
1/2 teaspoon ground cinnamon
1/2 teaspoon ground nutmeg
1/2 cup milk
1 tablespoon grated lemon peel
Flavored whipped cream, if desired

To make topping, preheat oven to 350F (175C). Place butter or margarine in a 9-inch-square baking pan; place in oven until melted. Stir brown sugar into melted butter or margarine; spread mixture evenly in pan. Arrange peach slices over brown-sugar mixture; set aside.

To make cake, beat butter or margarine and brown sugar in a medium bowl until creamy. Add eggs, 1 at a time, beating well after each addition. Blend cake flour, baking powder, salt, cloves, cinnamon and nutmeg. Stir into sugar mixture alternately with milk. Stir in lemon peel. Gently pour batter over peach slices; spread evenly into corners of pan. Bake 40 to 45 minutes or until a wooden pick inserted in center comes out clean. Cool in pan on a wire rack 2 minutes. Place a platter or cake plate over pan. Holding pan firmly to plate, invert pan and plate. Let stand 2 minutes; carefully remove pan. Serve warm or chilled, with whipped cream, if desired. Makes 1 cake.

On previous pages: Eggnog Gâteau, page 69.

To make cake, preheat oven to 350F (175C). Grease and flour 2 (8- or 9-inch) cake pans; set aside. In a large bowl, combine oil, sugar, eggs, molasses and vanilla; beat until blended. Blend flour, cocoa powder, baking soda, baking powder and salt. Stir into sugar mixture alternately with milk. Pour batter evenly into prepared pans; smooth tops. Bake 30 to 35 minutes or until a wooden pick inserted in center comes out clean. Cool in pans on wire racks 10 minutes. Remove from pans; cool on wire racks.

To make frosting, in a medium saucepan, combine sugar, water, cream of tartar and salt. Over medium heat, bring to a boil; stirring constantly, cook until sugar dissolves. Boil rapidly 1 minute without stirring; remove from heat. In a medium bowl, use an electric beater to beat egg whites until foamy. Slowly pour sugar syrup into egg whites in a steady stream, beating constantly until stiff peaks form. Beat in vanilla; use immediately.

To complete, place 1 cooled cake layer, bottom-side up, on a platter or cake plate. Spread with about 1/4 of frosting; top with remaining layer. Spread remaining frosting over side and top of cake. Makes 1 cake.

Chocolate-Almond Cake

Chocolate Cake:
6 eggs, separated
3/4 cup sugar
1/2 teaspoon almond extract
3/4 cup sifted cake flour
1/2 cup unsweetened cocoa powder
1/4 teaspoon salt

Chocolate-Almond Frosting:
4 oz. semisweet chocolate
1/2 cup butter or margarine
1-1/2 teaspoons almond extract
4 cups powdered sugar, sifted
1/2 cup chopped almonds

To make cake, preheat oven to 350F (175C). Grease and flour 2 (9-inch) cake pans; set aside. In a medium bowl, beat egg yolks, sugar and almond extract until creamy. In a sifter, combine cake flour, cocoa powder and salt. Gradually sift into egg-yolk mixture, folding while sifting. In a medium bowl, beat egg whites until stiff but not dry. Stir 3 heaping tablespoons beaten egg whites into batter until no white remains. Fold in remaining beaten egg whites. Pour batter evenly into prepared pans; smooth tops. Bake 30 to 35 minutes or until a wooden pick inserted in center comes out clean. Cool in pans on wire racks 10 minutes. Remove from pans; cool on wire racks.

To make frosting, in a medium saucepan, combine chocolate and butter or margarine. Over low heat, stir until melted and smooth; set aside to cool. Add almond extract. Stir in enough powdered sugar to make a good spreading consistency.

To complete, place 1 cake layer, bottom-side up, on a platter or cake plate. Spread with 1/4 of frosting; sprinkle with 1/4 cup chopped almonds. Top with remaining cake layer. Spread remaining frosting over side and top of cake. Sprinkle remaining 1/4 cup chopped almonds over top of cake. Makes 1 cake.

Cocoa Cake

Cake:
2/3 cup vegetable oil
1-1/4 cups sugar
2 eggs
2 tablespoons molasses
1 teaspoon vanilla extract
2 cups all-purpose flour
1/2 cup unsweetened cocoa powder
1 teaspoon baking soda
1 teaspoon baking powder
1/2 teaspoon salt
2/3 cup milk

Fluffy White Frosting:
1 cup sugar
1/3 cup water
1/2 teaspoon cream of tartar
1/8 teaspoon salt
2 egg whites
1 teaspoon vanilla extract

Othello Gâteau

1 recipe Chocolate Sponge Cake, page 48,
  prepared as directed below
3/4 cup ground toasted hazelnuts
6 tablespoons coffee-flavored liqueur

Mocha Butter Cream:
1 tablespoon instant-coffee powder
2 tablespoons hot water
1/2 cup butter, room temperature
2 oz. unsweetened chocolate, melted
1 (16-oz.) pkg. powdered sugar, sifted
2 to 3 tablespoons coffee-flavored liqueur

Decorations:
1/2 cup ground toasted hazelnuts
Marzipan cutouts, page 232
8 red candied cherries, halved

Prepare cake as directed, folding in 3/4 cup hazelnuts
with beaten egg whites. When cool, cut cake into 3 layers.
Sprinkle each layer with 2 tablespoons liqueur.

To make butter cream, dissolve coffee in hot water; set
aside to cool. In a medium bowl, beat butter until creamy.
Add chocolate and cooled coffee mixture; beat until
blended. Gradually beat in powdered sugar alternately
with liqueur. Continue beating until mixture is smooth
and of good spreading consistency. Refrigerate until
ready to use.

To complete, spoon 3/4 cup butter cream into a pastry
bag fitted with a star tip; set aside. Place bottom cake
layer, cut-side down, on a platter or cake plate. Spread
with a thin layer of remaining butter cream. Add middle
cake layer; spread with a thin layer of butter cream. Add
top cake layer, cut-side down. Spread remaining butter
cream over side and top of cake. Press hazelnuts around
side of cake. Pipe shells and rosettes of reserved butter
cream on top of cake, as shown. Decorate with marzipan
cutouts and candied cherries. Refrigerate until ready to
serve. Makes 1 cake.

Chocolate-Cherry Cake

Othello Gâteau

Chocolate-Cherry Cake

Cake:
1/2 cup butter or margarine, room temperature
1 cup sugar
2 teaspoons vanilla extract
2 eggs
1 cup all-purpose flour
1/4 cup unsweetened cocoa powder
1-1/2 teaspoons baking powder
1/2 teaspoon salt
1/2 cup milk
3 tablespoons kirsch or other cherry-flavored liqueur

Black & White Frosting:
1-1/2 cups whipping cream
3 tablespoons powdered sugar
2 to 3 tablespoons kirsch or other cherry-flavored liqueur
3 oz. semisweet chocolate, melted
16 maraschino cherries

To make cake, preheat oven to 350F (175C). Grease and
flour a 10-inch-square baking pan; set aside. In a medium
bowl, beat butter or margarine and sugar until creamy.
Add vanilla and eggs; beat until blended. Blend flour,
cocoa powder, baking powder and salt. Stir into sugar
mixture alternately with milk. Pour batter into prepared
pan; smooth top. Bake 20 to 25 minutes or until a wooden

Delicate Chocolate Cake

Chocolate Cake:
1 cup all-purpose flour
1 tablespoon unsweetened cocoa powder
1 teaspoon baking powder
2/3 cup butter or margarine, room temperature
1/2 cup sugar
2 eggs
4 eggs, separated
1 teaspoon vanilla extract
5 oz. semisweet chocolate, melted
2/3 cup seedless black-raspberry jam or jelly, melted

Chocolate Glaze:
4 oz. semisweet chocolate
5 tablespoons whipping cream

To make cake, preheat oven to 325F (165C). Grease a 10-inch cake pan or springform pan; set aside. In a small bowl, blend flour, cocoa powder and baking powder; set aside. In a large bowl, beat butter or margarine and sugar until creamy. Add 2 eggs, 4 egg yolks and vanilla; beat until blended. Stir in chocolate until blended. In a medium bowl, beat egg whites until stiff but not dry. Fold into sugar mixture alternately with flour mixture. Pour batter into prepared pan; smooth top. Bake 35 to 40 minutes or until a wooden pick inserted in center comes out clean. Cool in pan on a wire rack 10 minutes. Remove from pan; cool on wire rack. Cut cooled cake into 2 layers. Place bottom layer, cut-side down, on a platter or cake plate; brush with jam. Add remaining layer, cut-side down. Brush top and side of cake with jam; let stand until set.

To make glaze, in a small heavy saucepan, combine chocolate and whipping cream. Stir over low heat until melted and smooth. Spread glaze over top and side of cake; let stand until set. Do not refrigerate cake. Makes 1 cake.

pick inserted in center comes out clean. Cool in pan on a wire rack 10 minutes. Remove from pan; cool on wire rack. Place cooled cake, bottom-side up, on a platter or cake plate; poke several small holes in top of cake with tines of a fork or a small metal skewer. Sprinkle 3 tablespoons liqueur over cake; set aside.

To make frosting, in a medium bowl, whip cream until soft peaks form. Beat in powdered sugar and liqueur until stiff peaks form. Spoon 1/2 of whipped-cream mixture into a small bowl; fold in chocolate.

To complete, spread chocolate mixture over top of cake. Spoon remaining whipped-cream mixture into a pastry bag fitted with a star tip. Pipe whipped cream on top of cake in a trellis pattern. Pipe 1 rosette between each square in trellis pattern, as shown. Decorate each rosette with a cherry. Refrigerate until ready to serve. Makes 1 cake.

Delicate Chocolate Cake

Chocolate-Hazelnut Gâteau

Chocolate-Hazelnut Gâteau

Crisp Cake Layers:
2 cups all-purpose flour
1 cup finely ground hazelnuts
3/4 cup sugar
1 tablespoon unsweetened cocoa powder
2 teaspoons baking powder
1/2 teaspoon salt
1 cup butter or margarine, chilled
4 egg yolks, beaten
2 oz. milk chocolate
2 tablespoons whipping cream

Whipped-Cream Filling:
1 (1/4-oz.) envelope unflavored gelatin powder
3 tablespoons warm water
3 cups whipping cream (1-1/2 pints)
1 tablespoon vanilla extract
1/2 cup powdered sugar, sifted

To make cake layers, preheat oven to 375F (190C). Grease bottom of a 10-inch springform pan. In a medium bowl, blend flour, hazelnuts, sugar, cocoa powder, baking powder and salt. Use a pastry blender or 2 knives to cut in butter or margarine until mixture resembles coarse crumbs. Add egg yolks; toss with a fork until mixture binds together. Gather dough into a ball; divide into 4 equal pieces. Press 1 piece of dough evenly into bottom of prepared pan. Lightly prick with a fork. Bake 12 to 15 minutes or until edges are lightly browned. Cool in pan on a wire rack 5 minutes. Carefully remove from pan; cool on wire rack. Repeat with remaining dough, making 3 more layers. When last layer is taken from oven, immediately cut into 14 equal wedges. *Do not cool before cutting.* In a small heavy saucepan, heat chocolate and cream over low heat, stirring until smooth. Set aside to cool. Spread cooled chocolate mixture over top of each wedge. Place wedges, chocolate-side up, on a wire rack; let stand until chocolate sets.
To make filling, in a small saucepan, combine gelatin and water; let stand 3 minutes. Stir over low heat until gelatin dissolves; set aside to cool. In a large bowl, whip cream until soft peaks form. Stir in cooled gelatin mixture, vanilla and powdered sugar; beat until stiff peaks form. Spoon 1/2 of whipped-cream mixture into a large pastry bag fitted with a star tip.
To complete, place 1 cake layer on a flat surface. On top, pipe 14 spokes of whipped-cream mixture, starting at center and piping to outside edge. Arrange chocolate wedges at an angle between each spoke; set aside. Spoon remaining whipped-cream mixture into pastry bag. Pipe in spirals, starting from center and covering each layer. On a flat platter or pedestal cake dish, stack layers with decorated layer on top. Refrigerate until ready to serve. Makes 1 cake.

Variation

Substitute 2 oz. semisweet chocolate and 2 teaspoons vegetable shortening for milk chocolate and whipping cream used for coating wedges. Prepare as directed above.

Devil's Food Cake

Cake:
3/4 cup unsweetened cocoa powder
1/2 cup boiling water
1 cup butter or margarine, room temperature
2 cups sugar
4 eggs
2 teaspoons vanilla extract
2-1/4 cups cake flour
2 teaspoons baking soda
1/2 teaspoon baking powder
1 teaspoon salt
1 cup buttermilk

Mocha Frosting:
1/2 cup butter or margarine, room temperature
2 oz. semisweet chocolate, melted
1 tablespoon instant-coffee powder dissolved in
   2 tablespoons boiling water
4 cups powdered sugar, sifted

To make cake, preheat oven to 350F (175C). Grease and flour 2 (9-inch) cake pans; set aside. Dissolve cocoa powder in boiling water; set aside. In a large bowl, beat butter or margarine and sugar until creamy. Beat in eggs, 1 at a time, beating well after each addition. Stir in cocoa mixture and vanilla until blended. Blend cake flour, baking soda, baking powder and salt. Stir into sugar mixture alternately with buttermilk. Pour batter evenly into prepared pans; smooth tops. Bake 25 to 30 minutes or until a wooden pick inserted in center comes out clean. Cool in pans on wire racks 10 minutes. Remove from pans; cool on wire racks.
To make frosting, in a medium bowl, beat butter or margarine and chocolate until blended. Add coffee mixture. Stir in enough powdered sugar to make a good spreading consistency; beat until smooth.
To complete, place 1 cooled cake layer, bottom-side up, on a platter or cake plate. Spread with 1/4 of frosting; top with remaining layer. Spread remaining frosting over side and top of cake. Makes 1 cake.

Chocolate-Rum Gâteau

Rum Cake:
3/4 cup butter or margarine, room temperature
1 cup sugar
1 teaspoon vanilla extract
4 eggs
1-1/2 cups cake flour
1/4 cup unsweetened cocoa powder, sifted
2 teaspoons baking powder
3 tablespoons dark rum

Chocolate-Rum Butter Cream:
1/2 cup butter, room temperature
4 oz. unsweetened chocolate, melted
2 egg yolks
1 teaspoon vanilla extract
1 (16-oz.) pkg. powdered sugar, sifted
2 to 3 tablespoons dark rum
2 to 3 oz. semisweet chocolate, finely grated
8 small chocolate candies, if desired

To make cake, preheat oven to 350F (175C). Grease and flour a 10-inch springform pan or deep cake pan. In a large bowl, beat butter or margarine and sugar until creamy. Add vanilla and eggs; beat until blended. Blend cake flour, cocoa powder and baking powder. Stir into sugar mixture alternately with rum. Pour batter into prepared pan; smooth top. Bake 40 to 45 minutes or until a wooden pick inserted in center comes out clean. Cool in pan on a wire rack 10 minutes. Remove from pan; cool on wire rack. Cut cooled cake into 2 layers.

To make butter cream, in a medium bowl, combine butter, chocolate, egg yolks and vanilla; beat until blended. Gradually stir in powdered sugar alternately with rum, beating well after each addition. Continue beating until mixture is fluffy and of good spreading consistency.

To complete, spoon 1 cup butter cream into a pastry bag fitted with a star tip; set aside. Place bottom cake layer, cut-side down, on a platter or cake plate. Spread with 1/3 of remaining butter cream. Add remaining cake layer, cut-side down. Frost top and side with remaining butter cream. Press grated chocolate around side of cake. Pipe 16 spirals of reserved butter cream on top of cake. Decorate cake with small chocolate candies, if desired. Refrigerate until ready to serve. Makes 1 cake.

Chocolate-Rum Gâteau

Glazed Spice Cake

Spice Cake:
1/2 cup vegetable shortening
1-1/4 cups packed light-brown sugar
2 eggs
1-1/2 teaspoons vanilla extract
2 cups all-purpose flour
1-1/2 teaspoons baking powder
1/2 teaspoon baking soda
1/2 teaspoon salt
2 teaspoons ground cinnamon
1 teaspoon ground nutmeg
1/2 teaspoon ground cloves
1 cup evaporated milk

Glaze:
1-1/2 cups powdered sugar, sifted
1 to 2 tablespoons milk

To make cake, preheat oven to 350F (175C). Grease and flour a 13" x 9" baking pan. In a large bowl, beat shortening, brown sugar, eggs and vanilla until creamy. Blend flour, baking powder, baking soda, salt, cinnamon, nutmeg and cloves. Stir into egg mixture alternately with milk. Pour batter into prepared pan; smooth top. Bake 35 to 40 minutes or until a wooden pick inserted in center comes out clean. Cool in pan on a wire rack.

To make glaze, in a small bowl, blend powdered sugar and milk until smooth. Spread glaze over cake; let stand until glaze sets. Cut into squares; serve from pan. Makes 1 cake.

Chocolate-Apricot Gâteau

Chocolate-Apricot Gâteau

Shortbread:
1 cup sifted all-purpose flour
3 tablespoons sugar
6 tablespoons butter or margarine, chilled

Chocolate Genoise:
4 eggs
2/3 cup sugar
1 teaspoon vanilla extract
3/4 cup sifted cake flour
2 tablespoons unsweetened cocoa powder
1/4 cup Clarified Butter, page 232

Apricot Cream:
1 (30-oz.) can apricot halves
Water
2 tablespoons cornstarch
2 tablespoons granulated sugar
1 tablespoon lemon juice
2 teaspoons unflavored gelatin powder
2 tablespoons warm water
2 cups whipping cream (1 pint)
1-1/2 teaspoons vanilla extract
1/4 cup powdered sugar, sifted
3 tablespoons apricot jam, melted, cooled
1/2 cup finely chopped toasted almonds

To make shortbread, preheat oven to 400F (205C). Grease bottom of a 10-inch springform pan; set aside. In a medium bowl, blend flour and sugar. Use a pastry blender or 2 knives to cut in butter or margarine until mixture resembles coarse crumbs. Knead dough in bowl 10 strokes or until smooth. Pat or press dough into bottom of greased pan. Bake 10 to 12 minutes or until edges are golden. Cool in pan on a wire rack. Remove from pan; set aside. Wash and dry pan.

To make genoise, preheat oven to 350F (175C). Grease bottom of a 10-inch springform pan. Line bottom with waxed paper. Grease and flour paper and side of pan. Place eggs in a large bowl; set bowl over a pan of very hot water. Let stand until eggs are warm to the touch, about 5 minutes. Keeping bowl in hot water, beat eggs until thick and fluffy, about 5 minutes. Gradually beat in granulated sugar until mixture falls in thick ribbons from beaters, 10 to 12 minutes. Beat in vanilla; remove bowl from water. In a sifter, combine cake flour and cocoa powder. Gradually sift over egg mixture, folding in while sifting. Fold in clarified butter only until streaks of butter disappear. Spread batter in prepared pan; smooth top. Bake 25 to 30 minutes or until a wooden pick inserted in center comes out clean. Cool in pan on a wire rack 10 minutes. Remove from pan; peel off paper. Cool on wire rack. Cut cooled cake into 2 layers.

To make apricot cream, drain apricot syrup into a 1-cup measure. Reserve 12 apricot halves; set aside. Coarsely chop remaining apricots. Add enough water to apricot syrup to make 1 cup liquid; pour into a small saucepan. Stir in cornstarch and granulated sugar until mixture is smooth. Over low heat, cook, stirring constantly, until mixture thickens and comes to a boil. Stir in lemon juice and chopped apricots; cool to room temperature. In a small saucepan, combine gelatin and 2 tablespoons warm water; let stand 3 minutes. Stir over low heat until gelatin dissolves; set aside to cool. In a medium bowl, whip cream until soft peaks form. Stir in cooled gelatin mixture, vanilla and powdered sugar. Beat until stiff peaks form. Fold cooled apricot mixture into 1/2 of whipped-cream mixture. Spoon 3/4 cup remaining whipped-cream mixture into a pastry bag fitted with a star tip. Refrigerate apricot mixture and whipped-cream mixture.

To complete, place shortbread on a flat platter or cake plate; brush with jam. Let stand until set. Place bottom genoise layer, cut-side down, over shortbread base; spread with Apricot Cream. Add remaining genoise layer, cut-side down. Spread remaining whipped-cream mixture over side and top of cake. Press almonds onto side of cake. Pipe swirls and ripples of reserved whipped-cream mixture on top of cake. Decorate with reserved apricot halves. Refrigerate until ready to serve. Makes 1 cake.

Nutty Pound Cake

Nutty Pound Cake

Pound Cake:
1-1/4 cups butter or margarine, room temperature
1-3/4 cups sugar
6 eggs
2 teaspoons vanilla extract
2-1/2 cups sifted cake flour
2 teaspoons baking powder
1/2 cup milk
1-1/2 cups ground walnuts, pecans, almonds or hazelnuts
1 teaspoon rum extract

Chocolate Glaze:
5 oz. semisweet chocolate
4 teaspoons vegetable shortening

Decorator's Icing:
1 tablespoon stirred egg white
1 teaspoon water
1 cup powdered sugar, sifted
Silver or colored dragees

To make cake, preheat oven to 350F (175C). Grease and flour a 12-cup Bundt pan or similar cake pan. In a large bowl, beat butter or margarine and sugar until creamy. Add 5 eggs and vanilla; beat until blended. Blend cake flour and baking powder. Gradually stir into sugar mixture alternately with 1/4 cup milk. Pour batter into prepared pan. In a medium bowl, stir together remaining egg, remaining 1/4 cup milk, ground nuts and rum extract. Spoon over top of batter. Cut through batter with a small spatula to create a marbled effect; smooth top. Bake 55 to 60 minutes or until a wooden pick inserted in center comes out clean. Cool in pan on a wire rack 15 minutes. Remove from pan; cool on wire rack. Place cooled cake, top-side down, on a platter or cake plate.

To make glaze, in a small heavy saucepan, combine chocolate and shortening. Over low heat, stir until smooth. Spread glaze over cooled cake; let stand until set.

To make icing, in a small bowl, beat egg white and water until foamy. Gradually beat in powdered sugar until icing is very stiff. Spoon icing into a pastry bag fitted with a small plain writing tip. Pipe tiny dots in a decorative design over cake. Decorate dots with dragees. Makes 1 cake.

Cherry-Chocolate Slices

Cherry-Chocolate Slices

Shortbread Crust:
3/4 cup all-purpose flour
2 tablespoons sugar
1/2 teaspoon baking powder
6 tablespoons butter or margarine, chilled

Cake:
3 eggs, separated
1/4 cup warm water
1 teaspoon vanilla extract
1/2 cup sugar
3/4 cup sifted cake flour
1/4 cup unsweetened cocoa powder
1-1/2 teaspoons baking powder

Filling:
1 (16-oz.) can pitted tart red cherries
4 teaspoons cornstarch
1 tablespoon granulated sugar
1 teaspoon lemon juice
1 tablespoon kirsch or other cherry-flavored liqueur
1-1/2 cups whipping cream
1-1/2 teaspoons vanilla extract
3 tablespoons powdered sugar

To make crust, preheat oven to 375F (190C). Grease bottom of an 11'' x 7'' baking pan. In a medium bowl, blend flour, sugar and baking powder. Use a pastry blender or 2 knives to cut in butter or margarine until mixture resembles coarse crumbs. Press dough onto bottom of greased pan. Bake 10 to 12 minutes or until golden brown. Cool in pan on a wire rack 15 minutes. Carefully remove from pan; cool on wire rack. Wash and dry pan.

To make cake, preheat oven to 375F (190C). Grease and flour bottom and side of an 11'' x 7'' baking pan. In a medium bowl, beat egg yolks and water until foamy. Add vanilla and sugar; beat until thick and pale. In a sifter, combine cake flour, cocoa powder and baking powder. Gradually sift into egg-yolk mixture, folding in while sifting. In another medium bowl, beat egg whites until stiff but not dry; fold into batter. Pour batter into prepared pan; smooth top. Bake 15 to 20 minutes or until a wooden pick inserted in center comes out clean. Cool in pan on a wire rack 10 minutes. Remove from pan; cool on wire rack. Cut cooled cake into 2 layers.

To make filling, drain cherries, reserving syrup. Coarsely chop cherries; set aside. In a small saucepan, combine cornstarch, granulated sugar, lemon juice and reserved cherry syrup; stir until blended. Over low heat, cook, stirring, until mixture thickens and comes to a boil; set aside to cool. Stir in liqueur and chopped cherries. Cool before using.

To complete, in a medium bowl, whip cream until soft peaks form. Add vanilla and powdered sugar; beat until stiff peaks form. Refrigerate until ready to use. Reserve 1/4 cup cherry mixture and 3/4 cup whipped-cream mixture for decoration. Place shortbread crust on a flat platter or cake plate. Spread with remaining cherry filling. Place 1 cake layer, cut-side down, over cherry filling; spread with 1/2 of remaining whipped-cream mixture. Top with remaining cake layer, cut-side down; spread with remaining whipped-cream mixture. Spoon reserved whipped-cream mixture into a small pastry bag fitted with a star tip; pipe in swirls or rosettes on top of cake. Decorate swirls with reserved cherry mixture. Refrigerate until ready to serve. Makes 1 cake.

Chocolate-Cream Cake

Chocolate-Cream Cake

1 recipe 3-Egg Sponge Cake, page 68

Chocolate Glaze:
4 oz. semisweet chocolate
1 tablespoon vegetable shortening
3 oz. semisweet chocolate, melted

Cream Filling:
2 teaspoons unflavored gelatin powder
3 tablespoons warm water
2 cups whipping cream (1 pint)
1/4 cup powdered sugar, sifted
3 to 4 tablespoons white crème de cacao
2 tablespoons unsweetened cocoa powder, sifted
1 tablespoon powdered sugar
Chocolate curls

Prepare cake as directed. Cut cooled cake into 2 layers.
To make glaze, in a small heavy saucepan, melt chocolate and shortening over low heat. Stir until smooth; set aside to cool. Place bottom cake layer, cut-side down, on a wire rack. Spread glaze over layer, covering completely; let stand until set.
To make filling, in a small saucepan, combine gelatin and water; let stand 3 minutes. Stir over low heat until gelatin dissolves; set aside to cool. In a medium bowl, whip cream until soft peaks form. Add cooled gelatin mixture, 1/4 cup powdered sugar and crème de cacao; beat until stiff peaks form. Spoon 1 cup filling into a pastry bag fitted with a star tip. Fold chocolate into remaining filling.
To complete, place unglazed cake layer on a platter or cake plate; spread with about 1/4 of Cream Filling. Add glazed layer, chocolate-side up. Spread remaining Cream Filling over side of cake. In a small bowl, combine cocoa powder and 1 tablespoon powdered sugar; pat over side of cake. Pipe 12 swirls of Cream Filling on top of cake. Refrigerate until ready to serve. To serve, arrange chocolate curls on center of cake. Makes 1 cake.

Truffle Gâteau

Chocolate Sponge Cake:
4 eggs, separated
1/4 cup warm water
1 teaspoon vanilla extract
3/4 cup sugar
1-1/2 cups sifted cake flour
1/4 cup unsweetened cocoa powder
2 teaspoons baking powder
1/2 teaspoon baking soda

Chocolate-Truffle Filling:
3/4 cup butter or margarine, room temperature
3/4 cup unsweetened cocoa powder, sifted
1-1/2 cups sifted powdered sugar
1 egg, beaten
1 tablespoon dark rum
2 to 3 tablespoons warm water

Chocolate Glaze:
4 oz. semisweet chocolate
1 tablespoon butter or margarine
2 tablespoons whipping cream
Chocolate sprinkles

Truffle Gâteau

To make cake, preheat oven to 375F (190C). Grease and flour a 10-inch springform pan or deep cake pan; set aside. In a large bowl, beat egg yolks and water until foamy. Add vanilla and sugar; beat until thick and pale. In a sifter, combine cake flour, cocoa powder, baking powder and baking soda. Gradually sift over egg-yolk mixture, folding in while sifting. Beat egg whites until stiff but not dry; fold into batter. Pour batter into prepared pan; smooth top. Bake 20 to 25 minutes or until a wooden pick inserted in center comes out clean. Cool in pan on wire rack 10 minutes. Remove from pan; cool on wire rack. Cut cooled cake into 3 layers.

To make filling, in a medium bowl, beat butter or margarine until fluffy. Blend cocoa powder and powdered sugar; gradually add to butter alternately with egg and rum; beat until blended. Shape 16 teaspoons of filling into 16 small balls. Refrigerate until needed. Add 2 tablespoons warm water to remaining filling. Beat until blended and mixture is of spreading consistency. Add remaining 1 tablespoon water, if necessary.

To make glaze, in a small heavy saucepan, heat chocolate, butter or margarine and cream over low heat, stirring until smooth. Set aside to cool.

To complete, place bottom cake layer, cut-side down, on a platter or cake plate. Spread with 1/2 of filling. Add middle cake layer; spread with remaining filling. Add top layer, cut-side down. Pour Chocolate Glaze over cake; spread evenly over side and top of cake. Press chocolate sprinkles around side and top rim of cake. Roll reserved truffle balls in sprinkles; arrange on top of cake. Makes 1 cake.

Banana Layer Cake

Banana Cake:
1/2 cup butter or margarine, room temperature
3/4 cup granulated sugar
1/2 cup packed light-brown sugar
2 eggs
1-1/2 cups mashed ripe bananas (about 3 medium bananas)
1 teaspoon vanilla extract
2-1/2 cups all-purpose flour
2 teaspoons baking powder
1-1/4 teaspoons baking soda
1/2 teaspoon ground cloves
1/2 teaspoon ground nutmeg
1/2 teaspoon salt
1/2 cup buttermilk

Cream-Cheese Frosting:
1/4 cup butter or margarine, room temperature
1 (3-oz.) pkg. cream cheese, room temperature
1 teaspoon vanilla extract
3 tablespoons milk
4 cups powdered sugar, sifted

To make cake, preheat oven to 350F (175C). Grease and flour 2 (9-inch) cake pans; set aside. In a large bowl, beat butter or margarine and sugars until creamy. Beat in eggs until blended. Stir in bananas and vanilla. Blend flour, baking powder, baking soda, cloves, nutmeg and salt. Stir into sugar mixture alternately with buttermilk. Pour batter evenly into prepared pans; smooth tops. Bake 30 to 35 minutes or until a wooden pick inserted in center comes out clean. Cool in pans on wire racks 10 minutes. Remove from pans; cool on wire racks.

To make frosting, in a medium bowl, beat butter or margarine, cream cheese and vanilla until creamy. Stir in milk until blended. Gradually stir in enough powdered sugar to make a good spreading consistency; beat until smooth.

To complete, place 1 cake layer, bottom-side up, on a platter or cake plate. Spread cake layer with about 1/4 of frosting; top with remaining layer. Spread remaining frosting over side and top of cake. Makes 1 cake.

Black Forest Gâteau

Marble Cake

Black Forest Gâteau

1 recipe Chocolate Sponge Cake, page 48
6 tablespoons kirsch or other cherry-flavored liqueur

Cherry Filling:
2 (16-oz.) cans pitted tart red cherries
Water
2 tablespoons cornstarch
3 tablespoons sugar

Frosting:
2 teaspoons unflavored gelatin powder
2 tablespoons warm water
2 cups whipping cream (1 pint)
1/4 cup powdered sugar, sifted
2 to 3 tablespoons kirsch or other cherry-flavored liqueur
Chocolate curls

Prepare cake as directed. Cut cooled cake into 3 layers. Place layers on a flat surface; sprinkle each with 2 tablespoons liqueur. Let stand 2 hours.
To make filling, drain cherry syrup into a 2-cup measure. Cut drained cherries in half; set aside. Add enough water to cherry syrup to make 1-1/4 cups; pour into a small saucepan. Stir in cornstarch and sugar. Over low heat, cook, stirring, until mixture thickens and comes to a boil. Stir in reserved cut cherries; cook 1 minute. Cool to room temperature.
To make frosting, in a small saucepan, combine gelatin and water; let stand 3 minutes. Stir over low heat until gelatin dissolves; set aside to cool. In a medium bowl, whip cream until soft peaks form. Add cooled gelatin mixture, powdered sugar and liqueur; beat until stiff peaks form. Refrigerate until ready to use.
To complete, place bottom cake layer, cut-side down, on a platter or cake plate. Spread with 1/2 of Cherry Filling. Spread 1 cup frosting over Cherry Filling. Add middle layer; spread with remaining Cherry Filling and 1 cup frosting. Add top layer, cut-side down; spread remaining frosting over side and top of cake. Decorate with chocolate curls. Refrigerate until ready to serve. Makes 1 cake.

Marble Cake

3 oz. semisweet chocolate
1-1/4 cups milk or half and half
3/4 cup butter or margarine, room temperature
1-1/4 cups sugar
1 teaspoon rum extract or almond extract
3 eggs
2-1/2 cups all-purpose flour
2-1/2 teaspoons baking powder
1/2 teaspoon salt

Preheat oven to 350F (175C). Grease and flour a 10-cup turk's-head mold or 12-cup Bundt pan. In a small saucepan, combine chocolate and 1/4 cup milk or half and half. Stir over low heat until chocolate melts and mixture is smooth; set aside to cool. In a large bowl, beat butter or margarine and sugar until creamy. Add rum or almond extract and eggs; beat until blended. Blend flour, baking powder and salt. Stir into sugar mixture alternately with remaining 1 cup milk or half and half. Pour 2/3 of batter into prepared pan. Add cooled chocolate mixture to remaining batter; beat until blended. Spoon chocolate batter over plain batter in pan. To marble batter, swirl a small spatula through batters; smooth top. Bake 60 to 65 minutes or until a wooden pick inserted in center comes out clean. Cool in pan on a wire rack 10 minutes. Remove from pan; cool on wire rack. Place cooled cake, top-side down, on a platter or cake plate. Makes 1 cake.

Chocolate-Orange Gâteau

Choco-Pineapple Gâteau

Cake:
3 eggs, separated
3 tablespoons warm water
1 teaspoon vanilla extract
1/2 cup sugar
1 cup sifted cake flour
1 tablespoon unsweetened cocoa powder
1 teaspoon baking powder
4 oz. semisweet chocolate, grated
1/4 cup ground toasted hazelnuts or almonds

Chocolate Glaze:
3 oz. semisweet chocolate
1 tablespoon vegetable shortening

Pineapple Filling:
2 teaspoons unflavored gelatin powder
3 tablespoons warm water
1 (10-oz.) jar pineapple preserves or jam
3 tablespoons brandy or cognac
2 cups whipping cream (1 pint)
1/4 cup powdered sugar, sifted
1 (20-oz.) can pineapple tidbits, drained
1/3 cup ground toasted hazelnuts or almonds
Silver or gold dragees

Chocolate-Orange Gâteau

1 recipe Chocolate Genoise, page 44
6 tablespoons orange-flavored liqueur or orange juice
Orange marmalade

Orange Frosting:
2 teaspoons unflavored gelatin powder
3 tablespoons orange juice
2 cups whipping cream (1 pint)
1-1/2 teaspoons orange extract
1/4 cup powdered sugar, sifted
Candied orange peel

Prepare cake as directed. Cut cooled cake into 2 layers. Place layers on a flat surface; sprinkle each layer with 3 tablespoons liqueur or orange juice.

To make frosting, in a small saucepan, combine gelatin and orange juice; let stand 5 minutes. Stir over low heat until gelatin dissolves; set aside to cool. In a medium bowl, whip cream until soft peaks form. Add cooled gelatin mixture, orange extract and powdered sugar; beat until stiff peaks form. Refrigerate until ready to use. Spoon 1/2 of frosting into a pastry bag fitted with a large writing tip. Spoon 3/4 cup remaining frosting into a pastry bag fitted with a star tip; set aside.

To complete, place bottom cake layer, cut-side down, on a platter or cake plate. Spoon 1 tablespoon orange marmalade onto center of cake. Using large writing tip, pipe a thick circle of frosting around marmalade. Pipe 3 more thick circles of frosting around top of cake, about 1/2 inch apart. Fill spaces between circles with marmalade. Add remaining cake layer, cut-side down. Spread remaining frosting over side and top of cake. Using star tip, pipe 12 rosettes on top of cake. Decorate each rosette with a piece of candied orange peel. Refrigerate until ready to serve. Makes 1 cake.

To make cake, preheat oven to 350F (175C). Grease and flour a 10-inch springform pan or deep cake pan; set aside. In a medium bowl, beat egg yolks and water until foamy. Add vanilla and sugar; beat until thick and pale. In a sifter, combine cake flour, cocoa powder and baking powder. Gradually sift into egg-yolk mixture, folding in while sifting. In another medium bowl, beat egg whites until stiff but not dry; fold into batter. Carefully fold in chocolate and nuts. Pour batter into prepared pan; smooth top. Bake 25 to 30 minutes or until a wooden pick inserted in center comes out clean. Cool in pan on a wire rack 10 minutes. Remove from pan; cool on wire rack. Cut cooled cake into 2 layers.

To make glaze, in a small heavy saucepan, melt chocolate and shortening over low heat. Stir until smooth; set aside to cool. Place 1 cake layer, cut-side down, on a wire rack. Spread with Chocolate Glaze, covering completely. Let stand until glaze sets.

To make filling, in a small saucepan, combine gelatin and water; let stand 3 minutes. Stir over low heat until gelatin dissolves; set aside to cool. Press pineapple preserves or jam through a sieve into a small bowl. Stir in brandy or cognac and cooled gelatin mixture; set aside. In a medium bowl, whip cream until soft peaks form. Add powdered sugar; beat until stiff peaks form. Spoon 3/4 cup whipped-cream mixture into a pastry bag fitted with a star tip. Reserve another 1 cup whipped-cream mixture; refrigerate. Fold gelatin mixture into remaining whipped cream; refrigerate 30 minutes.

To complete, reserve 8 pineapple tidbits for decoration. Place unglazed cake layer on a platter or cake plate. Arrange remaining pineapple tidbits on top. Spread with pineapple mixture. Add chocolate-glazed cake layer, chocolate-side up. Frost side of cake with 1 cup reserved whipped-cream mixture. Press ground nuts onto frosted side of cake. Pipe whipped-cream rosettes around edge and on center top of cake. Arrange 8 reserved pineapple tidbits on center of cake. Decorate each rosette with a dragee. Refrigerate until ready to serve. Makes 1 cake.

Choco-Pineapple Gâteau

Rich Chocolate Cake

Chocolate Cake:
3/4 cup butter or margarine, room temperature
1-1/2 cups packed light-brown sugar
1 teaspoon vanilla extract
3 eggs
4 oz. unsweetened chocolate, melted
2 cups all-purpose flour
1-1/2 teaspoons baking soda
1/2 teaspoon baking powder
1/2 teaspoon salt
1 cup milk
1/2 cup raspberry or strawberry jam

Chocolate Frosting:
6 tablespoons butter or margarine, room temperature
2 oz. unsweetened chocolate, melted
1-1/2 teaspoons vanilla extract
3 tablespoons whipping cream
3 cups powdered sugar, sifted

To make cake, preheat oven to 350F (175C). Grease and flour 2 (9-inch) cake pans; set aside. In a large bowl, beat butter or margarine, brown sugar and vanilla until light and fluffy. Add eggs, 1 at a time, beating well after each addition. Stir in chocolate. Blend flour, baking soda, baking powder and salt. Stir into sugar mixture alternately with milk. Pour batter evenly into prepared pans; smooth tops. Bake 25 to 30 minutes or until a wooden pick inserted in center comes out clean. Cool in pans on wire racks 10 minutes. Remove from pans; cool on wire racks. Place 1 cooled cake layer, bottom-side up, on a platter or cake plate. Spread with jam; top with remaining layer.
To make frosting, in a medium bowl, combine butter or margarine, chocolate and vanilla; stir until blended. Stir in whipping cream. Stir in enough powdered sugar to make a good spreading consistency; beat until smooth. Spread frosting over side and top of cake. Makes 1 cake.

Chocolate-Marmalade Gâteau

1 recipe Chocolate Sponge Cake, page 48

Orange-Flavored Frosting:
1 (1/4-oz.) envelope unflavored gelatin powder
1/4 cup warm water
2-1/2 cups whipping cream
5 tablespoons powdered sugar, sifted
3 to 4 tablespoons orange-flavored liqueur
Grated peel of 1 orange, if desired
Orange marmalade
Orange segments

Prepare cake as directed. When cool, cut cake into 3 layers.
To make frosting, in a small saucepan, combine gelatin and water; let stand 3 minutes. Stir over low heat until gelatin dissolves; set aside to cool. In a large bowl, whip cream until soft peaks form. Add cooled gelatin mixture, powdered sugar and liqueur. Beat until stiff peaks form. Reserve 1 cup frosting in a pastry bag fitted with a star tip; refrigerate. Fold orange peel into remaining frosting. Refrigerate until ready to use.
To complete, place bottom layer, cut-side down, on a platter or cake plate. Spread with a thin layer of marmalade. Top with a thin layer of frosting. Add middle cake layer; spread with thin layers of marmalade and frosting. Add top cake layer, cut-side down. Spread frosting over side and top of cake. Pipe rosettes and small shells of reserved frosting on top of cake. Decorate with orange segments. Refrigerate until ready to serve. Makes 1 cake.

Chocolate-Marmalade Gâteau

Glazed Pound Cake

Glazed Pound Cake

Cake:
1-1/2 cups butter or margarine, room temperature
1-1/4 cups sugar
4 eggs
2 teaspoons vanilla extract or 1 teaspoon almond extract
2-3/4 cups cake flour
1-1/2 teaspoons baking powder

Chocolate Glaze:
5 oz. semisweet chocolate
1/4 cup vegetable shortening

Decorator's Icing:
1 tablespoon stirred egg white
1 teaspoon water
1 cup powdered sugar, sifted

To make cake, preheat oven to 325F (165C). Grease and flour a 9-cup gugelhupf pan or similar cake pan. In a large bowl, beat butter or margarine and sugar until creamy. Add eggs and vanilla or almond extract; beat until blended. Blend cake flour and baking powder; gradually stir into sugar mixture. Pour batter into prepared pan; smooth top. Bake 60 to 65 minutes or until a wooden pick inserted in center comes out clean. Cool in pan on a wire rack 15 minutes. Remove from pan; cool on wire rack. Place cooled cake, top-side down, on a platter or cake plate.
To make glaze, in a small heavy saucepan, combine chocolate and shortening. Over low heat, stir until melted and smooth. Spread glaze over cake; let stand until set.
To make icing, in a small bowl, beat egg white and water until foamy. Gradually beat in powdered sugar until icing is very stiff. Spoon icing into a pastry bag fitted with a small star tip. Pipe tiny rosettes on top and side of cake. Makes 1 cake.

Kirsch Cake

Sponge Cake:
1/2 cup butter or margarine, room temperature
1/2 cup sugar
1 teaspoon vanilla extract
2 eggs, separated
3/4 cup cake flour
1 teaspoon baking powder

Meringue Layers:
4 egg whites
1 cup sugar
1 teaspoon vanilla extract
1 cup ground almonds

Kirsch Syrup:
1/2 cup sugar
1/4 cup water
3 tablespoons kirsch or other cherry-flavored liqueur

Kirsch Butter Cream:
6 egg yolks
3/4 cup granulated sugar
1/2 cup water
1-1/2 cups butter
2 to 3 tablespoons kirsch or other cherry-flavored liqueur
1/2 cup sliced almonds
Powdered sugar

To make cake, preheat oven to 350F (175C). Grease bottom of a 9-inch springform pan. Line bottom with waxed paper. Grease and flour paper and side of pan. In a medium bowl, beat butter or margarine and sugar until creamy. Add vanilla and egg yolks; beat until blended. In a sifter, combine cake flour and baking powder. Gradually sift over egg mixture, folding in while sifting. In another medium bowl, beat egg whites until stiff but not dry; fold into batter. Pour batter into prepared pan; smooth top. Bake 20 to 25 minutes or until a wooden pick inserted in center comes out clean. Cool in pan on a wire rack 10 minutes. Remove from pan; cool on wire rack.
To make meringue layers, preheat oven to 225F (105C). Grease 2 round 9-inch cake pans. Line pan bottoms with parchment paper; grease paper. In a large bowl, beat egg whites until stiff but not dry. Gradually beat in sugar, 2 tablespoons at a time, beating well after each addition. Sugar should be dissolved before next addition. Continue beating until stiff, glossy peaks form. Beat in vanilla. Fold in almonds. Spread meringue mixture evenly in prepared pans. Bake 30 to 40 minutes or until golden. Turn off oven; leave meringues in closed oven 20 minutes. Cool in pans on wire racks. Remove from pans; peel off paper.
To make syrup, in a small saucepan, combine sugar and water. Stirring constantly over medium heat, bring to a boil. Continue stirring until sugar dissolves. Boil rapidly without stirring until mixture is syrupy, 3 to 5 minutes. Cool to room temperature. Stir in liqueur.
To make butter cream, in a medium bowl, beat egg yolks until smooth; set aside. In a medium saucepan, combine granulated sugar and water. Stirring constantly over medium heat, bring to a boil. Boil gently until syrup reaches 240F (115C) on a candy thermometer, about 5 minutes. Beating constantly, pour syrup into beaten egg yolks in a thin, steady stream. Beat until mixture is pale and cool; set aside. In another medium bowl, beat butter until creamy and fluffy. Gradually beat creamed butter into egg-yolk mixture until all butter has been added.

Add liqueur; beat until blended. Continue beating until mixture is fluffy and of good spreading consistency. Refrigerate until ready to use.

To complete, brush bottom, top and side of sponge cake with syrup. Place 1 meringue layer on a flat platter or cake plate; spread with 1/4 of butter cream. Place sponge cake on top. Spread with 1/4 of butter cream. Place remaining meringue layer on top. Spread remaining butter cream over side and top of cake. Press sliced almonds around side of cake; dust top with powdered sugar. Using blunt edge of a knife, score cake top in a trellis pattern. Refrigerate until ready to serve. Makes 1 cake.

Prince Regent Cake

Cake:
1 (7-oz.) pkg. marzipan or Marzipan, page 232, crumbled
1/2 cup butter, room temperature
1/4 cup half and half
1-1/2 teaspoons almond extract
1/2 cup sifted cake flour
6 tablespoons cornstarch
5 eggs, separated
1/2 cup sugar

Cocoa Butter Cream:
6 egg yolks
3/4 cup sugar
1/2 cup water
1-1/2 cups butter
1/4 cup unsweetened cocoa powder, sifted

Glaze:
4 oz. semisweet chocolate
4 teaspoons vegetable shortening
Thin chocolate wafers

To make cake, preheat oven to 400F (205C). Grease a 10-inch springform pan. Line bottom with parchment paper; grease paper. In a large bowl, beat marzipan, butter, half and half and almond extract until light and fluffy. In a sifter, combine cake flour and cornstarch. Gradually sift into marzipan mixture, folding in while sifting; set aside. In a medium bowl, beat egg yolks and sugar until pale and mixture falls in a thick ribbon from beaters. Fold egg-yolk mixture into marzipan mixture. In another medium bowl, beat egg whites until stiff but not dry; fold into marzipan mixture. Pour about 1/2 cup batter in bottom of prepared pan; smooth top. Bake 5 to 7 minutes or until edges are lightly browned. Cool in pan on a wire rack 3 minutes. Remove from pan; peel off paper. Cool on wire rack. Grease and line pan again. Use remaining batter to make 7 more layers.

To make butter cream, in a medium bowl, beat egg yolks until smooth; set aside. In a medium saucepan, combine sugar and water. Stir over medium heat until mixture comes to a boil. Boil gently until syrup reaches 240F (115C) on a candy thermometer, about 5 minutes. Beating constantly, pour syrup into beaten egg yolks in a thin, steady stream. Beat until mixture is pale and cool; set aside. In a medium bowl, beat butter until creamy and very fluffy. Beat fluffy butter into egg-yolk mixture, a little at a time. Sprinkle cocoa powder over butter mixture; beat until blended. Continue beating until mixture is very fluffy and of spreading consistency. Refrigerate until ready to use.

Prince Regent Cake

To make glaze, in a small heavy saucepan, combine chocolate and shortening. Stir over low heat until melted and smooth. Set aside to cool.

To complete, reserve 3/4 cup butter cream in a pastry bag fitted with a star tip. If cake layers differ in size, stack and trim edges so all are alike. Place 1 cake layer, bottom-side up, on a platter or cake plate. Spread with 1/2 cup butter cream. Top with a second layer, bottom-side up; spread with 1/2 cup butter cream. Repeat with remaining layers and butter cream. *Do not spread butter cream on top layer.* Pour glaze over cake; spread evenly over side and top. Let stand until glaze sets. Pipe rosettes or swirls of butter cream on top of cake. Decorate each rosette with a thin chocolate wafer. Makes 1 (8-layer) cake.

Ice Cream Cake

Ice Cream Cake

Cake:
3 eggs, separated
6 tablespoons warm water
1 teaspoon vanilla extract
3/4 cup granulated sugar
1 cup sifted cake flour
1 teaspoon baking powder
Powdered sugar

Filling:
2 teaspoons unflavored gelatin powder
3 tablespoons warm water
1-1/2 cups whipping cream
1 teaspoon vanilla extract
3 tablespoons powdered sugar
1/2 gallon square-packed Neapolitan ice cream
Chocolate curls

To make cake, preheat oven to 375F (190C). Grease a 15'' x 10'' jelly-roll pan. Line pan with waxed paper; grease paper. In a large bowl, beat egg yolks and water until foamy. Add vanilla and granulated sugar; beat until thick and pale. In a sifter, combine cake flour and baking powder. Gradually sift into egg-yolk mixture, folding in while sifting. In a medium bowl, beat egg whites until stiff but not dry; fold into batter. Pour batter into prepared pan; smooth top. Bake 15 to 20 minutes or until center springs back when pressed lightly. Sprinkle a clean towel with powdered sugar. Immediately invert cake onto sugar-coated towel. Peel off paper; trim edges. Cool; cut cake in half lengthwise. Place in freezer until frozen.

To make filling, in a small saucepan, combine gelatin and water; let stand 3 minutes. Stir over low heat until gelatin dissolves; set aside to cool. In a medium bowl, whip cream until soft peaks form. Add cooled gelatin mixture, vanilla and powdered sugar; beat until stiff peaks form. Refrigerate until ready to serve.

To complete, place 1 frozen cake layer on a long platter. Spread with a thin layer of filling. Remove ice cream from container. Dip blade of a sharp, thin knife into hot water. Use to cut ice cream in half horizontally. Place 1/2 of ice cream lengthwise on one end of filling-covered cake layer. Place remaining ice cream next to it, covering cake layer. Spread a thin layer of filling over ice cream. Top with remaining frozen cake layer. Spread remaining filling over side and top of cake. Freeze cake, unwrapped, 3 to 4 hours or until firm. Decorate with chocolate curls. Makes 1 cake.

Strawberry-Bavarian Cake

Cake:
3 eggs, separated
6 tablespoons warm water
1 teaspoon vanilla extract
3/4 cup granulated sugar
1 cup sifted cake flour
1 teaspoon baking powder
Powdered sugar, sifted

Strawberry-Bavarian Cream:
1 pint strawberries, washed, hulled
1 cup boiling water
1 (6-oz.) pkg. strawberry-flavored gelatin
1 cup cold water
2 cups whipping cream (1 pint)
1/4 cup powdered sugar, sifted
Shaved chocolate
Sugar-frosted strawberries or red currants

To make cake, preheat oven to 375F (190C). Grease a 15" x 10" jelly-roll pan. Line pan with waxed paper; grease paper. In a large bowl, beat egg yolks and water until foamy. Add vanilla and granulated sugar; beat until thick and pale. In a sifter, combine cake flour and baking powder. Gradually sift into egg-yolk mixture, folding in while sifting. In another medium bowl, beat egg whites until stiff but not dry; fold into batter. Pour batter into prepared pan; smooth top. Bake 15 to 20 minutes or until center springs back when pressed lightly. Sprinkle a clean towel with powdered sugar. Immediately invert cake onto sugar-coated towel. Peel off paper; trim edges of cake. Cool; cut cake in half lengthwise.

To make bavarian cream, reserve a few strawberries for decoration, if desired. Puree remaining strawberries in a food processor or blender. Press puree through a fine sieve; discard seeds. In a medium bowl, combine boiling water and gelatin; stir until dissolved. Stir in cold water. Refrigerate until gelatin is thick and syrupy, 30 to 45 minutes. In a large bowl, whip cream until soft peaks form. Add powdered sugar; beat until stiff peaks form. Fold strawberry puree and partially set gelatin into whipped cream until thoroughly blended. Refrigerate mixture until almost set.

To complete, place 1 cooled cake layer on a long platter. Spread with 2/3 of bavarian cream. Top with remaining cake layer. Spread with remaining bavarian cream. Place cake, unwrapped, in freezer 2 hours. Decorate with shaved chocolate and reserved strawberries, sugar-frosted strawberries or red currants. Makes 1 cake.

Strawberry-Bavarian Cake

Glazed Apple Cake

Apple Cake:
4 tart cooking apples, peeled, sliced
1 tablespoon lemon juice
1/2 teaspoon ground cinnamon
1 cup butter or margarine, room temperature
1 cup sugar
5 eggs
1 teaspoon vanilla extract
1-3/4 cups all-purpose flour
1-1/2 teaspoons baking powder

Glaze:
1 tablespoon lemon juice
1 teaspoon hot water
3/4 cup powdered sugar, sifted

To make cake, preheat oven to 350F (175C). Grease and flour a 10-inch cake pan or springform pan; set aside. Place apples in a bowl; add lemon juice and cinnamon. Toss gently; set aside. In a large bowl, beat butter or margarine and sugar until creamy. Add eggs and vanilla; beat until blended. Blend flour and baking powder; stir into sugar mixture until blended. Add apples to 1/2 of batter; pour into bottom of prepared pan. Pour remaining batter over top; smooth top. Bake 50 to 55 minutes or until a wooden pick inserted in center comes out clean. Cool in pan on a wire rack 10 minutes. Remove from pan; cool on wire rack. Place cooled cake, top-side up, on a platter or cake plate.

To make glaze, in a small bowl, combine lemon juice and hot water; stir in enough powdered sugar to make a good spreading consistency; beat until smooth. Spoon glaze over top of cake; let stand until glaze sets. Makes 1 cake.

Hazelnut Gâteau

Frosted Nut Cake

Hazelnut Gâteau

1 recipe 3-Egg Sponge Cake, page 68

Frosting:
2 teaspoons unflavored gelatin powder
2 tablespoons warm water
2 cups whipping cream (1 pint)
2 teaspoons vanilla extract or 1 teaspoon almond extract
1/4 cup powdered sugar, sifted
1-1/4 cups ground toasted hazelnuts
12 whole toasted hazelnuts

Prepare cake as directed. Cut cooled cake into 2 layers.
To make frosting, in a small saucepan, combine gelatin and water; let stand 3 minutes. Stir over low heat until gelatin dissolves; set aside to cool. In a medium bowl, whip cream until soft peaks form. Add cooled gelatin mixture, vanilla or almond extract and powdered sugar; beat until stiff peaks form. Refrigerate until ready to use.
To complete, fold 3/4 cup ground hazelnuts into 1/2 of frosting. Spoon 3/4 cup plain frosting into a pastry bag fitted with a star tip; set aside. Place bottom cake layer, cut-side down, on a platter or cake plate; spread with hazelnut mixture. Add remaining cake layer, cut-side down. Spread remaining plain frosting over side and top of cake. Press remaining 1/2 cup ground hazelnuts onto side of cake. Pipe 12 plain frosting rosettes around top edge of cake. Decorate each rosette with a hazelnut. Refrigerate until ready to serve. Makes 1 cake.

Frosted Nut Cake

Nut Cake:
3 eggs, separated
3 tablespoons warm water
1/2 cup granulated sugar
1 teaspoon vanilla extract
3/4 cup sifted cake flour
1 teaspoon baking powder
1/2 cup ground hazelnuts, pecans, walnuts or almonds
Powdered sugar

Frosting:
1-1/2 cups whipping cream
3 tablespoons powdered sugar
1-1/2 teaspoons vanilla extract or 1 teaspoon brandy extract
2 tablespoons apricot jam, melted
Whole hazelnuts or candied-cherry halves

To make cake, preheat oven to 400F (205C). Grease a 13" x 9" baking pan. Line pan with waxed paper; grease paper. In a medium bowl, beat egg yolks and warm water until foamy. Add granulated sugar and vanilla; beat until thick and pale. In a sifter, combine cake flour and baking powder. Gradually sift into egg-yolk mixture, folding in while sifting. In another medium bowl, beat egg whites until stiff but not dry; fold into batter. Fold in ground nuts. Spread batter in prepared pan; smooth top. Bake 12 to 15 minutes or until cake springs back when pressed lightly in center. Cover a wire rack with a clean towel. Sprinkle towel with powdered sugar. Immediately invert cake onto sugar-coated towel. Peel off paper; cool on wire rack. Trim edges of cooled cake; cut in half lengthwise.
To make frosting, in a medium bowl, whip cream until soft peaks form. Add powdered sugar and vanilla or brandy extract; beat until stiff peaks form. Spoon about 3/4 cup into a pastry bag fitted with a star tip; set aside.
To complete, place 1 cake layer on a long platter. Brush top with jam. Spread 1 cup frosting over bottom layer; top with remaining layer. Spread remaining frosting over side and top of cake. Pipe rosettes or scrolls of reserved frosting on top of cake. Decorate with hazelnuts or candied cherries. Makes 1 cake.

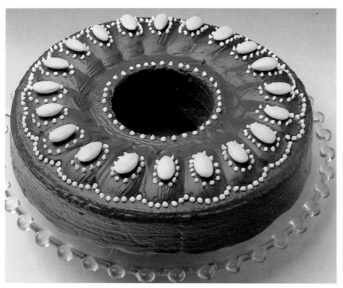

Nut-Rum Cake

Miniature Nut Cake

Nut-Rum Cake

Cake:
1 cup butter or margarine, room temperature
1-1/4 cups sugar
4 eggs
1 teaspoon rum extract
2 cups cake flour
2 teaspoons baking powder
1/2 cup milk
1 cup ground toasted almonds or walnuts
3 tablespoons milk

Chocolate Glaze:
4 oz. semisweet chocolate
1 tablespoon shortening

Decorator's Icing:
1 tablespoon stirred egg white
1 teaspoon water
1 cup powdered sugar, sifted
20 whole blanched almonds or walnuts

To make cake, preheat oven to 350F (175C). Grease and flour a 9-1/2-inch springform pan with a center tube and fluted bottom; set aside. In a large bowl, beat butter or margarine and sugar until creamy. Beat in eggs and rum extract until blended. Blend cake flour and baking powder. Stir into sugar mixture alternately with 1/2 cup milk. Pour batter into prepared pan. In a small bowl, blend nuts and 3 tablespoons milk, making a soft paste. Spoon over batter, then swirl through batter with a small spatula. Bake 50 to 55 minutes or until a wooden pick inserted in center comes out clean. Cool in pan on a wire rack 10 minutes. Remove from pan; cool on wire rack. Place cooled cake, top-side down, on a platter or cake plate.
To make glaze, in a small heavy saucepan, combine chocolate and shortening. Over low heat, stir until melted and smooth. Spread glaze over cake; let stand until set.
To make icing, in a small bowl, beat egg white and water until foamy. Gradually beat in enough powdered sugar to make a stiff icing. Spoon icing into a pastry bag fitted with a small plain tip. Pipe tiny dots on top of cake. Top with almonds or walnuts, as shown. Makes 1 cake.

Miniature Nut Cake

1/3 cup butter or margarine, room temperature
1/2 cup sugar
2 eggs
1 teaspoon almond extract or rum extract
1 cup sifted all-purpose flour
1 teaspoon baking powder
1/4 cup milk
1/2 cup toasted ground almonds, hazelnuts or walnuts

Preheat oven to 325F (165C). Grease and flour a 4-cup gugelhupf pan or decorative cake mold. In a medium bowl, beat butter or margarine and sugar until creamy. Add eggs and almond extract or rum extract; beat until blended. Blend flour and baking powder. Stir into sugar mixture alternately with milk. Fold in nuts. Pour batter into prepared pan; smooth top. Bake 50 to 55 minutes or until a wooden pick inserted in center comes out clean. Cool in pan on a wire rack 10 minutes. Remove from pan; cool on wire rack. Makes 1 cake.

Sylvia Cake

Chocolate-Chip Cake

Sylvia Cake

1-1/2 cups butter or margarine, room temperature
1-1/2 cups granulated sugar
2 teaspoons vanilla extract
4 eggs
2-1/3 cups cake flour
2 teaspoons baking powder
1/4 cup milk
Powdered sugar

Preheat oven to 350F (175C). Grease and flour a 12-cup Bundt pan or decorative cake mold. In a large bowl, beat butter or margarine and granulated sugar until creamy. Add vanilla and eggs; beat until blended. Blend cake flour and baking powder. Gradually stir into sugar mixture alternately with milk. Pour batter into prepared pan; smooth top. Bake 55 to 60 minutes or until a wooden pick inserted in center comes out clean. Cool in pan on a wire rack 15 minutes. Remove from pan; cool on wire rack. Place cooled cake, top-side down, on a platter or cake plate; dust with powdered sugar. Makes 1 cake.

Chocolate-Chip Cake

1 cup butter or margarine, room temperature
1-1/2 cups granulated sugar
2 teaspoons vanilla extract
4 eggs
3 cups sifted all-purpose flour
1 teaspoon baking powder
1 teaspoon baking soda
1/4 teaspoon salt
3/4 cup buttermilk
6 oz. semisweet chocolate, chopped, or
  6 oz. miniature semisweet chocolate pieces
Powdered sugar

Preheat oven to 350F (175C). Grease and flour a 10-cup turk's-head mold or 12-cup Bundt pan. In a large bowl, beat butter or margarine and granulated sugar until creamy. Add vanilla and eggs; beat until blended. Blend flour, baking powder, baking soda and salt. Stir into sugar mixture alternately with buttermilk. Fold in chocolate. Pour batter into prepared pan; smooth top. Bake 45 to 50 minutes or until a wooden pick inserted in center comes out clean. Cool in pan on a wire rack 15 minutes. Remove from pan; cool on wire rack. Place cooled cake, top-side down, on a platter or cake plate. Dust top with powdered sugar. Makes 1 cake.

Glazed Citrus Cake

Crowned Orange Cake

Glazed Citrus Cake

Citrus Cake:
1-1/4 cups butter or margarine, room temperature
1-1/2 cups sugar
1-1/2 teaspoons orange extract or lemon extract
5 eggs
3 cups sifted cake flour
2 teaspoons baking powder
Grated peel of 1 orange
Grated peel of 1 lemon

Apricot Glaze:
1/4 cup apricot jam
3 tablespoons apricot-flavored brandy
1 tablespoon warm water

Decorator's Icing:
1 tablespoon stirred egg white
1 teaspoon water
1 cup powdered sugar, sifted
Orange segments

To make cake, preheat oven to 350F (175C). Grease and flour a 9-1/2-inch springform pan with a center tube and fluted bottom; set aside. In a large bowl, beat butter or margarine and sugar until creamy. Add orange or lemon extract and eggs; beat until blended. Blend cake flour and baking powder; stir into sugar mixture. Fold in orange and lemon peels. Pour batter into prepared pan; smooth top. Bake 55 to 60 minutes or until a wooden pick inserted in center comes out clean. Cool in pan on a wire rack 10 minutes. Remove from pan; cool on wire rack. Place cooled cake, top-side down, on a platter or cake plate.
To make glaze, press jam through a fine sieve into a small heavy saucepan. Stir in brandy and water. Over low heat, cook, stirring constantly, until mixture comes to a boil. Set aside to cool; brush glaze over cake. Let stand until glaze sets.
To make icing, in a small bowl, beat egg white and water until foamy. Gradually beat in powdered sugar until icing is very stiff. Spoon into a pastry bag fitted with a small plain writing tip. Pipe tiny dots on top of cake. Decorate with orange segments. Makes 1 cake.

Crowned Orange Cake

1 cup butter or margarine, room temperature
1-1/2 cups sugar
1 teaspoon orange extract
6 eggs
1 tablespoon grated lemon peel
2 tablespoons grated orange peel
2-1/2 cups all-purpose flour
1 tablespoon baking powder
1/2 teaspoon salt
1 cup orange juice
1 large navel orange, cut in 8 sections, as shown

Preheat oven to 350F (175C). Grease and flour a 12-cup Bundt pan or decorative cake mold. In a large bowl, beat butter or margarine and sugar until creamy. Add orange extract and eggs; beat until blended. Stir in lemon and orange peels. Blend flour, baking powder and salt. Stir into sugar mixture alternately with orange juice. Pour batter into prepared pan; smooth top. Bake 55 to 60 minutes or until a wooden pick inserted in center comes out clean. Cool in pan on a wire rack 10 minutes. Remove from pan; cool on wire rack. Place cooled cake, top-side down, on a platter or cake plate. Decorate with orange sections, as shown. Makes 1 cake.

Martha Washington Ring

Martha Washington Ring

Cake:
1/2 cup butter or margarine, room temperature
3/4 cup sugar
1 teaspoon vanilla extract
3 eggs
1-1/2 cups sifted cake flour
2 teaspoons baking powder
1/2 teaspoon salt

Frosting:
2 cups whipping cream (1 pint)
1/4 cup powdered sugar, sifted
1 teaspoon rum extract or almond extract
1 cup toasted finely chopped almonds
    or 1 cup prepared nut topping
Maraschino cherries or red candied cherries

To make cake, preheat oven to 350F (175C). Grease and flour an 11- or 12-cup ring mold; set aside. In a medium bowl, beat butter or margarine and sugar until creamy. Add vanilla and eggs; beat until blended. Blend cake flour, baking powder and salt. Gradually stir into sugar mixture. Pour batter into prepared mold; smooth top. Bake 30 to 35 minutes or until a wooden pick inserted in center comes out clean. Cool in pan on a wire rack 10 minutes. Remove from pan; cool on wire rack. Cut cooled cake into 3 layers.

To make frosting, in a medium bowl, whip cream until soft peaks form. Beat in powdered sugar and rum extract or almond extract until stiff peaks form.

To complete, place bottom cake layer, cut-side down, on a platter or cake plate; spread with some of frosting. Add middle cake layer; spread with some of frosting. Add top cake layer, cut-side down. Spoon about 3/4 cup frosting into a small pastry bag fitted with a star tip; set aside. Spread remaining frosting over side and top of cake, covering completely. Sprinkle with almonds or nut topping; press into frosting. Pipe swirls or rosettes of reserved frosting on top of cake. Decorate each swirl with a cherry. Refrigerate until ready to serve. Makes 1 cake.

Chantilly Cake

Cake:
1 cup butter or margarine, room temperature
1-1/2 cups sugar
1/2 teaspoon almond extract
5 eggs, separated
1-2/3 cups cake flour
2 teaspoons baking powder
1/2 teaspoon salt
1/2 cup milk
1 teaspoon ground cinnamon
1/2 cup sliced almonds

Filling:
2 cups whipping cream (1 pint)
1 teaspoon almond extract
1/4 cup powdered sugar
1 cup coarsely chopped strawberries or 1 cup red currants

To make cake, preheat oven to 350F (175C). Grease and flour 4 (9-inch) cake pans with removable bottoms. In a

Chantilly Cake

large bowl, beat butter or margarine and 1 cup sugar until creamy. Add almond extract and egg yolks; beat until blended. Blend cake flour, baking powder and salt. Stir into sugar mixture alternately with milk. Spread about 1 cup cake batter in each prepared pan; smooth tops. In another large bowl, beat egg whites until stiff but not dry. Add cinnamon; beat in remaining 1/2 cup sugar, 2 tablespoons at a time, beating until stiff. Spoon egg-white mixture evenly into each pan; smooth tops. Sprinkle 2 tablespoons sliced almonds into each pan. Bake 30 to 35 minutes or until tops are lightly browned. Cool in pans on wire racks 10 minutes. Remove from pans; cool completely, almond-side up, on wire racks.

To make filling, in a medium bowl, whip cream until soft peaks form. Add almond extract and powdered sugar; beat until stiff peaks form. Fold in strawberries or red currants. Place 1 cake layer, almond-side up, on a platter or cake plate; spread with 1/3 of filling. Repeat with remaining layers and filling, ending with a cake layer. Refrigerate until ready to serve. Makes 1 cake.

Note: In place of 4 (9-inch) cake pans, bake 2 layers, cool and wash pans. Then bake remaining 2 layers. Divide egg whites in half; beat second half when ready to use batter.

Cherry Layer Cake

Cherry Layer Cake

Cake:
4 eggs, separated
3 tablespoons warm water
1 teaspoon vanilla extract
3/4 cup sugar
1-1/4 cups sifted cake flour
2 teaspoons baking powder
1 cup cherry preserves
1 tablespoon kirsch or other cherry-flavored liqueur, if desired

Kirsch Frosting:
1 (1/4-oz.) envelope unflavored gelatin powder
3 tablespoons warm water
2-1/2 cups whipping cream
5 tablespoons powdered sugar
2 to 3 tablespoons kirsch or other cherry-flavored liqueur
1/2 cup toasted sliced almonds
16 maraschino cherries

To make cake, preheat oven to 350F (175C). Grease bottom of a 10-inch springform pan or deep cake pan. Line bottom with waxed paper; grease and flour paper and side of pan. In a large bowl, beat egg yolks and water until foamy. Add vanilla and sugar; beat until thick and pale. In a sifter, combine cake flour and baking powder. Gradually sift into egg-yolk mixture, folding in while sifting. In a medium bowl, beat egg whites until stiff but not dry; fold into batter. Pour batter into prepared pan; smooth top. Bake 30 to 35 minutes or until a wooden pick inserted in center comes out clean. Cool in pan on a wire rack 10 minutes. Remove from pan; peel off paper. Cool on wire rack. Cut cooled cake into 3 layers. Press cherry preserves through a sieve into a small saucepan. Stir over low heat until melted. Set aside to cool 2 minutes. Stir in liqueur, if desired; cool to room temperature.

To make frosting, in a small saucepan, combine gelatin and water; let stand 3 minutes. Stir over low heat until gelatin dissolves; set aside to cool. In a large bowl, whip cream until soft peaks form. Add cooled gelatin mixture, powdered sugar and liqueur; beat until stiff peaks form. Refrigerate until ready to use.

To complete, spoon 1 cup frosting into a pastry bag fitted with a star tip; set aside. Place bottom cake layer, cut-side down, on a platter or cake plate; brush with sieved cherry preserves. Spread with 1 cup frosting. Add middle cake layer. Brush with preserves; spread with 1 cup frosting. Add top layer, cut-side down. Spread remaining frosting over side and top of cake. Spoon remaining preserves in a circle on top center of cake. Press almond slices onto side of cake. Pipe reserved frosting in dollops around preserves and on top of cake; decorate with maraschino cherries. Refrigerate until ready to serve. Makes 1 cake.

Little Orange Cakes

Cake:
3 eggs
1 teaspoon vanilla extract
1/8 teaspoon salt
3/4 cup sugar
1 cup sifted cake flour
2 tablespoons milk

Orange Syrup:
1/2 cup sugar
1/4 cup cold water
3/4 cup orange juice
4 to 5 tablespoons curaçao or other citrus-flavored liqueur

Orange Cream:
1-1/2 cups whipping cream
3 tablespoons powdered sugar
2 tablespoons curaçao or other citrus-flavored liqueur
1/2 cup finely chopped toasted almonds
Red candied cherries, halved
Marzipan cutouts, page 232
Small chocolate candies
1 slice unpeeled orange, cut in 6 wedges

To make cake, preheat oven to 350F (175C). Grease and flour 12 muffin cups. In a medium bowl, beat eggs until foamy. Stir in vanilla, salt and sugar; beat until thick and pale. Stir in cake flour alternately with milk. Spoon batter into prepared muffin cups, filling 2/3 full; smooth tops. Bake 18 to 20 minutes or until centers spring back when pressed lightly. Immediately remove from muffin cups; cool on wire racks. Wash and dry muffin cups. Cut very thin slices from top of each cake to let syrup soak in. Discard slices or save for another use. Trim sides of cakes to straighten, if desired. Return cakes to muffin cups.

To make syrup, in a small saucepan, stir sugar and water over low heat until sugar dissolves. Boil rapidly, without stirring, until mixture is syrupy, 3 to 5 minutes; set aside to cool. Stir in orange juice and liqueur. Spoon cooled syrup evenly over cakes. Let stand 1 to 2 hours.

To make orange cream, in a medium bowl, whip cream until soft peaks form. Add powdered sugar and liqueur; beat until stiff peaks form. Spoon 1/3 of cream mixture into a pastry bag fitted with a star tip; set aside.

To complete, remove cakes from muffin cups; cut 6 cakes in half horizontally. Fill and frost with remaining whipped-cream mixture. Press toasted almonds over sides and tops of frosted cakes. Decorate frosted cakes with cherry halves, marzipan cutouts or small chocolate candies. On tops of remaining 6 cakes, pipe an orange-cream rosette. Place an orange wedge, point-side down, in each rosette. Refrigerate until ready to serve. Makes 12 servings.

Little Orange Cakes

Florida Orange Cake

Orange Cake:
3/4 cup butter or margarine, room temperature
1-1/2 cups sugar
4 eggs, separated
2-1/2 cups all-purpose flour
2-1/2 teaspoons baking powder
1/2 teaspoon salt
1 cup orange juice
3 tablespoons grated orange peel

Orange Glaze:
2 tablespoons butter or margarine, melted
2 cups powdered sugar, sifted
1/4 cup orange juice
1 tablespoon grated orange peel

To make cake, preheat oven to 350F (175C). Grease and flour a 10-inch tube pan; set aside. In a large bowl, beat

Orange Pound Cake

Pound Cake:
1-1/2 cups butter or margarine, room temperature
1-1/4 cups sugar
6 eggs
2 tablespoons grated orange peel
2 teaspoons orange extract
2-1/2 cups cake flour
2 teaspoons baking powder
1/3 cup orange juice

Glaze:
1 teaspoon lemon juice
3 to 4 teaspoons orange juice
1 cup powdered sugar, sifted

To make cake, preheat oven to 325F (165C). Grease and flour a 9-cup gugelhupf pan or similar cake pan. In a large bowl, beat butter or margarine and sugar until creamy. Add eggs, orange peel and orange extract; beat until blended. Blend cake flour and baking powder. Stir into sugar mixture alternately with orange juice; beat until blended. Pour batter into prepared pan; smooth top. Bake 60 to 70 minutes or until a wooden pick inserted in center comes out clean. Cool in pan on a wire rack 10 minutes. Remove from pan; cool on wire rack. Place cooled cake, top-side down, on a platter or cake plate.
To make glaze, in a small bowl, combine lemon juice and orange juice. Stir in enough powdered sugar to make a good drizzling consistency; beat until smooth. Spoon glaze over cake; let stand until glaze sets. Makes 1 cake.

butter or margarine and sugar until creamy. Beat in egg yolks until blended. Blend flour, baking powder and salt. Stir into sugar mixture alternately with orange juice. Fold in orange peel. Beat egg whites until stiff but not dry; fold into cake batter. Pour batter into prepared pan; smooth top. Bake 50 to 60 minutes or until a wooden pick inserted in center comes out clean. Cool in pan on a wire rack 15 minutes. Remove from pan; cool on wire rack. Place cooled cake, top-side down, on a platter or cake plate.
To make glaze, in a small bowl, beat butter or margarine, powdered sugar and orange juice until smooth. Stir in orange peel. Spoon glaze over cake; let stand until set. Makes 1 cake.

Orange Pound Cake

Coffee "Rio" Gâteau

Shortbread:
1 cup sifted all-purpose flour
3 tablespoons sugar
6 tablespoons butter or margarine, chilled

Two-Egg Sponge Cake:
2 eggs, separated
3 tablespoons warm water
1 teaspoon vanilla extract
1/2 cup sugar
3/4 cup sifted cake flour
1 teaspoon baking powder

Cherry Filling:
1 (16-oz.) can dark sweet cherries, pitted
Water
2 tablespoons cornstarch
1 tablespoon sugar
2 teaspoons lemon juice

Coffee Frosting:
1 tablespoon instant-coffee powder
2 tablespoons boiling water
1 (1/4-oz.) envelope unflavored gelatin powder
3 tablespoons cold water
3 cups whipping cream (1-1/2 pints)
6 tablespoons powdered sugar, sifted
3 tablespoons red-currant jelly, melted
Candy coffee beans

Coffee "Rio" Gâteau

To make shortbread, preheat oven to 400F (205C). Grease bottom of a 10-inch springform pan; set aside. In a medium bowl, blend flour and sugar. Use a pastry blender or 2 knives to cut in butter or margarine until mixture resembles coarse crumbs. Knead dough in bowl 10 strokes or until smooth. Pat or press dough onto bottom of greased pan. Bake 10 to 12 minutes or until edges are golden. Cool in pan on a wire rack. Remove from pan; set aside. Wash and dry pan.

To make sponge cake, preheat oven to 375F (190C). Grease and flour a 10-inch springform pan or deep cake pan. In a medium bowl, beat egg yolks and water until foamy. Add vanilla and sugar; beat until thick and pale. In a sifter, combine cake flour and baking powder. Gradually sift over egg-yolk mixture, folding in while sifting. In another medium bowl, beat egg whites until stiff but not dry; fold into batter. Pour batter into prepared pan; smooth top. Bake 20 to 25 minutes or until a wooden pick inserted in center comes out clean. Cool in pan on a wire rack 10 minutes. Remove from pan; cool on wire rack. Cut cooled cake into 2 layers.

To make cherry filling, drain cherry juice into a 1-cup measure. Chop drained cherries; set aside. Add enough water to cherry juice to make 3/4 cup liquid; pour into a small saucepan. Add cornstarch and sugar; stir until smooth. Stirring constantly over low heat, cook until mixture thickens and comes to a boil. Add lemon juice and chopped cherries. Cook, stirring, 1 minute; cool to room temperature.

To make frosting, dissolve coffee powder in boiling water; set aside to cool. In a small saucepan, combine gelatin and cold water; let stand 3 minutes. Stir over low heat until gelatin dissolves; set aside to cool. In a large bowl, whip cream until soft peaks form. Add cooled gelatin mixture and powdered sugar; beat until stiff peaks form. Spoon 1/3 of whipped-cream mixture into a small bowl; stir in cooled coffee mixture. Spoon 3/4 cup plain whipped-cream mixture into a pastry bag fitted with a star tip. Refrigerate plain and coffee-flavored whipped-cream mixtures.

To complete, place shortbread base on a flat platter or cake plate. Brush with jelly; let stand until set. Place 1 sponge-cake layer, cut-side down, on shortbread base; spread with all of cherry filling. Let stand until set. Spread with all of coffee mixture. Top with remaining cake layer, cut-side down; press down lightly. Spread plain whipped-cream mixture over side and top of cake. Pipe 12 rosettes of plain whipped-cream mixture on top of cake. Decorate rosettes with candy coffee beans. Refrigerate until ready to serve. Makes 1 cake.

and baking powder. Gradually sift into chocolate mixture, folding in while sifting. In another medium bowl, beat egg whites until stiff but not dry; fold into batter. Fold in nuts. Pour batter into prepared pans; smooth tops. Bake 30 to 35 minutes or until a wooden pick inserted in center comes out clean. Cool in pans on wire racks 10 minutes. Remove from pans; cool on wire racks.

To make butter cream, in a small heavy saucepan, melt chocolate over low heat. Stir until smooth; set aside to cool. In a medium bowl, beat butter until creamy. Add melted chocolate and eggs; beat until blended. Gradually stir in enough powdered sugar to make a good spreading consistency; beat until smooth.

To complete, place 1 cake layer, bottom-side up, on a platter or cake plate. Spread about 1/4 of butter cream over top; add remaining cake layer, top-side up. Spread remaining butter cream over side and top of cake. Lightly press almonds onto side of cake. Use tines of a fork or an icing comb to make wavy lines on top of cake. Decorate cake with small chocolate candies, if desired. Makes 1 cake.

Panama Gâteau

Cake:
3/4 cup butter or margarine, room temperature
1 cup packed light-brown sugar
4 eggs, separated
5 oz. unsweetened chocolate, melted
1 cup all-purpose flour
1 teaspoon baking powder
3/4 cup ground hazelnuts, almonds or Brazil nuts

Chocolate Butter Cream:
4 oz. semisweet chocolate
2/3 cup butter, room temperature
2 eggs
About 3-1/2 cups powdered sugar, sifted
Toasted sliced almonds
Small chocolate candies, if desired

To make cake, preheat oven to 350F (175C). Grease and flour 2 round 9-inch cake pans; set aside. In a medium bowl, beat butter or margarine and brown sugar until creamy. Add egg yolks, 1 at a time, beating well after each addition. Stir in chocolate. In a sifter, combine flour

Panama Gâteau

Jelly Roll

Jelly Roll

5 eggs, separated
1 teaspoon vanilla extract
3/4 cup granulated sugar
1 cup sifted cake flour
1/2 teaspoon baking powder
1/4 teaspoon salt
Powdered sugar
1 (10-oz.) jar strawberry jelly or jam

Preheat oven to 375F (190C). Grease a 15" x 10" jelly-roll pan. Line pan with waxed paper; grease paper. In a medium bowl, beat egg yolks until foamy. Add vanilla and granulated sugar; beat until thick and pale. In a sifter, combine cake flour, baking powder and salt. Gradually sift over egg-yolk mixture, folding in while sifting. In another medium bowl, beat egg whites until stiff but not dry; fold into egg-yolk mixture. Pour batter into prepared pan; smooth top. Bake 12 to 15 minutes or until top springs back when pressed lightly. Sprinkle a clean towel with powdered sugar. Immediately invert cake onto sugar-coated towel. Peel off paper; trim edges. Starting at a short end, roll up cake and towel. Cool on a wire rack. Unroll cake; spread with jelly or jam. Reroll cake, without towel; place on a long platter, seam-side down. Dust with powdered sugar. To serve, cut in 1-inch slices. Makes 1 cake.

Lemon-Sponge Roll

Sponge Cake:
5 eggs, separated
1 teaspoon lemon extract
3/4 cup granulated sugar
1 cup sifted cake flour
1/2 teaspoon baking powder
1/4 teaspoon salt
1 tablespoon grated lemon peel
Powdered sugar

Lemon-Cream Frosting:
2 teaspoons unflavored gelatin powder
3 tablespoons warm water
2 cups whipping cream (1 pint)
1/4 cup powdered sugar, sifted
1-1/2 teaspoons lemon extract
2 teaspoons grated lemon peel, if desired

To make cake, preheat oven to 375F (190C). Grease a 15" x 10" jelly-roll pan. Line pan with waxed paper; grease paper. In a medium bowl, beat egg yolks until foamy. Add lemon extract; gradually beat in granulated sugar until thick and pale. In a sifter, combine cake flour, baking powder and salt. Gradually sift into egg-yolk mixture, folding in while sifting. Fold in lemon peel. In a large bowl, beat egg whites until stiff but not dry; fold into batter. Spread batter evenly in prepared pan; smooth top. Bake 12 to 15 minutes or until top springs back when pressed lightly. Sprinkle a clean towel with powdered sugar. Immediately invert cake onto sugar-coated towel. Peel off paper; trim edges. Starting at a short side, roll cake and towel. Cool on a wire rack.

To make frosting, in a small saucepan, combine gelatin and water; let stand 3 minutes. Stir over low heat until gelatin dissolves; set aside to cool. In a medium bowl, whip cream until soft peaks form. Stir in cooled gelatin mixture, powdered sugar and lemon extract; beat until stiff peaks form. Fold in lemon peel, if desired. Refrigerate until ready to use.

To complete, unroll cake; spread with 1/2 of frosting. Reroll cake without towel; place on a long platter, seam-side down. Spread remaining frosting over side and top of cake. Use tines of a fork or an icing comb to make a wavy pattern in frosting. Refrigerate until ready to serve. To serve, cut in 1-inch slices. Makes 1 cake.

Kirsch Bombe

Sponge Cake:
3 eggs, separated
6 tablespoons warm water
1 teaspoon vanilla extract
3/4 cup granulated sugar
1 cup sifted cake flour
1 teaspoon baking powder
Powdered sugar
1 cup cherry jelly

Cherry-Bavarian Filling:
2 lbs. fresh, dark sweet cherries
1/2 cup granulated sugar
Water
3 tablespoons cornstarch
6 tablespoons kirsch or other cherry-flavored liqueur
1 (1/4-oz.) envelope unflavored gelatin powder
1 cup whipping cream (1/2 pint)
2 tablespoons powdered sugar
Whipped cream

To make cake, preheat oven to 375F (190C). Grease a 15'' x 10'' jelly-roll pan. Line pan with waxed paper; grease paper. In a large bowl, beat egg yolks and water until foamy. Add vanilla and granulated sugar; beat until thick and pale. In a sifter, combine cake flour and baking powder. Gradually sift into egg-yolk mixture, folding in while sifting. In a medium bowl, beat egg whites until stiff but not dry; fold into batter. Pour batter into prepared pan; smooth top. Bake 15 to 20 minutes or until center springs back when pressed lightly. Sprinkle a clean towel with powdered sugar. Immediately invert cake onto sugar-coated towel. Peel off paper; trim edges. Starting at a short end, roll up cake and towel. Cool on a wire rack. Unroll cooled cake; spread with jelly. Reroll cake without towel; set aside.

To make filling, reserve 10 to 12 cherries to decorate cake. Remove pits from remaining cherries. In a medium saucepan, combine pitted cherries, granulated sugar and

Kirsch Bombe

Lemon-Sponge Roll

1/4 cup water. Bring to a boil over medium heat. Cover and simmer until cherries are soft but not mushy. Drain, reserving liquid in a 1-cup measure; set cooked cherries aside to cool. Add enough water to cherry liquid to make 1 cup. Return to saucepan; stir in cornstarch until blended. Stirring constantly, cook over low heat until mixture thickens and comes to a boil. Stir in liqueur and reserved cherries; set aside to cool. Pour 1/4 cup water into a small saucepan. Sprinkle gelatin over water; let stand 3 minutes. Stir over low heat until gelatin dissolves; set aside to cool. In a medium bowl, whip cream until soft peaks form. Add cooled gelatin mixture and powdered sugar; beat until stiff peaks form. Fold cooled cherry mixture into whipped-cream mixture. Refrigerate until needed.

To complete, cut cooled cake into 3/4-inch slices. Reserve 2 cake slices. Line a 1-1/2 to 2-quart bowl or charlotte mold with remaining cake slices. Press slices against each other to line bottom and side of mold. Spoon filling into cake-lined mold; smooth top. Cover filling with reserved cake slices. Refrigerate 3 to 4 hours. To serve, invert bombe onto a small, round platter. Decorate bombe with cherries and whipped cream. Makes 1 bombe.

Strawberry-Cream Gâteau

cooled cake into 2 layers. Cut 6 whole strawberries in half; reserve for decoration. Slice remaining strawberries; set aside.

To make frosting, in a small saucepan, combine gelatin and water; let stand 3 minutes. Stir over low heat until gelatin dissolves; set aside to cool. In a medium bowl, whip cream until soft peaks form. Add cooled gelatin mixture, vanilla or almond extract and powdered sugar; beat until stiff peaks form. Refrigerate until ready to use.

To complete, fold sliced strawberries into 1/2 of frosting. Spoon 3/4 cup remaining frosting into a pastry bag fitted with a star tip; set aside. Place bottom cake layer, cut-side down, on a platter or cake plate. Spread with strawberry mixture. Top with remaining layer, cut-side down. Spread remaining frosting over side and top of cake. Pipe 12 rosettes of frosting on top of cake. Decorate rosette with reserved strawberry halves. Refrigerate until ready to serve. Makes 1 cake.

Strawberry-Cream Gâteau

3-Egg Sponge Cake:
3 eggs, separated
3 tablespoons warm water
1 teaspoon vanilla extract
1/2 cup sugar
1 cup sifted cake flour
1 teaspoon baking powder
2 pints strawberries, washed, hulled

Whipped-Cream Frosting:
2 teaspoons unflavored gelatin powder
2 tablespoons warm water
2 cups whipping cream (1 pint)
2 teaspoons vanilla extract or 1 teaspoon almond extract
1/4 cup powdered sugar, sifted

To make cake, preheat oven to 350F (175C). Grease and flour a 10-inch springform pan or deep cake pan. In a medium bowl, beat egg yolks and water until foamy. Add vanilla and sugar; beat until thick and pale. In a sifter, combine cake flour and baking powder. Gradually sift into egg-yolk mixture, folding in while sifting. In another medium bowl, beat egg whites until stiff but not dry; fold into batter. Pour batter into prepared pan; smooth top. Bake 25 to 30 minutes or until a wooden pick inserted in center comes out clean. Cool in pan on a wire rack 10 minutes. Remove from pan; cool on wire rack. Cut

Pineapple Upside-Down Cake

Topping:
1/4 cup butter or margarine
1/2 cup packed light-brown sugar
1 (20-oz.) can sliced pineapple (9 slices), drained
9 maraschino cherries

Cake:
1/3 cup butter or margarine, room temperature
3/4 cup sugar
1 egg
1 teaspoon vanilla extract
1-1/3 cups all-purpose flour
2 teaspoons baking powder
1/2 teaspoon salt
2/3 cup milk
Flavored whipped cream, if desired

To make topping, preheat oven to 350F (175C). Place butter or margarine in a 9-inch-square baking pan; place in oven until melted. Stir brown sugar into melted butter or margarine; spread mixture evenly in pan. Arrange pineapple slices in 3 rows over brown-sugar mixture. Place a cherry in center of each pineapple slice; set aside.

To make cake, in a medium bowl, beat butter or margarine and sugar until creamy. Beat in egg and vanilla. Blend flour, baking powder and salt. Stir into sugar mixture alternately with milk. Gently pour batter over pineapple slices; spread evenly into corners of pan. Bake 40 to 45 minutes or until a wooden pick inserted in center comes out clean. Cool in pan on a wire rack 2 minutes. Place a platter or cake plate over pan. Holding pan firmly to plate, invert pan and plate. Let stand 2 minutes; carefully remove pan. Serve warm or chilled, with whipped cream, if desired. Makes 1 cake.

Spring Cake

Cake:
1 cup butter or margarine, room temperature
1 cup sugar
1 teaspoon vanilla extract
5 eggs
1 tablespoon grated lemon peel
1-2/3 cups sifted all-purpose flour
2 teaspoons baking powder

Cream-Cheese Frosting:
1 (8-oz.) pkg. cream cheese, room temperature
2 tablespoons half and half
1-1/2 teaspoons vanilla extract or 1 teaspoon almond extract
5 cups powdered sugar, sifted
5 tablespoons red-currant jelly, melted, cooled
1/2 cup finely chopped pistachios or almonds
2 tablespoons unsweetened cocoa powder blended with
   2 tablespoons powdered sugar

To make cake, preheat oven to 350F (175C). Grease and flour a 9-inch springform pan; set aside. In a large bowl, beat butter or margarine, sugar and vanilla until creamy. Gradually beat in eggs until blended. Stir in lemon peel. Blend flour and baking powder. Add a little at a time to sugar mixture, beating well after each addition. Pour batter into prepared pan; smooth top. Bake 45 to 50 minutes or until a wooden pick inserted in center comes out clean. Cool in pan on a wire rack 10 minutes. Remove from pan; cool on wire rack. Cut cooled cake into 3 layers.

To make frosting, in a medium bowl, beat cream cheese, half and half and vanilla or almond extract until blended. Gradually beat in enough powdered sugar to make a good spreading consistency.

To complete, place bottom cake layer, cut-side down, on a platter or cake plate. Brush with jelly; spread with about 1/4 of frosting. Add middle layer. Brush with jelly; spread with 1/4 of frosting. Add top layer, cut-side down. Spread remaining frosting over side and top of cake. Lightly press nuts into frosting on side of cake. Cut out several paper daisies; arrange on top of cake. Sprinkle cocoa mixture over top of cake; carefully remove paper flowers. Refrigerate until ready to serve. Makes 1 cake.

Spring Cake

Eggnog Gâteau

Eggnog Gâteau

Photo on pages 36-37.

Cake:
4 eggs, separated
3 tablespoons warm water
1 teaspoon vanilla extract
3/4 cup sugar
1-1/4 cups sifted cake flour
2 teaspoons baking powder

Eggnog Cream:
2 teaspoons unflavored gelatin powder
3 tablespoons warm water
2 cups whipping cream (1 pint)
1/4 cup powdered sugar, sifted
4 to 5 tablespoons Advocaat or other eggnog-flavored liqueur

To make cake, preheat oven to 350F (175C). Grease bottom of a 10-inch springform pan or deep cake pan. Line bottom with waxed paper. Grease and flour paper and side of pan. In a large bowl, beat egg yolks and water until foamy. Beat in vanilla and sugar until thick and pale. In a sifter, combine cake flour and baking powder. Gradually sift over egg-yolk mixture, folding in while sifting. In a medium bowl, beat egg whites until stiff but not dry; fold into batter. Pour batter into prepared pan; smooth top. Bake 30 to 35 minutes or until a wooden pick inserted in center comes out clean. Cool in pan on a wire rack 10 minutes. Remove from pan; cool on wire rack. Cut cooled cake into 2 layers.

To make cream mixture, in a small saucepan, combine gelatin and water; let stand 3 minutes. Stir over low heat until gelatin dissolves; set aside to cool. In a medium bowl, whip cream until soft peaks form. Stir in cooled gelatin mixture, powdered sugar and liqueur. Beat until stiff peaks form. Refrigerate until ready to use.

To complete, place bottom cake layer, cut-side down, on a platter or cake plate. Spread 1/3 of cream mixture over top. Add remaining cake layer, cut-side down. Spread remaining cream mixture over side and top of cake. Refrigerate until ready to serve. Makes 1 cake.

Chocolate-Frosted Vanilla Cake

Chocolate-Frosted Vanilla Cake

Vanilla Cake:
2 eggs, separated
1 tablespoon warm water
1 teaspoon vanilla extract
1/2 cup sugar
1 cup sifted cake flour
1 teaspoon baking powder
1/4 cup butter, melted

Creamy Chocolate Frosting:
6 tablespoons butter, room temperature
3 oz. semisweet chocolate, melted
1 teaspoon vanilla extract
3 cups sifted powdered sugar
1 egg yolk
Chocolate sprinkles

To make cake, preheat oven to 350F (175C). Grease and flour a 9" x 5" loaf pan; set aside. In a medium bowl, beat egg yolks and water until foamy. Add vanilla and sugar; beat until thick and pale. Blend cake flour and baking powder; add to egg-yolk mixture alternately with melted butter; beat until blended. In another medium bowl, beat egg whites until stiff but not dry; fold into batter. Pour batter into prepared pan; smooth top. Bake 25 to 30 minutes or until a wooden pick inserted in center comes out clean. Cool in pan on a wire rack 10 minutes. Remove from pan; cool on wire rack. Cut cooled cake into 2 layers.

To make frosting, in a medium bowl, beat butter or margarine until fluffy. Add chocolate and vanilla; beat until blended. Gradually beat in powdered sugar. Add egg yolk; beat until smooth and of spreading consistency. Spoon 1 cup frosting into a pastry bag fitted with a star tip; set aside.

To complete, place bottom cake layer, cut-side down, on an oval platter. Spread with 1/3 of remaining frosting. Add remaining cake layer, cut-side down. Spread remaining frosting over side and top of cake. Pipe frosting in rows on top of cake. Decorate side of bottom layer with chocolate sprinkles. Makes 1 cake.

Boston Cream Pie

Cake:
1/3 cup butter or margarine, room temperature
3/4 cup sugar
1 teaspoon vanilla extract
2 eggs
1-1/2 cups sifted cake flour
2 teaspoons baking powder
1/4 teaspoon salt
1/2 cup milk

Cream Filling:
2 tablespoons cornstarch
1 cup half and half (1/2 pint)
1/4 cup sugar
1 egg, slightly beaten
1 teaspoon vanilla extract

Chocolate Glaze:
3 oz. semisweet chocolate
1 tablespoon butter or margarine

To make cake, preheat oven to 375F (190C). Grease and flour 2 (8- or 9-inch) cake pans. In a large bowl, beat butter or margarine, sugar and vanilla until creamy. Beat in eggs, 1 at a time, beating well after each addition. Blend cake flour, baking powder and salt. Stir into sugar mixture alternately with milk until blended. Pour batter evenly into prepared pans; smooth tops. Bake 25 to 30 minutes or until a wooden pick inserted in center comes out clean. Cool in pans on wire racks 10 minutes. Remove from pans; cool on wire racks.

To make filling, in a small saucepan, combine cornstarch, half and half and sugar. Stirring constantly, cook over medium heat until mixture comes to a boil and thickens. Remove from heat. In a small bowl, beat egg; stir 1/4 cup hot mixture into beaten egg. Stirring constantly, slowly add egg mixture to remaining hot mixture. Stir constantly over low heat until thick and smooth. Set aside to cool; stir vanilla into cooled mixture. Place 1 cooled cake layer, bottom-side up, on a platter or cake plate. Spread with Cream Filling; top with remaining layer.

To make glaze, in a small heavy saucepan, melt chocolate and butter or margarine over low heat; stir until smooth. Spread glaze over top of cake; let stand until set. Refrigerate until ready to serve. Makes 1 cake.

Vanilla-Cream Gâteau

Vanilla-Cream Gâteau

Vanilla Genoise:
6 eggs
1 cup sugar
1 teaspoon vanilla extract
3/4 cup cake flour
1/2 cup cornstarch
6 tablespoons Clarified Butter, page 232

Vanilla Butter Cream:
6 egg yolks
3/4 cup sugar
1/2 cup water
1-1/2 cups unsalted butter
2 teaspoons vanilla extract

Fillings:
4 oz. semisweet chocolate, melted
3 tablespoons apricot jam, melted
Finely chopped semisweet chocolate or chocolate sprinkles

To make cake, preheat oven to 350F (175C). Grease bottom of a 10-inch springform pan. Line bottom with waxed paper; grease and flour paper and side of pan. Place eggs in a large bowl; set bowl over a pan of very hot water. Let stand until eggs are warm, about 5 minutes. With bowl in hot water, beat eggs until thick and fluffy, about 5 minutes. Gradually beat in sugar until mixture falls in thick ribbons from beaters, 10 to 12 minutes. Beat in vanilla. Remove bowl from water. In a sifter, combine cake flour and cornstarch. Gradually sift over egg mixture, folding in while sifting. Fold in clarified butter only until streaks of butter disappear. Spread batter in prepared pan; smooth top. Bake 25 to 30 minutes or until a wooden pick inserted in center comes out clean. Cool in pan on a wire rack 10 minutes. Remove from pan; peel off paper. Cool on wire rack. Cut cooled cake into 3 layers.

To make butter cream, in a medium bowl, beat egg yolks until smooth; set aside. Combine sugar and water in a medium saucepan. Stirring constantly, bring to a boil over medium heat. Boil gently until syrup reaches 240F (115C) on a candy thermometer, about 5 minutes. Beating constantly, pour syrup into egg yolks in a thin, steady stream. Beat until mixture is pale yellow and cool; set aside. In a small bowl, beat butter until creamy and fluffy. Gradually beat creamed butter into egg-yolk mixture until all butter has been incorporated. Beat in vanilla. Continue beating until mixture is fluffy and of spreading consistency. Refrigerate until ready to use.

To complete, spoon 1 cup butter cream into a pastry bag fitted with a star tip; set aside. Place bottom cake layer, cut-side down, on a platter or cake plate; spread with melted chocolate. Spread a thin layer of remaining butter cream over chocolate. Add middle cake layer; brush with apricot jam. Spread a thin layer of butter cream over jam. Add remaining cake layer, cut-side down. Spread remaining butter cream over side and top of cake. Press chopped chocolate or chocolate sprinkles onto side of cake. Pipe reserved butter cream in a lattice pattern on top of cake. Pipe small rosettes around outside edge of cake. Makes 1 cake.

Glazed Honey Cake

Glazed Honey Cake

Delicate Spice Cake:
1/2 cup vegetable shortening
1/2 cup packed light-brown sugar
2 eggs
1 cup honey
1 tablespoon grated orange peel
1 teaspoon baking soda
1 cup hot water
2-1/2 cups all-purpose flour
1 tablespoon ground cinnamon
1/2 teaspoon ground cardamom
1/2 teaspoon ground cloves
1/2 teaspoon salt
1/2 cup chopped almonds

Chocolate Glaze:
6 oz. semisweet chocolate
1 tablespoon butter or margarine
Blanched almond halves

To make cake, preheat oven to 350F (175C). Grease and flour a 15'' x 10'' jelly-roll pan; set aside. In a large bowl, beat shortening and brown sugar until creamy. Add eggs, honey and orange peel; beat until blended. Dissolve baking soda in water; set aside. Blend flour, cinnamon, cardamom, cloves and salt. Add to honey mixture alternately with reserved soda-water mixture. Fold in almonds. Pour batter into prepared pan; smooth top. Bake 35 to 40 minutes or until a wooden pick inserted in center comes out clean. Cool in pan on a wire rack.
To make glaze, melt chocolate and butter or margarine in a small heavy saucepan over low heat; stir until smooth. Spread glaze over cake. Cut into squares; top each square with an almond half. Makes 1 cake.

Fruity Pound Cake

Pound Cake:
1 cup butter or margarine, room temperature
1-1/4 cups sugar
1-1/2 teaspoons vanilla extract
4 eggs
2-3/4 cups sifted all-purpose flour
2-1/2 teaspoons baking powder
1/2 teaspoon salt
1/2 cup half and half or milk
1 cup raisins
1/2 cup currants or chopped raisins

Cocoa Glaze:
2 cups powdered sugar, sifted
3 tablespoons unsweetened cocoa powder
3 tablespoons butter or margarine, melted
3 to 4 tablespoons hot water

To make cake, preheat oven to 350F (175C). Grease and flour a 9-cup gugelhupf pan or similar cake pan. In a large bowl, beat butter or margarine and sugar until creamy. Add vanilla and eggs; beat until blended. Blend flour, baking powder and salt. Stir into sugar mixture alternately with half and half or milk. Fold in raisins and currants or chopped raisins. Pour batter into prepared pan; smooth top. Bake 45 to 50 minutes or until a wooden pick inserted in center comes out clean. Cool in pan on a wire rack 15 minutes. Remove from pan; cool on wire rack. Place cooled cake, top-side down, on a platter or cake plate.
To make glaze, in a medium bowl, combine powdered sugar and cocoa powder. Add butter or margarine. Add hot water, 1 tablespoon at a time, stirring until glaze is spreadable. Spread glaze over cake; let stand until set. Makes 1 cake.

Fruity Pound Cake

Mandarin-Ricotta Cake

Mandarin-Ricotta Cake

Cake:
1 egg
3 tablespoons warm water
1/2 teaspoon vanilla extract
1/3 cup sugar
1/2 cup sifted all-purpose flour
3/4 teaspoon baking powder

Mandarin-Ricotta Filling:
2 (11-oz.) cans mandarin oranges
2 (1/4-oz.) envelopes unflavored gelatin powder
2 cups ricotta cheese (16 oz.)
1 cup sugar
2 teaspoons vanilla extract
2 cups whipping cream (1 pint)

To make cake, preheat oven to 350F (175C). Grease and flour a 10-inch springform pan. In a medium bowl, beat egg and water until foamy. Add vanilla and sugar; beat until thick and pale. In a sifter, combine flour and baking powder. Gradually sift into egg mixture, folding in while sifting. Pour batter into prepared pan; smooth top. Bake 20 to 25 minutes or until a wooden pick inserted in center comes out clean. Cool in pan on a wire rack.

To make filling, drain oranges, reserving 1/2 cup juice in a small saucepan. Reserve 24 orange segments to decorate cake. Cut each remaining orange segment into 3 pieces; set aside. Sprinkle gelatin over orange juice in saucepan; let stand 5 minutes. Stir over low heat until gelatin dissolves; set aside to cool. In a medium bowl, combine cheese, sugar and vanilla; stir until blended. Stir in cooled gelatin mixture. In another medium bowl, whip cream until stiff peaks form. Spoon 3/4 cup whipped cream into a small pastry bag fitted with a star tip. Refrigerate until ready to use. Fold remaining whipped cream into cheese mixture. Fold in orange pieces.

To complete, spoon filling over cake in pan; smooth top. Refrigerate 4 hours or until filling sets. Run tip of sharp knife around inside edge of pan. Release side of pan; place cake on a platter or cake plate. Pipe reserved whipped cream decoratively on top of cake. Decorate with reserved orange segments. Makes 1 cake.

Sand Cake

Pound Cake:
1 cup butter or margarine, room temperature
1 cup sugar
1 teaspoon vanilla extract or lemon extract
4 eggs
1-3/4 cups cake flour
1/2 teaspoon baking powder
1/4 teaspoon salt

Chocolate Glaze:
4 oz. semisweet chocolate
1 tablespoon butter or margarine

To make cake, preheat oven to 350F (175C). Grease a 9" x 5" loaf pan. Line pan with waxed paper; grease paper. In a large bowl, beat butter or margarine, sugar and vanilla or lemon extract until creamy. Add eggs, 1 at a time, beating well after each addition. Blend cake flour, baking powder and salt; gradually stir into sugar mixture. Pour batter into prepared pan; smooth top. Bake 65 to 70 minutes or until a wooden pick inserted in center comes out clean. Cool in pan on a wire rack 10 minutes. Remove from pan; cool on wire rack. Place cooled cake, top-side up, on a platter or cake plate.

To make glaze, in small heavy saucepan, combine chocolate and butter or margarine. Stir over low heat until melted and smooth; set aside to cool. Spread glaze over side and top of cake except for crack in top. Let stand until glaze sets. Makes 1 cake.

Sand Cake

Lucky Star

Lucky Star

Cake:
3 eggs, separated
3 tablespoons warm water
1 teaspoon vanilla extract
1/2 cup sugar
1 cup cake flour
5 tablespoons butter or margarine, melted

Chocolate Glaze:
4 oz. semisweet chocolate
1 tablespoon vegetable shortening

Decorator's Icing:
1 tablespoon stirred egg white
1 teaspoon water
1 cup powdered sugar, sifted
Food coloring, if desired

Decorations:
Chocolate covered candy coins
Red candied cherries or maraschino cherries
Whole nuts
Candy flowers
Sweetened whipped cream

To make cake, preheat oven to 350F (175C). Grease and flour a 12-point-star mold or a deep, round, 10-inch cake pan; set aside. In a medium bowl, beat egg yolks and water until foamy. Add vanilla and sugar; beat until thick and pale. Gradually sift cake flour over egg-yolk mixture, folding in while sifting. In another medium bowl, beat egg whites until stiff but not dry; fold into batter. Fold in butter or margarine only until no streaks remain. Pour batter into prepared pan; smooth top. Bake 30 to 35 minutes or until a wooden pick inserted in center comes out clean. Cool in pan on a wire rack 10 minutes. Remove from pan; cool on wire rack.

To make glaze, in a small heavy saucepan, melt chocolate and shortening over low heat. Stir until smooth; set aside to cool.

To make icing, in a small bowl, beat egg white and water until foamy. Gradually stir in enough powdered sugar to make a stiff icing. Tint with food coloring, if desired. Spoon icing into a pastry bag fitted with a plain writing tip.

To complete, place cake, bottom-side up, on a wire rack. If a round pan was used, cut 12 evenly spaced points in cake to make a 12-point star. Spread glaze over cake, covering completely. Let stand until glaze sets. Place glazed cake on a platter or cake plate, glazed-side up. Pipe icing decoratively on top of cake. Decorate as desired. Makes 1 cake.

English Cherry Cake

Mocha-Cream Ring

Cake:
2 eggs, separated
3 tablespoons warm water
1/2 cup sugar
1 teaspoon vanilla extract
1/2 cup cake flour
1/4 cup cornstarch
1 teaspoon baking powder

Mocha Cream:
2 cups whipping cream (1 pint)
1/4 cup powdered sugar, sifted
2 teaspoons instant-coffee powder
1 teaspoon vanilla extract

Decorations:
Chocolate-cookie crumbs or chocolate sprinkles
Maraschino cherries
Small fancy chocolate-coated cookies

To make cake, preheat oven to 350F (175C). Grease and flour a 9-inch (6-cup) ring mold; set aside. In a medium bowl, beat egg yolks and water until foamy. Add sugar and vanilla; beat until thick and pale. In a sifter, combine cake flour, cornstarch and baking powder. Gradually sift over egg-yolk mixture, folding in while sifting. In another medium bowl, beat egg whites until stiff but not dry; fold into batter. Pour batter into prepared pan; smooth top. Bake 20 to 25 minutes or until a wooden pick inserted in center comes out clean. Cool in pan on a wire rack 10 minutes. Remove from pan; cool on wire rack. Cut cooled cake into 2 layers.
To make mocha cream, in a medium bowl, whip cream until soft peaks form. Add powdered sugar, coffee powder and vanilla; beat until stiff peaks form. Spoon 1 cup Mocha Cream into a pastry bag fitted with a star tip; set aside.
To complete, fill and frost cake with remaining Mocha Cream. Sprinkle top and side of cake with chocolate-cookie crumbs or chocolate sprinkles. Pipe swirls of reserved Mocha Cream on top of cake. Decorate with maraschino cherries and cookies. Makes 1 cake.

English Cherry Cake

1 (16-oz.) can pitted tart red cherries, drained, halved
2 tablespoons kirsch or other cherry-flavored liqueur
1 cup butter or margarine, room temperature
1 cup sugar
1 teaspoon vanilla extract
5 eggs
2 cups all-purpose flour
2 teaspoons baking powder
1/2 teaspoon salt
1 cup raisins
1/2 cup currants or chopped raisins

Place cherries in a small bowl; sprinkle with liqueur. Set aside. Preheat oven to 325F (165C). Grease an 11'' x 4'' loaf pan. Line pan with waxed paper; grease paper. In a large bowl, beat butter or margarine and sugar until creamy. Add vanilla and eggs; beat until blended. Blend flour, baking powder and salt. Stir into sugar mixture; beat until blended. Fold cherry mixture, raisins and currants or chopped raisins into batter. Pour batter into prepared pan; smooth top. Bake 80 to 85 minutes or until a wooden pick inserted in center comes out clean. Cool in pan on a wire rack 10 minutes. Remove from pan; cool on wire rack. Makes 1 cake.

Mocha-Cream Ring

Pineapple-Marzipan Cake

Pineapple-Marzipan Cake

Cake:
1 (7-oz.) pkg. marzipan or Marzipan, page 232, crumbled
3/4 cup butter or margarine, room temperature
3/4 cup sugar
3 eggs
2 cups all-purpose flour
2 teaspoons baking powder
1 (8-oz.) can crushed pineapple, drained

Chocolate Glaze:
4 oz. semisweet chocolate
1 tablespoon butter or margarine
Pineapple tidbits, if desired

To make cake, preheat oven to 350F (175C). Grease and flour a 9" x 5" loaf pan; set aside. In a large bowl, combine marzipan, butter or margarine, sugar and eggs; beat until creamy. In a sifter, combine flour and baking powder. Gradually sift into marzipan mixture, folding in while sifting. Stir in crushed pineapple until blended. Spread batter in prepared pan; smooth top. Bake 60 to 65 minutes or until a wooden pick inserted in center comes out clean. Cool in pan on a wire rack 10 minutes. Remove from pan; cool on wire rack. Place cooled cake, top-side up, on a platter or cake plate.

To make glaze, in a small heavy saucepan, combine chocolate and butter or margarine. Stir over low heat until melted and smooth. Spread glaze over cake; let stand until set. Decorate with pineapple tidbits, if desired. Makes 1 cake.

Pecan Party Roll

Sponge Cake:
6 eggs, separated
1/2 cup granulated sugar
1 cup finely chopped pecans
2 tablespoons all-purpose flour
1/2 teaspoon baking powder
1/4 teaspoon salt
Powdered sugar, sifted

Filling:
1-1/2 cups whipping cream
3 tablespoons powdered sugar
1 tablespoon brandy, if desired
1/2 cup finely ground pecans
Powdered sugar, sifted
Pecan halves

To make sponge cake, preheat oven to 350F (175C). Grease a 15" x 10" jelly-roll pan. Line pan with waxed paper; grease paper. In top of a double boiler, combine egg yolks and granulated sugar; beat until thick and pale. Place over simmering water. Beat until mixture falls in thick ribbons when beater is lifted, about 5 minutes. Pour mixture into a large bowl; continue beating until mixture cools, about 4 minutes. Fold in chopped pecans; set aside. Beat egg whites until stiff. Stir 2 heaping tablespoons beaten egg whites into egg-yolk mixture until no white remains. Fold in remaining beaten egg whites. In a sifter, combine flour, baking powder and salt. Gradually sift over egg mixture, folding in while sifting. Pour batter into prepared pan; smooth top. Bake 18 to 20 minutes or until top springs back when pressed lightly. Meanwhile, sprinkle a clean towel with powdered sugar. Invert hot cake onto sugar-coated towel. Peel off paper; trim cake edges. Starting at a short end, roll up hot cake in towel. Cool on a wire rack.

To make filling, whip cream until soft peaks form. Beat in 3 tablespoons powdered sugar and brandy until stiff peaks form. Fold in ground pecans.

To complete, unroll cooled cake; spread filling over cake to within 1/4 inch of edges. Reroll cake without towel. Place rolled cake, seam-side down, on a platter or cake plate. Dust with powdered sugar; decorate with pecan halves. Refrigerate until ready to serve. To serve, cut in 1-inch slices. Makes 10 servings.

Caracas Gâteau

French Pound Cake

Caracas Gâteau

Cake:
1/2 cup butter or margarine, room temperature
1/2 (7-oz.) pkg. marzipan or 1/2 recipe Marzipan, page 232
6 eggs, separated
3/4 cup sugar
1 teaspoon vanilla extract
1 cup all-purpose flour
2 teaspoons baking powder
1/2 teaspoon ground cinnamon
1/2 cup finely chopped almonds

Chocolate-Cream Frosting:
2 cups whipping cream (1 pint)
4 oz. semisweet chocolate, melted
2 teaspoons vanilla extract or 1 teaspoon almond extract
1/4 cup powdered sugar, sifted
12 thin chocolate candies
Toasted sliced almonds, if desired

To make cake, preheat oven to 350F (175C). Grease and flour a 10-inch springform pan or deep cake pan; set aside. In a large bowl, beat butter or margarine, marzipan, egg yolks, sugar and vanilla until creamy. Blend flour, baking powder and cinnamon; gradually stir into marzipan mixture, beating until blended. Fold in chopped almonds. In another large bowl, beat egg whites until stiff but not dry; fold into marzipan mixture. Pour batter into prepared pan; smooth top. Bake 30 to 35 minutes or until a wooden pick inserted in center comes out clean. Cool in pan on a wire rack 10 minutes. Remove from pan; cool on wire rack. Cut cooled cake into 2 layers.
To make frosting, in a medium bowl, whip cream until soft peaks form. Add chocolate, vanilla or almond extract and powdered sugar; beat until stiff peaks form.
To complete, spoon 3/4 cup frosting into a pastry bag fitted with a plain tip; set aside. Place bottom cake layer, cut-side down, on a platter or cake plate. Spread with 1/4 of remaining frosting. Add remaining cake layer, cut-side down. Spread remaining frosting over side and top of cake. Press sliced almonds onto side of cake, if desired. With reserved frosting, pipe 12 small spirals around edge of cake. Place a candy piece in each spiral. Refrigerate cake until ready to serve. Makes 1 cake.

French Pound Cake

Cake:
1 cup butter or margarine, room temperature
1 cup packed light-brown sugar
1 teaspoon almond extract
6 eggs
1-3/4 cups all-purpose flour
2 teaspoons baking powder
1/2 cup ground toasted almonds
6 oz. semisweet chocolate, grated

Decorator's Icing:
1 tablespoon stirred egg white
1 teaspoon water
1 cup powdered sugar
Small red candies, if desired

To make cake, preheat oven to 350F (175C). Grease and flour a 10-cup turk's-head mold or 12-cup Bundt pan. In a large bowl, beat butter or margarine, brown sugar and almond extract until creamy. Add eggs, 1 at a time, beating well after each addition. Blend flour and baking powder. Stir into sugar mixture. Fold in almonds and chocolate. Pour batter into prepared pan; smooth top. Bake 50 to 55 minutes or until a wooden pick inserted in center comes out clean. Cool in pan on a wire rack 15 minutes Remove from pan; cool on wire rack. Place cooled cake, top-side down, on a platter or cake plate.
To make icing, in a small bowl, beat egg white and water until foamy. Gradually beat in powdered sugar until icing is very stiff. Spoon icing into a pastry bag fitted with a small plain writing tip. Pipe small dollops of icing on top of cake; pipe lines down side of cake. Decorate with candy, if desired. Makes 1 cake.

Tarts & Flans

Rhubarb-Meringue Tart

Rhubarb-Meringue Tart

Sponge:
1 cup butter or margarine, room temperature
3/4 cup sugar
2 eggs
1 teaspoon vanilla extract
2 cups all-purpose flour
2 teaspoons baking powder

Filling:
2 (28-oz.) pkgs. frozen sliced rhubarb, thawed
2 teaspoons grated orange peel
1 cup powdered sugar

Meringue Topping:
3 egg whites
1/2 cup sugar

To make sponge, preheat oven to 350F (175C). Grease a 15'' x 10'' jelly-roll pan. In a medium bowl, beat butter or margarine, sugar, eggs, and vanilla until creamy. Blend flour and baking powder; stir into sugar mixture. Spread batter in greased pan.

To make filling, in a medium bowl, toss rhubarb with orange peel and powdered sugar; arrange in rows over batter. Bake 20 to 25 minutes or until lightly browned. Cool in pan on a wire rack 20 to 30 minutes. Increase oven heat to 400F (205C).

To make meringue topping, beat egg whites until stiff but not dry. Beat in sugar, 2 tablespoons at a time. Beat until stiff peaks form. Spoon meringue into a pastry tube fitted with a serrated-ribbon tip or a medium star tip. Pipe meringue decoratively over rhubarb. Bake 8 to 10 minutes or until meringue is lightly browned. Cool in pan on wire rack. Cut into squares. Makes about 20 servings.

Apple Flan

Flan Base:
2 eggs, separated
3 tablespoons hot water
1/2 cup sugar
1 teaspoon vanilla extract
1 cup sifted cake flour
1 teaspoon baking powder

Topping:
1 cup sweet white wine
1/2 cup water
4 large, tart baking apples (about 2 lbs.), peeled, cored, sliced
1/4 cup sugar
1 (3-inch) cinnamon stick
4 teaspoons cornstarch
Sweetened whipped cream

To make base, preheat oven to 350F (175C). Grease bottom and side of a 10-inch springform pan. Line side of pan with waxed paper; grease paper. In a medium bowl, beat egg yolks and water until foamy. Beat in sugar and vanilla until thick and pale. In another medium bowl, beat egg whites until stiff but not dry. Fold beaten egg whites into sugar mixture. In a sifter, combine cake flour and baking powder; slowly sift over egg mixture, folding in while sifting. Pour batter into lined pan. Bake 25 to 30 minutes or until top is golden and springs back when pressed lightly. Cool on a wire rack.

To make topping, place wine, water, apples, sugar and cinnamon stick in a large saucepan. Cook over low heat until apples are soft but not mushy. Set aside to cool. Drain apples, reserving liquid; discard cinnamon stick. In a small bowl, blend cornstarch and 1/4 cup reserved apple liquid until smooth; set aside. Return remaining apple liquid to saucepan; bring to a boil. Boil rapidly 5 minutes. Slowly stir in cornstarch mixture; cook over low heat, stirring, until mixture is clear and thick. Use to brush over cake. Arrange cooked apples, pinwheel fashion, over glaze. Generously brush apples with remaining glaze. Refrigerate 3 to 4 hours or until glaze sets. Remove from pan; peel off paper. Decorate with whipped cream. Makes 1 flan.

Apple Flan

On previous pages: Fruit Flan, page 86.

Wine & Apple Flan

Wine & Apple Flan

Flan Sponge:
1/3 cup butter or margarine, room temperature
1/2 cup sugar
2 eggs
1 teaspoon vanilla extract
1 cup all-purpose flour
1 teaspoon baking powder
1/2 teaspoon salt
1/4 cup milk

Filling:
1/2 cup sugar
1/2 cup sweet white wine or sweet sherry
1/2 cup water
4 Golden Delicious apples, peeled, quartered, cored
1 (3-inch) cinnamon stick
1/3 cup golden raisins
1/3 cup dark raisins
1/4 cup slivered almonds
3 tablespoons sugar
1/2 teaspoon ground cinnamon
Sweetened whipped cream, if desired

To make sponge, preheat oven to 400F (205C). Grease a 10-inch flan pan. In a medium bowl, beat butter or margarine, sugar, eggs and vanilla until creamy. Blend flour, baking powder and salt; stir into sugar mixture alternately with milk. Spread in greased pan. Bake 18 to 20 minutes or until lightly browned. Let stand in pan on a wire rack 10 minutes. Remove from pan; cool on wire rack.

To make filling, in a medium saucepan, combine 1/2 cup sugar, wine or sherry and water. Bring to a boil over medium heat; add apples and cinnamon stick. Reduce heat; cover and cook 5 minutes or until apples are crisp-tender. Drain apples, reserving liquid; discard cinnamon stick. Sprinkle 1/4 cup reserved apple liquid over sponge. Return remaining apple liquid to saucepan; bring to a boil. Boil rapidly until reduced to 1/3 cup; set aside to cool. Arrange cooked apples, cut-side down, over sponge; brush with reduced apple liquid. In a small bowl, combine raisins, almonds, 3 tablespoons sugar and ground cinnamon. Sprinkle over apples. If desired, top with sweetened whipped cream. Makes 1 flan.

Plum Tart

Plum Tart

Pastry:
1-1/2 cups all-purpose flour
1-1/2 teaspoons baking powder
1/3 cup sugar
1/2 cup butter or margarine, chilled
1 egg, slightly beaten

Filling:
3 tablespoons butter or margarine
1/3 cup sugar
1 tablespoon cornstarch
2 tablespoons milk
1 cup ricotta cheese (8 oz.)
1 egg
1 teaspoon lemon extract
1-3/4 lbs. small purple plums or Italian prunes, halved,
   pitted, or 2 (29-oz.) cans purple plums, drained, halved,
   pitted

Topping:
2 tablespoons butter, melted
2 tablespoons sugar
1/4 teaspoon ground cinnamon
1/4 cup sliced blanched almonds

To make pastry, preheat oven to 350F (175C). In a medium bowl, blend flour, baking powder and sugar. Use a pastry blender or 2 knives to cut in butter or margarine until mixture resembles coarse crumbs. Add egg; toss until mixture binds together. Pat or press dough into an ungreased 15" x 10" jelly-roll pan; prick pastry with tines of a fork. Bake 15 minutes; set aside to cool.

To make filling, in a medium bowl, beat butter or margarine and sugar until creamy. Beat in cornstarch and milk. Add ricotta cheese, egg and lemon extract; beat until blended. Spread filling over baked crust. Arrange plums, skin-side down, over filling. Bake 30 minutes or until browned. Cool in pan on a wire rack.

To make topping, drizzle butter over plums. In a small bowl, combine sugar, cinnamon and almonds; sprinkle over plums. Makes 16 to 20 servings.

On previous pages: Plum Tart.

Blueberry-Cheese Flan

Blueberry-Cheese Flan

Pastry:
1 (3-oz.) pkg. cream cheese, room temperature
3 tablespoons sugar
1/4 cup vegetable oil
1 tablespoon milk
1 egg
1-3/4 cups all-purpose flour
2 teaspoons baking powder

Filling:
5 cups fresh or frozen blueberries, thawed, drained
1/2 cup sugar
3 tablespoons cornstarch
1 (8-oz.) pkg. cream cheese, room temperature
3 tablespoons butter, room temperature
1/3 cup sugar
1/3 cup milk
1 egg
2 teaspoons vanilla extract
1 egg yolk beaten with 1 tablespoon milk for glaze

To make pastry, preheat oven to 325F (165C). Grease a 10-inch springform pan. In a medium bowl, beat cream cheese, sugar, oil, milk and egg until blended. Blend flour and baking powder; fold into sugar mixture, 1/2 cup at a time. Gather dough into a ball. On a lightly floured surface, roll out dough to a 14-inch circle. Use to line greased pan, pressing dough 1-1/2 inches up side of pan.
To make filling, toss blueberries with 1/2 cup sugar and cornstarch. Spread over bottom crust. In a medium bowl, beat cream cheese, butter, 1/3 cup sugar, milk, egg and vanilla until blended. Pour over blueberries; smooth surface. Lightly brush top with egg-yolk glaze. Bake 1 hour 15 minutes or until top is lightly browned and center is set. Cool in pan on a wire rack. When cool, remove from pan. Makes 1 flan.

Fruit Flan

Photo on pages 78-79.

1 Flan Sponge, page 81

Filling:
4 or 5 kiwifruit or 1 pint strawberries, raspberries or
  other fresh fruit
1 teaspoon lemon juice for kiwifruit
1/3 cup apple jelly or red-currant jelly
1 cup whipping cream (1/2 pint)
1 teaspoon vanilla extract
2 tablespoons powdered sugar

Prepare Flan Sponge.

To make filling, peel and thinly slice kiwifruit; brush
with lemon juice. Or wash and hull strawberries; wash
other fresh fruit. Melt jelly in a small saucepan over low
heat; set aside to cool. Whip cream until soft peaks form.
Beat in vanilla and powdered sugar. Beat until stiff peaks
form. Spread 1/2 of whipped-cream mixture over sponge.
Arrange sliced fruit in slightly overlapping circles over
top. Brush melted jelly over fruit; let stand until set.
Serve with remaining whipped-cream mixture. Makes 1
flan.

Red-Currant Tart

Fruit Flan

Red-Currant Tart

Cake:
1 cup butter or margarine, room temperature
2/3 cup sugar
2 eggs
1 teaspoon vanilla extract
2 cups all-purpose flour
2 teaspoons baking powder
1/2 teaspoon salt
1/3 cup milk

Filling:
3 eggs
2 egg yolks
2 cups ricotta cheese (16 oz.)
1-1/4 cups sugar
1/2 cup all-purpose flour
1 tablespoon grated orange peel
2 cups red currants or blueberries

Meringue:
2 egg whites
5 tablespoons sugar
2 tablespoons sliced blanched almonds

Cherry & Almond Tart

Pastry:
1-1/4 cups all-purpose flour
3 tablespoons sugar
1/2 teaspoon salt
1/2 cup butter or margarine, chilled
1 egg, slightly beaten
2 tablespoons dry breadcrumbs

Filling:
1 (17-oz.) can pitted, dark sweet cherries, drained, halved
1/4 cup whipping cream
1/3 cup sugar
1 egg
1 tablespoon cornstarch
1/2 teaspoon almond extract
1/2 cup finely chopped, blanched almonds

To make pastry, preheat oven to 325F (165C). In a medium bowl, blend flour, sugar and salt. Use a pastry blender or 2 knives to cut in butter or margarine until mixture resembles coarse crumbs. Add egg; toss until mixture binds together. Gather dough together; shape into a flat ball. On a lightly floured surface, roll out dough to a 12-inch circle. Use to line an ungreased 9-inch springform pan, pressing dough 1 inch up side of pan. Sprinkle breadcrumbs over bottom crust.

To make filling, arrange cherries over breadcrumbs. In a small bowl, beat cream, sugar, egg, cornstarch and almond extract only until blended. Stir in almonds. Carefully pour mixture over cherries. Bake 40 to 45 minutes or until center is set. Cool in pan on a wire rack. When cool, remove from pan. Makes 1 tart.

To make cake, preheat oven to 350F (175C). Grease an 18" x 12" jelly-roll pan or sheet pan. In a medium bowl, beat butter or margarine, sugar, eggs and vanilla until creamy. Blend flour, baking powder and salt; stir into sugar mixture alternately with milk. Spread batter evenly in greased pan.

To make filling, in a medium bowl, beat eggs, egg yolks, ricotta cheese, sugar, flour and orange peel until blended. Fold in currants or blueberries. Pour filling over batter in pan. Bake 35 to 40 minutes or until a wooden pick inserted in center comes out clean. Cool in pan on a wire rack 15 minutes.

To make meringue, increase oven heat to 400F (205C). Beat egg whites until stiff but not dry. Beat in sugar, 1 tablespoon at a time, until stiff peaks form. Spread meringue over baked filling. Sprinkle with almonds. Bake 6 to 8 minutes or until meringue is golden. Cool in pan on wire rack. Makes about 48 servings.

Bohemian Apple Flan

Bohemian Apple Flan

Pastry:
1-1/2 cups all-purpose flour
1/4 cup packed light-brown sugar
1/2 teaspoon baking powder
3/4 cup butter or margarine, chilled
1 egg, beaten

Filling:
1/2 cup raisins
2 tablespoons dark rum
2 tablespoons butter or margarine
2 tablespoons dry breadcrumbs
1 tablespoon sugar
1 teaspoon ground cinnamon
2 tart red apples (about 1 lb.), peeled, cored, sliced
2 (8-oz.) pkgs. cream cheese, room temperature
1/2 cup sugar
1/4 cup all-purpose flour
2 eggs, separated
1 tablespoon grated lemon peel
1 cup dairy sour cream (1/2 pint)
1 egg yolk beaten with 1 tablespoon milk for glaze

To make pastry, in a medium bowl, blend flour, brown sugar and baking powder. Use a pastry blender or 2 knives to cut in butter or margarine until mixture resembles coarse crumbs. Add egg; toss to distribute. Shape dough into a flat ball. Cover; refrigerate 1 hour. Roll out dough to a 13-inch circle. Use to line an ungreased 9-inch springform pan, pressing pastry 2 inches up side of pan. Preheat oven to 300F (150C).
To make filling, in a small bowl, combine raisins and rum; set aside. Melt butter or margarine in a small skillet. Stir in breadcrumbs, 1 tablespoon sugar and cinnamon. Stir until crumbs are lightly browned. Sprinkle over bottom of pastry. Sprinkle with raisin mixture. Arrange apple slices over top. In a medium bowl, beat cream cheese, 1/2 cup sugar, flour, egg yolks and lemon peel. Fold in sour cream. Beat egg whites until stiff but not dry. Fold into cream-cheese mixture. Pour over apples. Brush egg-yolk glaze over top of filling. Bake 1 hour and 15 to 25 minutes or until top is lightly browned and center is set. Cool in pan on a wire rack. When cool, remove from pan. Makes 1 flan.

Fruit-Filled Meringues

Meringue Cases:
3 egg whites, room temperature
Pinch of cream of tartar
3/4 cup sugar

Fruit Filling:
3 cups seedless green grapes
1/3 cup sugar
1 cup water

Glaze:
1/2 cup apple jelly or red-currant jelly

To make meringue cases, preheat oven to 250F (120C). Line a baking sheet with parchment paper. Draw 6 (3-1/2-inch) circles on parchment paper. In a medium bowl, beat egg whites and cream of tartar until foamy. Beat in sugar, 2 tablespoons at a time. Beat at high speed with an electric mixer about 15 minutes or until stiff peaks form and sugar is completely dissolved. Rub a little meringue between your fingertips. If it feels grainy, continue beating until mixture is smooth. Spoon meringue into a large pastry bag fitted with a large star tip. Starting in center of each circle, pipe meringue in a continuous spiral, filling in each circle. Pipe a ring of meringue on top edge of each circle. If desired, pipe 6 dollops of meringue onto parchment paper for decoration. Bake 50 minutes. Turn off oven; leave meringues in oven 2 to 3 hours to dry. Remove from oven; cool completely on pan on a wire rack. When cool, peel off parchment paper. Store in a container with a tight-fitting lid until ready to use.

To make filling, in a medium saucepan, cook grapes, sugar and water over low heat, stirring gently, until grapes are soft. Do not let skins pop or break open. Drain; discard liquid. Cool completely. Spoon cooled grapes into meringue cases.

To glaze, melt jelly in a small saucepan over low heat; set aside to cool. Brush over grapes. Top with meringue dollops, if desired. Makes 6 meringue cases.

Fruit-Filled Meringues

Variations

To make rhubarb filling, trim 1-1/2 lbs. fresh rhubarb; cut into 1-inch pieces. In a medium saucepan, combine rhubarb pieces, 3/4 cup sugar, 1 tablespoon grated orange peel and 1/4 cup water. Cook over low heat, stirring occasionally, until rhubarb is tender. Set aside to cool. When cool, drain and spoon into meringue cases; glaze as above.

To make strawberry filling, wash, hull and slice 1 pint fresh strawberries. Place in a medium bowl; sprinkle with 2 tablespoons sugar, if desired. Let stand 30 minutes. Spoon into meringue cases; glaze as above.

To make ice-cream filling, fill meringue cases with ice cream. Top with a sweet sauce or fresh or canned fruit.

Fruit-Filled Meringues

Apple & Marzipan Flan

Pastry:
1 cup all-purpose flour
2/3 cup ground almonds
1/3 cup sugar
1/2 teaspoon baking powder
1/2 teaspoon ground cinnamon
1/2 cup butter or margarine, chilled
1 egg yolk
2 to 3 tablespoons ice water

Marzipan Filling:
1 (7-oz.) pkg. marzipan or Marzipan, page 232, crumbled
1/2 cup butter or margarine, room temperature
3/4 cup powdered sugar, sifted
2 eggs
1 egg white
3/4 cup all-purpose flour
1 teaspoon baking powder
3 medium, tart cooking apples, peeled, cored

To make pastry, in a medium bowl, blend flour, almonds, sugar, baking powder and cinnamon. Use a pastry blender or 2 knives to cut in butter or margarine until mixture resembles coarse crumbs. In a small bowl, beat egg yolk and 2 tablespoons water until blended. Sprinkle over flour mixture; toss with a fork until mixture binds together. Add remaining 1 tablespoon water, if necessary. Shape dough into a slightly flat ball. Cover; refrigerate 30 minutes. Roll out 2/3 of dough to a 10-inch circle. Place in bottom of an ungreased 10-inch springform pan. Roll out remaining dough; press around inside rim of pan so pastry comes 1 inch up side of pan. Press side and bottom pastries together. Preheat oven to 375F (190C).

To make filling, in a medium bowl, beat marzipan and butter or margarine until creamy. Beat in powdered sugar, eggs and egg white. Blend flour and baking powder; gradually stir into marzipan mixture. Chop 2 apples; stir into marzipan mixture. Spoon mixture evenly into pastry-lined pan. Thinly slice remaining apple; arrange slices over filling, like spokes of a wheel. Bake 40 to 45 minutes or until top is golden brown. Cool in pan on a wire rack. Remove from pan; place on a serving plate. Makes 1 flan.

Apple & Marzipan Flan

Latticed Apple Tart

Pastry:
1 cup butter or margarine, room temperature
1 (8-oz.) pkg. cream cheese, room temperature
2 tablespoons sugar
1/2 teaspoon salt
2-1/4 cups all-purpose flour

Filling:
6 medium, red apples (about 3 lbs.) peeled, cored, sliced
3/4 cup raisins
1/2 cup sugar
2 tablespoons grated lemon peel
Milk
Sugar

To make pastry, in a medium bowl, beat butter or margarine, cream cheese, sugar and salt until creamy. Gradually stir in flour. Shape dough into a flat ball. Cover; refrigerate 1 hour. Preheat oven to 350F (175C). Grease a 15" x 10" jelly-roll pan. On a lightly floured surface, roll out 2/3 of dough to a 17" x 12" rectangle about 1/4 inch thick. Use to line greased pan. Roll out remaining dough to a rectangle 1/4 inch thick. Cut in 1/2-inch-wide strips.

To make filling, in a large bowl, combine apples, raisins, sugar and lemon peel. Pour into dough-lined pan. Arrange pastry strips in a lattice pattern over apples. Brush pastry strips with milk; sprinkle with sugar. Bake 40 to 45 minutes or until top is golden brown. Cool in pan on a wire rack. Cut into squares. Makes about 20 servings.

Latticed Apple Tart

Linzer Torte

2 cups sifted all-purpose flour
2/3 cup sugar
1 teaspoon baking powder
1 teaspoon ground cinnamon
1/8 teaspoon ground cloves
3/4 cup butter or margarine, chilled
1 egg, slightly beaten
1/2 cup ground almonds
3/4 cup raspberry jam or preserves
1 egg yolk blended with 1 tablespoon milk for glaze

In a medium bowl, blend flour, sugar, baking powder, cinnamon and cloves. Use a pastry blender or 2 knives to cut in butter or margarine until mixture resembles coarse crumbs. Add egg and almonds; toss until mixture binds together. Divide dough in half. Cover 1/2 of dough; refrigerate 30 minutes. Roll out remaining dough to an 11-inch circle; use to line an ungreased 10-inch springform pan, pressing dough about 1/2 inch up side of pan. Refrigerate crust 30 minutes. Preheat oven to 350F (175C). Roll out remaining 1/2 of dough to a rectangle 1/4 inch thick; cut into 14 (1/2-inch-wide) strips. Spread raspberry jam over refrigerated crust. Arrange 10 dough strips over jam, making a lattice top. Carefully brush pastry edge with egg-yolk glaze. Place remaining 4 pastry strips around top outer edge of torte; brush strips with egg-yolk glaze. Bake 30 to 35 minutes or until top is browned. Cool in pan on a wire rack. When cool, remove from pan. Makes 1 torte.

Linzer Torte

Apple-Custard Tart

Apple-Custard Tart

Custard Filling:
2 eggs
3 egg yolks
2/3 cup sugar
1/2 cup all-purpose flour
1/2 teaspoon salt
3 cups milk, scalded, cooled
2 teaspoons vanilla extract

Pastry:
2 (3-oz.) pkgs. cream cheese, room temperature
1/3 cup sugar
1/4 cup milk
1/4 cup vegetable oil
2-1/2 cups all-purpose flour
2 teaspoons baking powder
1 teaspoon salt

Topping:
7 medium baking apples, peeled, cored, sliced 1/2 inch thick
2 tablespoons apricot jam
1 tablespoon water
2 tablespoons apricot-flavored brandy

To make custard filling, in top of a double boiler, beat eggs, egg yolks and sugar until thick and pale. Beat in flour and salt until blended. Gradually stir in milk. Place top of double boiler over pan of simmering water. Stirring constantly, cook until custard is smooth and thick. Pour custard into a medium bowl. Stir in vanilla. Cover surface of custard with waxed paper; set aside to cool.

To make pastry, preheat oven to 375F (190C). Grease a 15'' x 10'' jelly-roll pan. In a medium bowl, beat cream cheese, sugar, milk and oil until blended. Blend flour, baking powder and salt; fold into cream-cheese mixture, 1/2 cup at a time. On a lightly floured surface, roll out dough to a 16'' x 11'' rectangle. Use to line greased pan. Spread cooled custard evenly over crust.

To make topping, arrange apple slices in overlapping rows over custard. Bake 45 to 55 minutes or until apples are tender and crust is lightly browned. Place pan on a wire rack. Press jam through a sieve into a small saucepan; add water and brandy. Over low heat, cook, stirring, until mixture comes to a boil. Use to brush over apples while tart is still warm. Cool completely in pan on a wire rack. Refrigerate 1 hour before serving. Makes about 20 servings.

Pear & Black-Cherry Flan

Shortbread Crust:
1-3/4 cups all-purpose flour
1/3 cup sugar
3/4 cup butter or margarine, chilled
1 egg yolk, slightly beaten

Filling:
1 (3-oz.) pkg. black-cherry-flavored gelatin
3/4 cup boiling water
1/2 cup cold water
1 cup whipping cream (1/2 pint)
2 tablespoons sugar
1 (16-oz.) can sliced pears, drained

To Decorate:
1/2 cup whipping cream
1 tablespoon sugar
Grated chocolate

To make crust, preheat oven to 375F (190C). Grease a 10-inch springform pan. In a medium bowl, blend flour and sugar. Use a pastry blender or 2 knives to cut in butter or margarine until mixture resembles coarse crumbs. Add egg yolk; toss to distribute. Press dough onto bottom and 1-1/2 inches up side of greased pan. Prick bottom with tines of a fork. Bake 15 to 18 minutes or until golden. Cool in pan on a wire rack.

To make filling, dissolve gelatin in boiling water. Stir in cold water; refrigerate until gelatin is syrupy, about 45 minutes. Whip cream until soft peaks form. Add sugar; beat until stiff peaks form. Fold whipped-cream mixture into partially set gelatin. Arrange pears on bottom of cooled crust. Pour gelatin mixture over pears; refrigerate 3 to 4 hours or until set. When set, remove from pan.

To decorate, whip cream until soft peaks form. Beat in sugar until stiff peaks form. Spoon into a pastry bag fitted with a star tip; pipe dollops on top of flan while rotating tip. Sprinkle chocolate over dollops. Makes 1 flan.

Starburst Apricot Tart

Starburst Apricot Tart

Pastry:
2 cups all-purpose flour
5 tablespoons sugar
1-1/2 teaspoons baking powder
1 teaspoon salt
3/4 cup butter or margarine, chilled
1 egg
1 egg yolk

Filling:
1/2 cup whipping cream
1/2 cup sugar
2 eggs
3/4 cup ground almonds
1 (30-oz.) can apricot halves, drained
Whole blanched almonds

To make pastry, in a medium bowl, blend flour, sugar, baking powder and salt. Use a pastry blender or 2 knives to cut in butter or margarine until mixture resembles coarse crumbs. In a small bowl, beat egg and egg yolk. Add to flour mixture; toss until mixture binds together. Shape dough into a flat ball. Cover; refrigerate 30 minutes. On a lightly floured surface, roll out dough to a 12-inch circle. Use to line an ungreased 10-inch springform pan, pressing dough 1 inch up side of pan. Preheat oven to 350F (175C).
To make filling, in a medium bowl, beat cream, sugar and eggs until blended. Stir in ground almonds. Pour mixture into pastry-lined pan. Arrange apricot halves, rounded-side down, over egg mixture. Place a whole almond in center of each apricot. Bake 55 to 65 minutes or until top is lightly browned. Cool in pan on a wire rack. When cool, remove from pan. Makes 1 tart.

Quick Breads & Coffeecakes

Peach-Crumb Coffeecake

2/3 cup butter or margarine, room temperature
3/4 cup sugar
1 teaspoon vanilla extract
4 eggs
2 cups all-purpose flour
1 teaspoon baking powder
1/2 teaspoon salt
1 (29-oz.) can sliced peaches, drained

Crumb Topping:
1 cup all-purpose flour
1/2 cup sugar
1/2 teaspoon ground cinnamon
1/2 cup butter or margarine, chilled

Glaze:
1 cup powdered sugar, sifted
1 to 2 tablespoons lemon juice

Preheat oven to 350F (175C). Grease a 15'' x 10'' jelly-roll pan. In a medium bowl, beat butter or margarine, sugar, vanilla and eggs until creamy. Blend flour, baking powder and salt; stir into sugar mixture. Spread batter in greased pan. Arrange peaches in rows on top of batter.

To make topping, in a small bowl, blend flour, sugar and cinnamon. Use a pastry blender or 2 knives to cut in butter or margarine until mixture resembles coarse crumbs; sprinkle over peaches. Bake 30 to 35 minutes or until a wooden pick inserted in center comes out clean. Cool in pan on a wire rack.

To make glaze, in a small bowl, blend powdered sugar and lemon juice until smooth; spoon over top of cake. Cut cake into squares; serve from pan. Makes about 20 servings.

Peach-Crumb Coffeecake

Candied-Fruit Loaf

2 cups all-purpose flour
1-1/2 teaspoons baking powder
1/2 teaspoon baking soda
1/2 teaspoon salt
1/2 cup chopped walnuts, pecans or almonds
1/2 cup currants
1/2 cup raisins
1/2 cup chopped mixed candied fruit
3/4 cup orange juice
3/4 cup sugar
1/4 cup vegetable oil
1 egg, beaten
1 teaspoon orange extract

Preheat oven to 350F (175C). Grease an 8'' x 4'' loaf pan. In a medium bowl, blend flour, baking powder, baking soda, salt, nuts, currants, raisins and candied fruit. In a small bowl, combine orange juice, sugar, oil, egg and orange extract. Stir into flour mixture. Pour into greased pan. Bake 60 to 65 minutes or until a wooden pick inserted in center comes out clean. Let stand in pan on a wire rack 10 minutes. Remove from pan; cool on wire rack. Makes 1 loaf.

On previous pages: Cherry-Raisin Coffeecake, page 102.

Grandma's Nut Loaf

3 cups all-purpose flour
1 cup sugar
3-1/2 teaspoons baking powder
1 teaspoon salt
2 eggs, beaten
1-1/4 cups milk
1/4 cup vegetable oil
1-1/2 cups finely chopped pecans, walnuts or almonds
1/4 cup apricot jam
2 tablespoons water

Preheat oven to 325F (165C). Grease a 9'' x 5'' loaf pan. In a large bowl, blend flour, sugar, baking powder and salt. In a small bowl, combine eggs, milk and oil. Stir into flour mixture; fold in nuts. Pour batter into greased pan. Bake 65 to 75 minutes or until a wooden pick inserted in center comes out clean. Let stand in pan on a wire rack 10 minutes. Remove from pan; cool on wire rack. Press jam through a sieve into a small saucepan. Add water; bring to a boil. Set aside to cool. Brush cooled jam mixture over top of bread. Makes 1 loaf.

Cinnamon-Nut Coffeecake

1/3 cup butter or margarine, room temperature
1/2 cup granulated sugar
1 teaspoon vanilla extract
2 eggs
1-1/2 cups all-purpose flour
2 teaspoons baking powder
1/2 cup milk
1/2 cup chopped walnuts, pecans or almonds
1/4 cup packed light-brown sugar
1 teaspoon ground cinnamon

Glaze:
3/4 cup powdered sugar
3 to 4 teaspoons milk

Preheat oven to 350F (175C). Grease a 9-inch-square baking pan. In a medium bowl, beat butter or margarine, granulated sugar and vanilla until creamy. Beat in eggs, 1 at a time. Blend flour and baking powder; stir into sugar mixture alternately with milk. Spread 1/2 of batter in greased pan. Combine nuts, brown sugar and cinnamon. Sprinkle 1/2 of nut mixture over batter in pan. Carefully top with remaining batter. Sprinkle with remaining nut mixture. Bake 30 to 35 minutes or until a wooden pick inserted in center comes out clean. Cool in pan on a wire rack.

To make glaze, in a small bowl, blend powdered sugar and milk until smooth; drizzle over coffeecake. Let stand until glaze sets. Slice and serve directly from pan. Makes about 12 servings.

Orange-Sponge Waffles

3 eggs
1/4 cup sugar
1-3/4 cups cake flour
2 teaspoons baking powder
3/4 teaspoon salt
1-1/4 cups milk
1/3 cup butter or margarine, melted, cooled
2 tablespoons grated orange peel

In a medium bowl, beat eggs and sugar until thick and pale. Blend cake flour, baking powder and salt; stir into sugar mixture alternately with milk. Fold in melted butter or margarine and orange peel. Preheat a waffle iron. Using 1/2 to 1 cup batter, bake according to manufacturer's directions. Serve with ice cream. Makes 6 to 12 waffles.

Cinnamon-Nut Coffeecake

Sour-Cream Coffeecake

Sour-Cream Coffeecake

1 cup sugar
1/2 cup butter or margarine, room temperature
2 eggs
1 teaspoon vanilla extract
2 cups all-purpose flour
1-1/2 teaspoons baking powder
1 teaspoon baking soda
1/4 teaspoon salt
1 cup dairy sour cream (1/2 pint)
1/2 cup currants or chopped raisins
2 tablespoons butter or margarine, melted
2/3 cup sliced almonds

Preheat oven to 350F (175C). Grease a 15" x 10" jelly-roll pan. Reserve 1/4 cup sugar. In a medium bowl, beat 1/2 cup butter or margarine, 3/4 cup sugar, eggs and vanilla until creamy. Blend flour, baking powder, baking soda and salt; stir into sugar mixture alternately with sour cream. Fold in currants or raisins. Spread batter in greased pan. Brush 2 tablespoons butter or margarine over batter. Sprinkle reserved 1/4 cup sugar over cake; sprinkle with almonds. Bake 25 to 30 minutes or until a wooden pick inserted in center comes out clean. Cool in pan on a wire rack. Cut into squares. Makes about 20 servings.

Rich Cream Waffles

3 eggs, separated
1 cup half and half (1/2 pint)
5 tablespoons butter or margarine, melted
3 tablespoons sugar
1-1/2 cups cake flour
2 teaspoons baking powder
1/2 teaspoon salt

In a medium bowl, beat egg yolks, half and half, butter or margarine and sugar until smooth. Blend cake flour, baking powder and salt; stir into sugar mixture. In another medium bowl, beat egg whites until stiff but not dry. Fold beaten egg whites into batter. Preheat a waffle iron. Using 1/2 to 1 cup batter, bake according to manufacturer's directions. Serve with sweetened butter, hot maple syrup or honey. Makes 4 to 8 waffles.

Rich Cream Waffles

Hazelnut Waffles

Hazelnut Waffles

2 eggs, separated
3 tablespoons sugar
1/3 cup butter or margarine, melted
1-1/2 cups milk
2 cups sifted all-purpose flour
2 teaspoons baking powder
1/2 teaspoon salt
1/2 cup ground hazelnuts
Sweetened whipped cream and hazelnuts

In a medium bowl, beat egg yolks, sugar, butter or margarine and milk until blended. Blend flour, baking powder and salt; stir into sugar mixture. In another medium bowl, beat egg whites until stiff but not dry. Fold beaten egg whites into batter. Fold in ground hazelnuts. Preheat a waffle iron. Using 1/2 to 1 cup batter, bake according to manufacturer's directions. Serve with sweetened whipped cream and hazelnuts. Makes 6 to 12 waffles.

Raisin-Bread Special

2 cups boiling water
1 lb. raisins
1/2 cup butter or margarine, room temperature
1-1/2 cups sugar
2 eggs, beaten
1 teaspoon vanilla extract
4 cups all-purpose flour
1 teaspoon salt
2 teaspoons baking soda
1/2 cup chopped walnuts, if desired

Collect 5 empty cans similar to 16-ounce vegetable cans; set aside. In a medium bowl, pour boiling water over raisins. Let stand overnight. Grease insides of cans. Cut 5 (7'' x 6'') pieces of waxed paper. Grease 1 side of each paper; roll into a tube, greased-side in. Carefully insert into cans, spreading tubes to fit against sides of cans. Preheat oven to 350F (175C). In a large bowl, beat butter or margarine and sugar until creamy. Beat in eggs and vanilla. Stir in raisins with water. Blend flour, salt and baking soda. Stir into raisin mixture. Stir in walnuts, if desired. Spoon evenly into prepared cans, filling each can at least 2/3 full. Bake 1 hour. Remove from oven. Let cool on a wire rack 10 minutes. Remove bread and waxed paper from cans. Remove waxed paper from bread. Serve warm or cold. Makes 5 small loaves.

Cherry-Raisin Coffeecake

Cherry-Raisin Coffeecake
Photo on cover and pages 96-97.

1/2 cup butter or margarine, room temperature
1 cup granulated sugar
4 eggs
1-1/2 teaspoons lemon extract
2-1/4 cups all-purpose flour
2-1/2 teaspoons baking powder
1/2 teaspoon salt
3/4 cup milk
1 tablespoon grated lemon peel
1/2 cup raisins
1/2 cup coarsely chopped red candied cherries
Powdered sugar

Preheat oven to 325F (165C). Grease and flour a 9-cup gugelhupf pan or similar cake pan. In a large bowl, beat butter or margarine and granulated sugar until creamy. Add eggs and lemon extract; beat until blended. Blend flour, baking powder and salt; stir into sugar mixture alternately with milk. Fold in lemon peel, raisins and cherries. Pour batter into prepared pan; smooth top. Bake 50 to 55 minutes or until a wooden pick inserted in center comes out clean. Cool in pan on a wire rack 10 minutes. Remove from pan; cool on wire rack. Place cake, top-side down, on a platter or cake plate. Dust with powdered sugar. Makes 1 cake.

Sour-Cream Waffles

Sour-Cream Waffles

2 eggs, separated
3 tablespoons sugar
2 cups dairy sour cream (1 pint)
1/4 cup butter or margarine, melted
2 cups sifted all-purpose flour
1-1/2 teaspoons baking powder
1 teaspoon baking soda
1/2 teaspoon salt

Cranberry Cream:
1 cup whipping cream (1/2 pint)
2 tablespoons sugar
1/4 to 1/2 cup coarsely chopped cranberries

In a medium bowl, beat egg yolks and sugar until pale. Stir in sour cream and butter or margarine. Blend flour, baking powder, baking soda and salt; stir into sugar mixture. In a small bowl, beat egg whites until stiff but not dry. Fold beaten egg whites into batter. Preheat a waffle iron. Using 1/2 to 1 cup batter, bake according to manufacturer's directions.
To make cranberry cream, whip cream until soft peaks form. Beat in sugar until stiff peaks form; fold in cranberries. Spoon Cranberry Cream over baked waffles. Makes 4 to 8 waffles.

Fruity Quick Bread

1/4 cup butter or margarine, room temperature
1 cup sugar
3 eggs
2-1/2 cups sifted all-purpose flour
2 teaspoons baking powder
1/2 teaspoon baking soda
1/2 teaspoon salt
3/4 cup milk
1 cup golden raisins
1 cup dark raisins
1/2 cup chopped candied citron

Preheat oven to 350F (175C). Grease a 9" x 5" loaf pan. In a medium bowl, beat butter or margarine and sugar until creamy. Beat in eggs, 1 at a time. Blend flour, baking powder, baking soda and salt; stir into sugar mixture alternately with milk. Fold in raisins and citron. Pour batter into greased pan. Bake 65 to 70 minutes or until a wooden pick inserted in center comes out clean. Let stand in pan on a wire rack 10 minutes. Remove from pan; cool on wire rack. Makes 1 loaf.

Spicy Beet Bread

Bread:
4 cups all-purpose flour
1 teaspoon baking powder
1/2 teaspoon baking soda
1/2 teaspoon salt
2 teaspoons ground cinnamon
1/2 teaspoon ground cloves
1/2 teaspoon ground ginger
1 teaspoon grated lemon peel
2/3 cup vegetable shortening
1/2 cup granulated sugar
1 cup packed light-brown sugar
2 eggs, beaten
1 (16-oz.) can cut beets

Beet Glaze:
1/2 cup packed light-brown sugar
1/4 cup orange juice

To make bread, preheat oven to 325F (165C). Grease a 9" x 5" loaf pan; set aside. In a medium bowl, blend flour, baking powder, baking soda, salt, cinnamon, cloves, ginger and lemon peel; set aside. In a large bowl, cream shortening and sugars; add eggs. Beat until light and fluffy, about 4 minutes. Drain beets, reserving 1/2 cup liquid. Puree drained beets in a blender or food processor or by pressing through a fine sieve. Stir puree into egg mixture. Fold in 3 cups flour mixture. Stir in 1/4 cup reserved beet liquid; reserve remaining liquid for glaze. Fold remaining flour mixture into beet mixture. Spoon batter into prepared pan; smooth top. Bake about 50 minutes or until a wooden pick inserted in center comes out clean. While bread bakes, prepare glaze.

Fruity Quick Bread

To make glaze, in a small saucepan, combine brown sugar, orange juice and 1/4 cup reserved beet liquid. Simmer over medium heat until mixture reaches 170F (75C) on a candy thermometer and is slightly thickened. Cover; keep warm.

To complete, place a wire rack over a piece of waxed paper on a flat surface. Remove baked bread from pan; place on wire rack. Pierce loaf several times with a wooden skewer. Brush glaze over top of loaf. Serve warm or cold. Makes 1 loaf.

Apple-Crumb Cake

1/2 cup butter or margarine, room temperature
1 cup sugar
2 eggs
2 cups all-purpose flour
1-1/2 teaspoons baking powder
1/2 teaspoon ground cinnamon
1 tablespoon grated lemon peel
1/2 cup milk
2 large Golden Delicious apples, peeled, cored, thinly sliced

Crumb Topping:
1-1/4 cups all-purpose flour
3/4 cup sugar
1/2 teaspoon ground cinnamon
3/4 cup butter or margarine, chilled

Preheat oven to 350F (175C). Grease a 13'' x 9'' baking pan. In a medium bowl, beat butter or margarine, sugar and eggs until creamy. Blend flour, baking powder, cinnamon and lemon peel; stir into sugar mixture alternately with milk. Spread batter in greased pan. Arrange apple slices on top of batter in slightly overlapping rows.
To make topping, in a small bowl, combine flour, sugar and cinnamon. Use a pastry blender or 2 knives to cut in butter or margarine until mixture resembles coarse crumbs. Sprinkle topping over apples. Bake 40 to 45 minutes or until a wooden pick inserted in center comes out clean. Cool in pan on a wire rack. Makes about 16 servings.

Apple-Crumb Cake

Buttermilk Waffles

2 eggs, separated
1 tablespoon sugar
6 tablespoons butter or margarine, melted
2 cups buttermilk
1-3/4 cups all-purpose flour
1-1/2 teaspoons baking powder
1 teaspoon baking soda
1/2 teaspoon salt

In a medium bowl, beat egg yolks, sugar, butter or margarine and buttermilk until creamy. Blend flour, baking powder, baking soda and salt; stir into sugar mixture. Beat egg whites until stiff but not dry. Fold beaten egg whites into batter. Preheat a waffle iron. Using 1/2 to 1 cup batter, bake according to manufacturer's directions. Serve with honey butter. Makes 4 to 8 waffles.

Cinnamon-Raisin Cake

3/4 cup butter or margarine, room temperature
1 cup sugar
2 eggs
2-1/4 cups all-purpose flour
3-1/2 teaspoons baking powder
2 teaspoons ground cinnamon
1/2 teaspoon salt
3/4 cup milk
3/4 cup golden raisins
3/4 dark raisins
1/2 cup chopped walnuts, pecans or almonds
1 tablespoon grated lemon peel

Preheat oven to 350F (175C). Grease and flour a 9-cup Bundt pan. In a medium bowl, beat butter or margarine, sugar and eggs until creamy. Blend flour, baking powder, cinnamon and salt; stir into sugar mixture alternately with milk, starting with flour mixture and ending with milk. Fold in raisins, nuts and lemon peel. Pour batter into prepared pan. Bake 55 to 60 minutes or until a wooden pick inserted 2 inches from edge of pan comes out clean. Let stand in pan on a wire rack 15 to 20 minutes. Remove from pan; cool on wire rack. Makes 1 cake.

Delicate Apple Cake

4 to 5 small Golden Delicious apples, peeled, quartered, cored
1 tablespoon lemon juice
1/2 cup butter or margarine, room temperature
3/4 cup granulated sugar
2 eggs
1 teaspoon lemon extract
1-3/4 cups all-purpose flour
1-1/2 teaspoons baking powder
1/2 teaspoon salt
1/2 cup milk
Powdered sugar

Preheat oven to 350F (175C). Grease bottom and side of a 10-inch springform pan. Cut several deep slashes lengthwise in each apple quarter. Brush cut apples with lemon juice; set aside. In a medium bowl, beat butter or margarine, granulated sugar, eggs and lemon extract until creamy. Blend flour, baking powder and salt; stir into sugar mixture alternately with milk. Spread batter in greased pan. Arrange apple quarters, slashed-side up, on top of batter, as shown. Bake 50 to 55 minutes or until a wooden pick inserted in center comes out clean. Cool in pan on a wire rack. Remove cake from pan; dust with powdered sugar. Makes 1 cake.

Delicate Apple Cake

Cinnamon-Raisin Cake

Carrot-Nut Bread

1 cup sugar
1/3 cup vegetable oil
2 eggs
1 cup all-purpose flour
1/2 cup graham or whole-wheat flour
1/2 teaspoon salt
1 teaspoon baking soda
1 teaspoon baking powder
1 teaspoon ground cinnamon
1 cup shredded carrot
1/2 cup chopped walnuts or pecans

Preheat oven to 375F (190C). Grease an 8'' x 4'' loaf pan; set aside. In a medium bowl, combine sugar, oil and eggs. Stir to blend. Blend flours, salt, baking soda, baking powder and cinnamon. Stir into egg mixture until dry ingredients are moistened. Stir in carrots and nuts. Spoon mixture into greased pan; smooth top. Bake 50 to 55 minutes or until a wooden pick inserted in center comes out clean. Cool on a wire rack 5 minutes. Remove from pan; cool on rack. Makes 1 loaf.

Macaroon Loaf

3/4 cup butter or margarine, room temperature
2/3 cup granulated sugar
2 whole eggs
2 eggs, separated
1 teaspoon vanilla extract
2 cups all-purpose flour
2 teaspoons baking powder
1/2 teaspoon salt
1/2 cup milk
1/3 cup powdered sugar
1/2 teaspoon almond extract
1 cup ground almonds

Preheat oven to 325F (165C). Grease a 9" x 5" loaf pan. In a medium bowl, beat butter or margarine, granulated sugar, 2 eggs, 2 egg yolks and vanilla until creamy. Blend flour, baking powder and salt; stir into sugar mixture alternately with milk. Spread batter in greased pan. In another medium bowl, beat egg whites until stiff but not dry. Beat in powdered sugar until stiff peaks form. Fold in almond extract and ground almonds. Using the back of a spoon, make a deep trough, 2 inches wide, down center of batter in pan. Quickly spoon almond mixture into trough. Bake 60 to 65 minutes or until a wooden pick inserted in center comes out clean. Let stand in pan on a wire rack 10 minutes. Remove from pan; cool on wire rack. Makes 1 loaf.

Macaroon Loaf

Winter-Squash Bread

2/3 cup vegetable shortening
1-1/2 cups sugar
2 eggs, beaten
1-3/4 cups cooked, mashed winter squash
1/3 cup molasses
4 cups all-purpose flour
1 teaspoon baking powder
1/2 teaspoon baking soda
1/2 teaspoon salt
1 tablespoon ground cinnamon
1/4 teaspoon ground ginger
1/2 teaspoon ground cloves
1/2 teaspoon grated lemon peel
2/3 cup milk
1 cup chopped walnuts or pecans, if desired

Grease 2 (9" x 5") loaf pans. Line each greased pan with waxed paper, letting paper extend 2 to 3 inches above long sides of pans. Preheat oven to 350F (175C). In a large bowl, cream together shortening and sugar. Beat in eggs, squash and molasses. Blend flour, baking powder, baking soda, salt, cinnamon, ginger, cloves and lemon peel. Stir flour mixture into squash mixture alternately with milk, beginning and ending with flour mixture. Stir in nuts, if desired. Pour into prepared pans. Bake about 1 hour or until golden brown. Remove from pans; remove waxed paper from bread. Cool top-side up on a wire rack. Makes 2 loaves.

Yorkshire Parkin

1-1/3 cups rolled oats
3/4 cup whole-wheat flour
1/2 teaspoon baking soda
1/2 teaspoon ground ginger
1/8 teaspoon ground allspice
1/2 cup raisins
1/3 cup packed dark-brown sugar
1/2 cup molasses
1/4 cup butter or margarine
1 egg
1 cup milk

Preheat oven to 350F (175C). Grease an 8-inch-square baking pan; set aside. In a large bowl, combine rolled oats, flour, baking soda, ginger, allspice and raisins. Mix well; set aside. In a small saucepan, combine brown sugar, molasses and butter or margarine. Stir over low heat until butter or margarine melts. In a small bowl, beat egg and milk until blended. Stir into molasses mixture. Stir milk mixture into flour mixture. Pour batter into greased pan; smooth top. Bake 1 hour. Cool in pan on a wire rack 20 minutes. Cut into bars. Makes 10 to 16 servings.

Coconut-Lemon Loaf

1 cup butter or margarine, room temperature
1 cup sugar
3 eggs
2-1/2 cups all-purpose flour
1 tablespoon baking powder
1/2 teaspoon salt
3/4 cup milk
1 cup flaked or shredded coconut
2 tablespoons grated lemon peel
1 teaspoon lemon extract
3 to 4 drops yellow food coloring

Nut Topping:
3 tablespoons butter or margarine
3 tablespoons milk
1/4 cup packed light-brown sugar
1/4 cup finely chopped almonds

Preheat oven to 350F (175C). Grease and flour an 11" x 4" or 9" x 5" loaf pan. In a medium bowl, beat butter or margarine and sugar until creamy. Beat in eggs, 1 at a time. Blend flour, baking powder and salt; stir into sugar mixture alternately with milk. Fold in coconut. Spoon 2/3 of batter into prepared pan. To remaining batter, add lemon peel, lemon extract and food coloring. Stir until blended. Spoon lemon batter over batter in pan.
To make topping, melt butter or margarine in a small saucepan. Stir in milk, brown sugar and almonds. Carefully pour topping over cake. Bake 55 to 60 minutes or until a wooden pick inserted in center comes out clean. Let stand in pan on a wire rack 10 minutes. Remove from pan; cool on wire rack. Makes 1 loaf.

Coconut-Lemon Loaf

Lemon Loaf

1/2 cup butter or margarine, room temperature
1 cup sugar
2 eggs
1/4 cup lemon juice
2 tablespoons grated lemon peel
2-1/4 cups all-purpose flour
1 tablespoon baking powder
1/2 teaspoon salt
1/2 cup milk
1/2 cup ground almonds

Lemon Glaze:
1 cup sifted powdered sugar
2 to 3 tablespoons lemon juice

Preheat oven to 350F (175C). Grease a 9" x 5" loaf pan. In a medium bowl, beat butter or margarine, sugar and eggs until creamy. Stir in lemon juice and lemon peel. Blend flour, baking powder and salt; stir into sugar mixture alternately with milk. Fold in almonds. Pour batter into greased pan. Bake 55 to 60 minutes or until a wooden pick inserted in center comes out clean. Let stand in pan on a wire rack 10 minutes. Remove from pan; cool on wire rack.
To make lemon glaze, in a small bowl, blend powdered sugar and lemon juice until smooth. Spoon glaze over top of loaf. Makes 1 loaf.

Chocolate-Almond Loaf

1 cup sugar
2 eggs
1 teaspoon almond extract
2-1/4 cups all-purpose flour
1 teaspoon baking soda
1/2 teaspoon salt
1 cup dairy sour cream (1/2 pint)
2 oz. unsweetened chocolate, melted
3/4 cup ground almonds

Preheat oven to 350F (175C). Grease a 9" x 5" loaf pan. In a medium bowl, beat sugar, eggs and almond extract until blended. Blend flour, baking soda and salt; stir into sugar mixture alternately with sour cream. Stir in chocolate. Fold in almonds. Pour batter into greased pan. Bake 65 to 70 minutes or until a wooden pick inserted in center comes out clean. Let stand in pan on a wire rack 10 minutes. Remove from pan; cool on wire rack. Makes 1 loaf.

Yeast Baking

Clam Pizza

Clam Pizza

Basic Pizza Dough, opposite

Topping:
2 tablespoons butter or margarine
1/2 lb. mushrooms
2 cups homemade or prepared pizza sauce
2 (6-oz.) cans minced clams, drained
1 large, red bell pepper, cut in thin strips
6 jumbo pimiento-stuffed green olives, sliced
1 teaspoon dried leaf oregano
1 teaspoon dried leaf basil
1 teaspoon dried leaf rosemary
2 tablespoons olive oil
1 lb. mozzarella cheese, sliced
2 small red chilies, if desired

Prepare Basic Pizza Dough. Preheat oven to 450F (230C). **To make topping,** melt butter or margarine in a medium skillet. Add mushrooms; sauté until tender. Spoon 1 cup sauce over each pizza base, spreading sauce evenly. Over each pizza, sprinkle 1/2 of sautéed mushrooms, clams, bell-pepper strips, olives, oregano, basil and rosemary. Drizzle 1 tablespoon olive oil over top of each. Top each with cheese. Bake 18 to 22 minutes or until cheese is hot and bubbly, and crust is lightly browned. Top each with a chili, if desired. Serve hot from pan. Makes 2 pizzas.

On previous pages: Savory Artichoke Pizza.

Salami & Onion Pizza

Basic Pizza Dough, below

Topping:
1/4 cup vegetable oil
3 to 4 large onions, cut in thin rings
2 cups homemade or prepared pizza sauce
1/4 lb. thinly sliced Genoa salami
1 red or green bell pepper, cut in thin strips
1 teaspoon dried leaf oregano
1 teaspoon dried leaf thyme
1 teaspoon dried leaf rosemary
1 lb. mozzarella cheese, shredded (4 cups)

Prepare Basic Pizza Dough. Preheat oven to 450F (230C). **To make topping,** heat vegetable oil in a large skillet. Add onions; sauté until transparent. Remove from heat. Spoon 1 cup sauce over each pizza base, spreading sauce evenly. Over each pizza, sprinkle 1/2 of sautéed onion rings, salami slices, bell-pepper strips, oregano, thyme and rosemary. Top each with cheese. Bake 18 to 22 minutes or until cheese is hot and bubbly, and crust is lightly browned. Serve hot from pan. Makes 2 pizzas.

Savory Artichoke Pizza

Photo on pages 108-109.

Basic Pizza Dough:
1 (1/4-oz.) pkg. active dry yeast (1 tablespoon)
1 teaspoon sugar
1-1/4 cups warm water (110F, 45C)
1 tablespoon vegetable oil
2 teaspoons salt
About 3-1/2 cups all-purpose or bread flour

Topping:
2 cups homemade or prepared pizza sauce
1 teaspoon dried leaf oregano
1 teaspoon dried leaf basil
1 (14-1/2-oz.) can artichoke hearts, drained, quartered
10 jumbo pimiento-stuffed green olives, halved
2 tablespoons drained capers
1 lb. mozzarella cheese, shredded (4 cups)

To make basic pizza dough, in a large bowl, combine yeast, 1 teaspoon sugar and water. Let stand until foamy, 5 to 10 minutes. Stir in vegetable oil. Add salt and 2 cups flour; beat vigorously. Stir in enough remaining flour to make a stiff dough. Turn out dough onto a lightly floured surface; knead until smooth and elastic, 8 to 10 minutes. Clean and grease bowl; place dough in greased bowl, turning to coat all sides. Cover; let rise in a warm place, free from drafts, until doubled in bulk. Grease 2 (12-inch) pizza pans. Punch down dough; divide in half. Roll out each piece of dough to a 13-inch circle; place on greased pans. Pinch up edges of dough to make rims. **To make topping,** preheat oven to 450F (230C). Spoon 1 cup sauce over each pizza base, spreading sauce evenly. Sprinkle 1/2 of oregano, basil, artichoke hearts, olives and capers over each pizza base. Top each with cheese. Bake 18 to 22 minutes or until cheese is hot and bubbly, and crust is lightly browned. Serve hot from pan. Makes 2 pizzas.

Buttermilk Bread

1 cup buttermilk
1/4 cup butter or margarine
3 tablespoons sugar
1/2 teaspoon salt
1 (1/4-oz.) pkg. active dry yeast (1 tablespoon)
1 teaspoon sugar
1/4 cup warm water (110F, 45C)
About 3-1/4 cups all-purpose or bread flour
1/4 teaspoon baking soda
1 egg yolk blended with 1 tablespoon milk for glaze

In a small saucepan, combine buttermilk, butter or margarine, 3 tablespoons sugar and salt. Stir constantly over low heat until butter or margarine melts. Set aside to cool. In a large bowl, combine yeast, 1 teaspoon sugar and water. Let stand until foamy, 5 to 10 minutes. Stir buttermilk mixture into yeast mixture. Blend 2 cups flour and baking soda; stir into yeast mixture. Stir in enough remaining flour to make a stiff dough. Turn out dough onto a lightly floured surface; knead until dough is smooth and elastic, 8 to 10 minutes. Clean and grease bowl; place dough in greased bowl, turning to coat all sides. Let rise in a warm place, free from drafts, until doubled in bulk. Grease a 9" x 5" loaf pan. Punch down dough.

To complete, shape dough into a loaf, pinching and tucking ends under; place in greased pan. Cover; let rise until almost doubled. Preheat oven to 375F (190C). Brush top of loaf with egg-yolk glaze. Bake 45 to 50 minutes or until bread sounds hollow when tapped on bottom. Remove from pan; cool on a wire rack. Makes 1 loaf.

Hearty Pizza

Pizza Sauce:
1/4 cup chopped onion
1 (8-oz.) can tomato sauce
1/2 teaspoon salt
Pepper
Pinch of ground cumin
Pinch of ground marjoram
Pinch of celery salt
1 teaspoon Worcestershire sauce

Pizza Crust:
About 3/4 cup warm water or milk
1 (1/4-oz.) pkg. active dry yeast (1 tablespoon)
2-1/2 cups buttermilk baking mix
1-1/2 cups shredded mozzarella cheese (6 oz.)
1-1/2 cups cooked crumbled sausage or ground beef
1 teaspoon dried leaf oregano, crushed

To make sauce, combine all ingredients; set aside.
To make crust, preheat oven to 400F (205C). Pour water or milk into a medium bowl. Sprinkle yeast over top. Let stand 5 minutes or until foamy. Stir in baking mix. Turn out onto a lightly floured surface. Knead about 15 strokes. Divide dough in half. Roll out each half to a 12-inch circle, 1/8 inch thick. Place each circle in an ungreased 12-inch pizza pan.
To complete, Spread sauce evenly over each dough circle. Top each with 1/2 of cheese and 1/2 of meat. Sprinkle evenly with oregano. Bake 15 to 20 minutes until dough browns. Makes 2 (12-inch) pizzas or 8 to 12 servings.

Sesame Ring

1 (1/4-oz.) pkg. active dry yeast (1 tablespoon)
1 teaspoon sugar
1/4 cup warm water (110F, 45C)
2 tablespoons butter or margarine, room temperature
2 tablespoons sugar
1 teaspoon salt
1 cup whipping cream (1 pint), scalded
2 eggs, beaten
1 egg white
About 4 cups all-purpose or bread flour
1 egg yolk blended with 1 tablespoon milk for glaze
Sesame seeds
Small Brie-cheese wheel, if desired
10 parsley sprigs, 10 radishes, 12 Swiss-cheese strips,
    1 butter curl and 4 dill sprigs, if desired

In a large bowl, combine yeast, 1 teaspoon sugar and water. Let stand until foamy, 5 to 10 minutes. In a small bowl, combine butter or margarine, 2 tablespoons sugar, salt and cream; cool to room temperature. Stir cream mixture into yeast mixture. Add eggs, egg white and 2-1/2 cups flour; beat vigorously. Stir in enough remaining flour to make a stiff dough. Turn out dough onto a lightly floured surface; knead until dough is smooth and elastic, 8 to 10 minutes. Clean and grease bowl; place dough in greased bowl, turning to coat all sides. Cover; let rise in a warm place, free from drafts, until doubled in bulk. Grease a baking sheet. Punch down dough.

To complete, divide dough in half. Shape each piece into a 22-inch rope. Brush egg-yolk glaze over each rope. Sprinkle with sesame seeds. Twist ropes together; place on greased baking sheet, making a large ring. Pinch ends together to seal. Cover; let rise until doubled. Preheat oven to 375F (190C). Bake 35 to 40 minutes or until golden brown and bread sounds hollow when tapped on bottom. Remove from baking sheet; cool on a wire rack.

To serve, insert a small wheel of Brie in center of loaf, if desired. Garnish with parsley, radishes, Swiss cheese, a butter curl and sprigs of dill, if desired. Makes 1 loaf.

Sesame Ring

Breakfast Raisin Bread

2 (1/4-oz.) pkgs. active dry yeast (2 tablespoons)
1 teaspoon sugar
1/2 cup warm water (110F, 45C)
1/2 cup butter or margarine, room temperature
1/2 cup sugar
2 teaspoons salt
1-1/4 cups milk, scalded
3 eggs, beaten
About 5-1/4 cups all-purpose or bread flour
1-1/2 cups raisins
2 tablespoons grated lemon peel
1 egg white blended with 1 tablespoon water for glaze

In a large bowl, combine yeast, 1 teaspoon sugar and water. Let stand until foamy, 5 to 10 minutes. In a small bowl, combine butter or margarine, 1/2 cup sugar, salt and milk; cool to room temperature. Stir milk mixture into yeast mixture. Stir in eggs, 3 cups flour, raisins and lemon peel. Stir in enough remaining flour to make a stiff dough. Turn out dough onto a lightly floured surface; knead until smooth and elastic, 8 to 10 minutes. Clean and grease bowl; place dough in greased bowl, turning to coat all sides. Cover; let rise in a warm place, free from drafts, until doubled in bulk. Grease 2 (9" x 5") loaf pans. Punch down dough.

To complete, divide dough in half. Shape each half into a loaf, pinching and tucking ends under. Place in greased pans. Cover; let rise until doubled in bulk. Preheat oven to 375F (190C). Slash top of each loaf lengthwise. Brush with egg-white glaze. Bake 40 to 45 minutes or until bread sounds hollow when tapped on bottom. Cool on wire racks. Makes 2 loaves.

Breakfast Raisin Bread

Prune Plait

Filling:
1 cup coarsely chopped pitted prunes
1/2 cup chopped walnuts, pecans or almonds
1/2 teaspoon ground cinnamon
2 tablespoons brandy

Base:
1 (1/4-oz.) pkg. active dry yeast (1 tablespoon)
1 teaspoon sugar
1/4 cup warm water (110F, 45C)
1/4 cup butter or margarine, room temperature
1/3 cup sugar
1/2 teaspoon salt
3/4 cup milk, scalded
1 egg, beaten
About 3 cups all-purpose flour
1 tablespoon grated orange peel
1 tablespoon butter or margarine, melted

Icing:
2 teaspoons milk
1/2 cup powdered sugar, sifted

To make filling, in a small bowl, combine prunes, nuts and cinnamon. Stir in brandy; set aside.

To make base, in a large bowl, combine yeast, 1 teaspoon sugar and water. Let stand until foamy, 5 to 10 minutes. In a small bowl, combine 1/4 cup butter or margarine, 1/3 cup sugar, salt and milk; cool to room temperature. Add milk mixture to yeast mixture. Add egg, 2 cups flour and orange peel; beat vigorously. Stir in enough remaining flour to make a stiff dough. Turn out dough onto a lightly floured surface; knead until dough is smooth and elastic, 8 to 10 minutes. Clean and grease bowl; place dough in greased bowl, turning to coat all sides. Cover; let rise in a warm place, free from drafts, until doubled in bulk. Grease a 15" x 10" jelly-roll pan. Punch down dough. Roll out dough to a 15" x 10" rectangle. Place dough in greased pan. Spoon prune mixture lengthwise down center of rectangle. Cut 3 diagonal slashes through dough on each side of filling. Alternating sides, fold strips of dough over filling, covering completely. Cover; let rise until doubled in bulk. Preheat oven to 350F (175C). Brush 1 tablespoon melted butter or margarine over loaf. Bake 30 to 35 minutes or until golden brown. Remove from pan; cool on a wire rack.

To make icing, in a small bowl, blend milk and powdered sugar until smooth. Drizzle over cooled coffeecake. Let stand until icing sets. Makes 1 coffeecake.

Wheat & Honey Bread

1 (1/4-oz.) pkg. active dry yeast (1 tablespoon)
1 teaspoon sugar
1/4 cup warm water (110F, 45C)
2 tablespoons vegetable oil
1/4 cup honey
1-1/2 teaspoons salt
1 cup milk, scalded
About 1-3/4 cups whole-wheat flour
About 1-3/4 cups all-purpose or bread flour
1 tablespoon butter or margarine, melted

In a large bowl, combine yeast, sugar and water. Let stand until foamy, 5 to 10 minutes. In a small bowl, combine oil, molasses, salt and milk; cool to room temperature. Stir milk mixture into yeast mixture. Stir in 1-1/2 cups whole-wheat flour and 1 cup all-purpose or bread flour. Turn out dough onto a lightly floured surface; knead in enough of remaining flours to make a stiff dough. Knead until smooth and elastic, 8 to 10 minutes. Clean and grease bowl; place dough in greased bowl, turning to coat all sides. Cover; let rise in a warm place, free from drafts, until doubled in bulk. Grease a 9" x 5" loaf pan. Punch down dough.

To complete, shape dough into a loaf, pinching and tucking ends under; place in greased loaf pan. Cover; let rise until doubled. Preheat oven to 375F (190C). Brush top of loaf with butter or margarine. Bake 35 to 40 minutes or until bread sounds hollow when tapped on bottom. Cool on a wire rack. Makes 1 loaf.

Poinsettia Coffeecake

1/3 Holiday Sweet Bread dough, page 118
3 tablespoons butter or margarine, melted
2 tablespoons sugar
1/2 cup mixed candied fruits and peels or
  finely chopped candied cherries

Icing:
3/4 cup powdered sugar, sifted
4 to 5 teaspoons hot water

Grease a large baking sheet or 18-inch pizza pan; set aside. Roll out dough to a 16" x 12" rectangle, about 1/4 inch thick. Brush butter or margarine over surface except for a 1/2-inch strip along 1 long side. In a small bowl, combine sugar and candied fruits and peels or chopped cherries. Arrange over buttered area of dough. Roll dough, jelly-roll fashion, from long buttered edge toward unbuttered edge. Pinch edge to seal. Use a sharp knife to cut ends of roll on a diagonal. Place end pieces in center of greased baking sheet or pan. Cut remaining dough in 1-inch diagonal slices. Dough will flatter slightly into pointed oval slices. Arrange slices, cut-side down and touching, in a circle around end pieces. Place slices so upper points are to center and lower points are to outside of circle. Cover; let rise until doubled in bulk. Preheat oven to 350F (175C). Bake 25 minutes or until lightly browned. Cool on pan on a wire rack.

To make icing, in a small bowl, combine powdered sugar and enough water to make an icing of drizzling consistency. Drizzle icing over cooled coffeecake. Makes 1 coffeecake.

Holiday Cinnamon Rolls

1/3 recipe Holiday Sweet Bread dough, page 118
3 tablespoons butter or margarine, melted
1/2 cup light-brown sugar
1/2 cup granulated sugar
2 teaspoons ground cinnamon
3/4 to 1 cup raisins, if desired

Icing:
1-1/2 cups powdered sugar, sifted
Hot water

Butter a large baking sheet, pizza pan or 13" x 9" baking pan; set aside. Roll out dough to a 16" x 12" rectangle, about 1/4 inch thick. Brush butter or margarine over surface except for a 1/2-inch strip along 1 long side. In a small bowl, combine sugars and cinnamon; sprinkle over buttered area of dough. Sprinkle with raisins, if desired. Roll dough, jelly-roll fashion, from long buttered edge toward unbuttered edge. Pinch edge to seal. Use a sharp knife or a thread placed around dough, crossed, then pulled tight to cut rolled dough into 1-inch slices. Arrange slices, cut-side down, in buttered pan. Cover; let rise until doubled in bulk. Preheat oven to 350F (175C). Bake 25 minutes or until lightly browned. Cool in pan on a wire rack 10 minutes. Remove from pan; cool on wire rack.

To make icing, in a small bowl, combine powdered sugar and enough water to make an icing of drizzling consistency. Drizzle icing over cooled cinnamon rolls. Makes about 16 rolls.

Dinner Casserole Loaf

3/4 cup warm water
1/2 teaspoon sugar
1 (1/4-oz.) pkg. active dry yeast (1 tablespoon)
1 cup ricotta cheese or cottage cheese (8 oz.)
1 egg, beaten
1 teaspoon salt
1/4 cup vegetable oil
1/2 teaspoon celery seeds
1/4 teaspoon celery salt
1 teaspoon dried leaf rosemary, crushed
3/4 teaspoon dried leaf basil, crushed
2 tablespoons dried minced onion, if desired
2-1/2 to 3 cups all-purpose flour
1/4 teaspoon celery seeds

Generously grease a deep, round, 1-1/2-quart casserole with straight sides; set aside. In a large bowl, combine warm water and sugar. Sprinkle yeast over surface. Let stand until foamy 5 to 10 minutes. In a small saucepan, heat ricotta or cottage cheese until warmed. Stir until smooth. Set aside to cool slightly. Stir in egg, salt, oil, 1/2 teaspoon celery seeds, celery salt, rosemary and basil. Add onion, if desired. Stir cheese mixture into yeast mixture until blended. Stir in 2-1/2 cups flour until blended. Add more flour if needed to make a soft dough. Turn out onto a lightly floured surface. Knead gently about 5 minutes. Dough will be very soft, but not sticky. Place in greased casserole, turning to grease all sides. Sprinkle with 1/4 teaspoon celery seeds. Cover and let rise in a warm place, free from drafts, until doubled in bulk, about 45 minutes. Preheat oven to 425F (220C). Place raised dough in oven. Bake 10 minutes. Reduce heat to 350F (175C). Bake 15 to 20 minutes longer or until loaf is golden brown and sounds hollow when tapped on bottom. Remove from casserole; cool, top-side up, on a wire rack 10 to 15 minutes before cutting with a serrated knife. Makes 1 large loaf.

Pecan-Raisin Sweet Buns

Pecan-Raisin Sweet Buns

1 (1/4-oz.) pkg. active dry yeast (1 tablespoon)
1 teaspoon granulated sugar
1/4 cup warm water (110F, 45C)
1/3 cup butter or margarine, room temperature
1/4 cup granulated sugar
1 teaspoon salt
3/4 cup milk, scalded
2 eggs, beaten
About 3-3/4 cups all-purpose flour
2 tablespoons grated orange peel
2 tablespoons butter or margarine, melted
1/2 cup packed light-brown sugar
1/2 cup raisins
1/3 cup chopped pecans
1 teaspoon ground cinnamon
1 egg yolk blended with 1 tablespoon milk for glaze

In a large bowl, combine yeast, 1 teaspoon granulated sugar and water. Let stand until foamy, 5 to 10 minutes. In a small bowl, combine 1/3 cup butter or margarine, 1/4 cup granulated sugar, salt and milk; cool to room temperature. Stir milk mixture into yeast mixture. Add eggs, 2-1/2 cups flour and orange peel; beat vigorously. Stir in enough remaining flour to make soft dough. Turn out dough onto a lightly floured surface; knead in enough remaining flour to make a stiff dough. Knead until dough is smooth and elastic, 8 to 10 minutes. Clean and grease bowl; place dough in bowl, turning to coat all sides. Cover; let rise in a warm place, free from drafts, until doubled in bulk. Grease 2 round 9-inch cake pans. Punch down dough. On a lightly floured surface, roll out dough to an 18" x 12" rectangle. Brush with 2 tablespoons butter or margarine. In a small bowl, combine brown sugar, raisins, pecans and cinnamon; sprinkle over dough. Starting on a long side, roll up dough jelly-roll fashion. Cut into 16 slices. Place 8 slices, cut-side down, in each greased pan. Cover; let rise 30 minutes. Preheat oven to 375F (190C). Brush tops of raised rolls with egg-yolk glaze. Bake 25 to 30 minutes or until golden brown. Remove from pans; cool on wire racks. Makes 16 buns.

Almond Spirals

Almond Spirals

1 (1/4-oz.) pkg. active dry yeast (1 tablespoon)
1 teaspoon sugar
1/4 cup warm water (110F, 45C)
1/2 cup butter or margarine, room temperature
1/3 cup sugar
1-1/2 teaspoons salt
1/2 cup milk, scalded
2 eggs, beaten
About 3-1/2 cups all-purpose flour

Almond Filling:
1 (7-oz.) pkg. marzipan or Marzipan, page 232
1/3 cup finely chopped almonds
1/3 cup sugar

Apricot Glaze:
1/4 cup apricot jam
3 tablespoons water

In a large bowl, combine yeast, 1 teaspoon sugar and water. Let stand until foamy, 5 to 10 minutes. In a small bowl, combine butter or margarine, 1/3 cup sugar, salt and milk; cool to room temperature. Stir milk mixture into yeast mixture. Add eggs and 2-1/2 cups flour; beat vigorously. Stir in enough remaining flour to make a soft dough. Turn out dough onto a lightly floured surface; knead in enough remaining flour to make a stiff dough. Clean and grease bowl; place dough in greased bowl, turning to coat all sides. Cover; let rise in a warm place, free from drafts, until doubled in bulk. Grease 2 large baking sheets; set aside. Punch down dough. On a lightly floured surface, roll out dough to a 20'' x 16'' rectangle.

To make filling, crumble marzipan into a small bowl. Stir in almonds and sugar. Sprinkle over dough. Starting at a short side, roll up dough jelly-roll fashion. Cut into 1-inch slices; place, cut-side up and 2 inches apart, on greased baking sheets. Cut 2 slashes on top of each slice; spread open slightly. Cover; let rise until almost doubled in bulk. Preheat oven to 375F (190C). Bake 15 to 18 minutes or until golden brown. Remove from baking sheets; cool on wire racks.

To make glaze, press jam through a sieve into a small saucepan. Add water; cook over low heat, stirring constantly until jam is melted and mixture is smooth. Spoon over warm buns. Makes 16 buns.

Filled Half-Moons

1 (1/4-oz.) pkg. active dry yeast (1 tablespoon)
1 teaspoon granulated sugar
1/4 cup warm water (110F, 45C)
1/2 cup buttermilk
3 tablespoons butter or margarine, room temperature
1/4 cup granulated sugar
1/2 teaspoon salt
1 egg, beaten
2-1/4 cups all-purpose flour
1/4 teaspoon ground nutmeg
Vegetable oil for deep-frying
Powdered sugar

Filling:
1 cup whipping cream (1/2 pint)
2 tablespoons sugar
1 teaspoon vanilla extract

In a large bowl, combine yeast, 1 teaspoon granulated sugar and water. Let stand until foamy, 5 to 10 minutes. In a small saucepan, combine buttermilk, butter or margarine, 1/4 cup granulated sugar and salt. Stir over low heat until butter or margarine melts; cool to room temperature. Stir cooled buttermilk mixture into yeast mixture. Beat in egg, 1-1/2 cups flour and nutmeg. Stir in enough remaining flour to make a soft dough. Cover; let rise in a warm place, free from drafts, until doubled in bulk. Flour baking sheets. Punch down dough. On a lightly floured surface, sprinkle flour over dough; roll out until 1/2 inch thick. Flour a round 3-inch biscuit cutter; use to cut dough. Cut each 3-inch circle in half. Place 1-1/2 inches apart on floured baking sheets. Cover; let rise until doubled in bulk. Heat oil in a deep-fryer to 350F (175C) or until a 1-inch cube of bread turns golden brown in 65 seconds. Gently lower 4 or 5 pieces of raised dough into hot oil; do not crowd. Deep-fry 1 minute on each side or until deep golden brown. Use a slotted spoon to remove from oil; drain on paper towels. Repeat with remaining dough. Cut slit in each half-moon on curved side.

To make filling, whip cream until soft peaks form. Beat in sugar and vanilla until stiff peaks form. Spoon into a pastry bag fitted with a medium, round tip; pipe filling into baked half-moons. Dust filled half-moons with powdered sugar. Makes about 24 filled pastries.

Filled Half-Moons

Crusty Rolls

1 (1/4-oz.) pkg. active dry yeast (1 tablespoon)
1 teaspoon sugar
1/4 cup warm water (110F, 45C)
1/4 cup vegetable oil
1 teaspoon salt
1 cup milk, scalded
About 3 cups all-purpose or bread flour
1 egg white blended with 1 tablespoon water for glaze
1 to 2 tablespoons poppy seeds

In a large bowl, combine yeast, 1 teaspoon sugar and 1/4 cup water. Let stand until foamy, 5 to 10 minutes. In a small bowl, combine oil, salt and milk; cool to room temperature. Stir milk mixture into yeast mixture. Stir in 2 cups flour; beat vigorously. Stir in enough remaining flour to make a stiff dough. Turn out dough onto a lightly floured surface; knead until dough is smooth and elastic, 8 to 10 minutes. Clean and grease bowl; place dough in greased bowl, turning to coat all sides. Cover; let rise in a warm place, free from drafts, until doubled. Grease a large baking sheet; set aside. Punch down dough.

To complete, divide dough into 8 equal pieces. Shape each piece into a flat ball, pinching and tucking sides under. Place balls, seam-side down, 2 to 3 inches apart on greased baking sheet. Cover; let rise until doubled in bulk. Preheat oven to 400F (205C). Use a razor blade to cut an **X** in top of each roll. Brush egg-white glaze over rolls; sprinkle with poppy seeds. Bake 15 to 20 minutes or until rolls sound hollow when tapped on bottom. Remove from baking sheet; cool on a wire rack. Makes 8 rolls.

Almond-Currant Snails

Almond-Currant Snails

1 (1/4-oz.) pkg. active dry yeast (1 tablespoon)
1 teaspoon sugar
1/4 cup warm water (110F, 45C)
1/4 cup butter or margarine, room temperature
6 tablespoons sugar
1 teaspoon salt
1/2 cup milk, scalded
2 eggs, beaten
2 teaspoons almond extract
About 2-3/4 cups all-purpose flour
2 tablespoons butter or margarine, melted
1/2 cup chopped almonds
1/2 cup currants or chopped raisins

Icing:
1-1/2 cups powdered sugar, sifted
1/2 teaspoon almond extract
2 to 3 tablespoons milk

In a large bowl, combine yeast, 1 teaspoon sugar and water. Let stand until foamy, 5 to 10 minutes. In a small bowl, combine 1/4 cup butter or margarine, 3 tablespoons sugar, salt and milk; cool to room temperature. Stir milk mixture into yeast mixture. Add eggs, almond extract and 2 cups flour; beat vigorously. Stir in enough remaining flour to make a stiff dough. Turn out dough onto a lightly floured surface; knead until dough is smooth and elastic, 8 to 10 minutes. Clean and grease bowl; place dough in greased bowl, turning to coat all sides. Cover; let rise in a warm place, free from drafts, until doubled in bulk. Grease 2 large baking sheets. Punch down dough.

To shape dough, on a lightly floured surface, roll out dough to an 18" x 14" rectangle. Brush with 2 tablespoons melted butter or margarine. Combine almonds, currants or chopped raisins and remaining 3 tablespoons sugar. Sprinkle over dough. Starting on a short side, roll up dough jelly-roll fashion. Pinch seam to seal; cut into 1-inch slices. Place slices, cut-side up, on greased baking sheets. Using a wide spatula, flatten slices slightly. Cover; let rise 30 minutes. Preheat oven to 375F (190C). Bake 20 to 25 minutes or until golden brown. Remove from baking sheets; cool on wire racks.

To make icing, in a small bowl, blend powdered sugar, almond extract and 2 tablespoons milk until smooth. Stir in enough milk to make a drizzling consistency. Drizzle icing over snails; let stand until icing sets. Makes 14 snails.

Fresian Nuggets

1 (1/4-oz.) pkg. active dry yeast (1 tablespoon)
1 teaspoon sugar
1/4 cup warm water (110F, 45C)
1/3 cup butter or margarine, room temperature
3 tablespoons sugar
1 teaspoon salt
1/2 cup milk, scalded
2 eggs, beaten
About 2-1/4 cups all-purpose flour
1 tablespoon grated lemon peel
Vegetable oil for deep-frying
1/4 cup sugar
1 teaspoon ground cinnamon

In a large bowl, combine yeast, 1 teaspoon sugar and water. Let stand until foamy, 5 to 10 minutes. In a small bowl, combine butter or margarine, 3 tablespoons sugar, salt and milk; cool to room temperature. Stir milk mixture into yeast mixture. Add eggs, 1-1/2 cups flour and lemon peel; beat vigorously. Stir in enough remaining flour to make a soft dough. Cover; let rise in a warm place, free from drafts, until doubled in bulk. Heat oil in a deep-fryer to 350F (175C) or until a 1-inch cube of bread turns golden brown in 65 seconds. Punch down dough. Drop by rounded teaspoons into hot oil. Fry 4 or 5 balls of dough at a time, 1 minute on each side or until browned. Use a slotted spoon to remove from oil; drain on paper towels. Repeat with remaining dough. In a small bowl, combine 1/4 cup sugar and cinnamon. Roll nuggets in sugar-cinnamon mixture to coat. Makes about 48 nuggets.

Fruit & Nut Ring

Fruit & Nut Ring

1 recipe Basic Sweet Dough, page 126
2 tablespoons butter or margarine, melted
1 egg yolk blended with 1 tablespoon milk for glaze

Fruit & Nut Filling:
1/2 cup raisins
1/4 cup currants or chopped raisins
1/4 cup chopped walnuts, pecans or almonds
1/4 cup sugar
2 tablespoons chopped candied orange peel, if desired

Prepare Basic Sweet Dough through first rising. Grease a large baking sheet. Punch down dough. On a lightly floured surface, roll out dough to a 20" x 16" rectangle. Brush dough with butter or margarine; cut in half lengthwise.
To make filling, in a medium bowl, combine all ingredients. Sprinkle mixture evenly over dough pieces. Starting on a long side, roll up each piece of dough jelly-roll fashion. Pinch seams to seal. Place filled rolls on greased baking sheet; twist rolls together. Shape twisted roll into a ring; pinch ends together to seal. Use a razor blade to cut 1/4-inch-deep slashes around outside of ring, about 2 inches apart. Cover; let rise until almost doubled in bulk. Preheat oven to 350F (175C). Brush ring with egg-yolk glaze. Bake 30 to 35 minutes or until browned. Remove from baking sheet; cool on a wire rack. Makes 1 coffeecake.

French Bread

2 cups warm water
1/2 teaspoon sugar
1 (1/4-oz.) pkg. active dry yeast (1 tablespoon)
2 teaspoons salt
2 tablespoons vegetable oil
4 to 4-1/2 cups all-purpose flour
2 tablespoons cornmeal

In a large bowl, combine water and sugar. Sprinkle yeast over surface. Let stand until foamy 5 to 10 minutes. Stir in salt, oil and 2-1/2 cups flour. Beat 100 strokes by hand or 2 minutes with electric mixer. Stir in enough remaining flour to make a stiff sticky dough. Cover with a wet cloth; let rise in a warm place, free from drafts, until doubled in bulk, about 1 hour. Grease a large baking sheet. Sprinkle with cornmeal; set aside. Stir down dough. Turn out 1/2 of dough onto a floured board. Sprinkle dough with flour, if needed. Roll out to a 12-inch square. Roll up from 1 side, jelly-roll fashion. Dampen edges with water, if necessary; pinch edges to seal. Shape ends narrower than rest of loaf. Repeat with remaining dough. Place loaves side by side on prepared baking sheet. Use a sharp knife to cut 3 diagonal slashes across top of each loaf. Cover; let rise until almost doubled in bulk. Preheat oven to 425F (220C). Brush water over tops and sides of loaves. Bake loaves 12 minutes. Reduce heat to 325F (165C). Again brush tops of loaves with water. Bake 35 minutes longer or until browned and firm to the touch. Cool on a wire rack. **To freeze unbaked loaves,** shape loaves and arrange on baking sheet. Place uncovered loaves in freezer until firm, about 2 hours. Wrap each loaf in heavy foil or freezer wrap, making an airtight seal. Store in freezer up to 2 months. **To bake frozen loaves,** sprinkle cornmeal on a large baking sheet. Place frozen loaves on cornmeal. Cover with plastic wrap; let thaw about 2 hours. Then let rise in a warm place, free from drafts, until doubled in bulk. Bake as directed above. Makes 2 loaves.

Holiday Sweet Bread

1/2 cup warm water
2 (1/4-oz.) pkgs. active dry yeast (2 tablespoons)
1/2 teaspoon granulated sugar
2 cups hot water
1 cup butter, margarine or vegetable shortening
1/2 cup granulated sugar, packed brown sugar or honey
1 teaspoon ground cinnamon
2 teaspoons grated lemon peel or lime peel
1/2 teaspoon ground nutmeg
2 teaspoons salt
3 eggs, beaten
2/3 cup instant milk powder
8 to 10 cups all-purpose or whole-wheat flour

In a small bowl, combine 1/2 cup warm water, yeast and 1/2 teaspoon granulated sugar. Let stand until foamy. In a large bowl, combine water and butter, margarine or shortening, stirring until fat is melted. Stir in 1/2 cup sugar or honey, cinnamon, lemon or lime peel, nutmeg, salt, eggs and milk powder. Cool to warm. Stir in yeast mixture. Stir in about 3 cups flour. Beat 100 strokes by hand or 2-1/2 minutes with electric mixer. Stir in enough remaining flour to make a stiff but tender dough. Turn out on a lightly floured surface. Let rest 5 minutes. Clean and grease bowl. Knead dough until smooth and elastic and small bubbles form under surface. Place in greased bowl, turning to grease all sides. Cover; let rise in a warm place, free from drafts, until doubled in bulk. Punch down dough. For a finer texture, let dough rest 30 minutes before shaping. Divide into 3 or 4 equal pieces. Shape into braids, rings, coffeecakes, cinnamon rolls or Christmas wreaths. Makes 3 or 4 large loaves.

Cinnamon-Crumb Cake

1 (1/4-oz.) pkg. active dry yeast (1 tablespoon)
1 teaspoon sugar
1/4 cup warm water (110F, 45C)
1/3 cup butter or margarine, room temperature
1/3 cup sugar
1 teaspoon salt
3/4 cup milk, scalded
About 3 cups all-purpose flour
1 teaspoon ground cinnamon

Crumb Topping:
2 cups all-purpose flour
3/4 cup packed light-brown sugar
2 teaspoons ground cinnamon
1 cup butter or margarine, chilled
1 tablespoon butter or margarine, melted
1/4 cup powdered sugar

In a large bowl, combine yeast, 1 teaspoon sugar and water. Let stand until foamy, 5 to 10 minutes. In a small bowl, combine 1/3 cup butter or margarine, 1/3 cup sugar, salt and milk; cool to room temperature. Stir milk mixture into yeast mixture. Add 2 cups flour and cinnamon; beat vigorously. Stir in enough remaining flour to make a soft dough. Turn out dough onto a lightly floured surface; knead in enough remaining flour to make a stiff dough. Knead until dough is smooth and elastic, 8 to 10 minutes. Clean and grease bowl; place dough in greased bowl, turning to coat all sides. Cover; let rise in a warm place, free from drafts, until doubled in bulk. Grease a 13" x 9" baking pan. Punch down dough. Pat dough into greased pan.

To make crumb topping, in a small bowl, combine flour, brown sugar and cinnamon. Use a pastry blender or 2 knives to cut in 1 cup butter or margarine until mixture resembles coarse crumbs. Brush 1 tablespoon butter or margarine over dough. Sprinkle crumb topping over dough. Cover; let rise until almost doubled in bulk. Preheat oven to 375F (190C). Bake 25 to 30 minutes or until a wooden pick inserted in center comes out clean. Cool in pan on a wire rack. Sprinkle with powdered sugar; serve directly from pan. Makes about 15 servings.

Almond-Spice Braid

1 (1/4-oz.) pkg. active dry yeast (1 tablespoon)
1 teaspoon sugar
1/4 cup warm water (110F, 45C)
1/2 cup butter or margarine, room temperature
1/3 cup sugar
1 teaspoon salt
3/4 cup milk, scalded
2 eggs, beaten
About 3-1/2 cups all-purpose flour
1/2 teaspoon ground cinnamon
1/2 teaspoon ground mace or coriander
1 tablespoon grated lemon peel
3/4 cup raisins
1/2 cup currants or chopped raisins
1/4 cup ground almonds
1/4 cup finely chopped citron
1 egg yolk blended with 1 tablespoon milk for glaze

Almond-Spice Braid

In a large bowl, combine yeast, 1 teaspoon sugar and water. Let stand until foamy, 5 to 10 minutes. In a small bowl, combine butter or margarine, 1/3 cup sugar, salt and milk; cool to room temperature. Stir milk mixture into yeast mixture. Add eggs, 2-1/2 cups flour, cinnamon, mace or coriander and lemon peel; beat vigorously. Stir in raisins, currants or chopped raisins, almonds, citron and enough remaining flour to make a soft dough. Turn out dough onto a lightly floured surface; knead in enough remaining flour to make a stiff dough. Knead until dough is smooth and elastic, 8 to 10 minutes. Clean and grease bowl; place dough in greased bowl, turning to coat all sides. Cover; let rise in a warm place, free from drafts, until doubled in bulk. Grease a large baking sheet; set aside. Punch down dough.

To complete, cut 2/3 of dough into 3 equal pieces. Shape each piece into a 16-inch rope. Place ropes on greased baking sheet; braid, pinching ends to seal. Brush with egg-yolk glaze. Cut remaining dough into 3 equal pieces. Shape each piece into a 14-inch rope. Braid ropes, pinching ends to seal. Place small braid on top of large braid. Cover; let rise until doubled in bulk. Preheat oven to 350F (175C). Brush bread with egg-yolk glaze. Bake 30 to 35 minutes or until bread sounds hollow when tapped on bottom. Remove from baking sheet; cool on a wire rack. Makes 1 large loaf.

Star Hazelnut Ring

Star Hazelnut Ring

1 recipe Basic Sweet Dough, page 126
2 tablespoons butter or margarine, melted
1 egg yolk blended with 1 tablespoon milk for glaze

Filling:
1-1/2 cups ground hazelnuts
3/4 cup sugar
1 egg, beaten
1/4 cup milk
1/2 teaspoon almond extract

Prepare Basic Sweet Dough through first rising. Grease a large baking sheet. Punch down dough. Roll out dough to an 18'' x 14'' rectangle. Brush with butter or margarine.
To make filling, in a small bowl, combine all ingredients; stir until blended. Spread over dough. Starting on a long side, roll up dough jelly-roll fashion. Pinch seam to seal. Place on greased baking sheet, seam-side down, making a ring. Pinch ends together to seal. Use a razor blade to cut 8 connected **Vs**, making 16 diagonal lines around outside curve of ring. This will create an 8-point star around center top of ring. Cover; let rise in a warm place, free from drafts, until doubled in bulk. Preheat oven to 350F (175C). Brush with egg-yolk glaze. Bake 35 to 40 minutes or until browned. Remove from baking sheet; cool on a wire rack. Makes 1 coffeecake.

Savarin

1 (1/4-oz.) pkg. active dry yeast (1 tablespoon)
1 teaspoon sugar
1/4 cup warm water (110F, 45C)
2 cups all-purpose flour
3 tablespoons sugar
1/2 teaspoon salt
1 egg, beaten
2 egg yolks, beaten
1/4 cup milk
1/4 cup butter or margarine, melted
Sweetened whipped cream
Fresh strawberries or other fresh fruit

Syrup:
1 cup sugar
1/2 cup water
1/2 cup sweet sherry or dark rum

Glaze:
1/2 cup apricot jam
1 tablespoon dark rum

Grease a 9-inch ring mold; set aside. In a large bowl, combine yeast, 1 teaspoon sugar and water. Let stand until foamy, 5 to 10 minutes. Stir in 1 cup flour, 3 tablespoons sugar and salt; beat vigorously. Add egg, egg yolks, milk and remaining 1 cup flour; beat vigorously until smooth. Beat in butter or margarine. Spoon dough into greased mold. Cover; let rise in a warm place, free from drafts, until dough has risen to within 1 inch of rim of mold, about 1 hour. Preheat oven to 375F (190C). Bake 25 to 30 minutes or until a wooden pick inserted in center comes out clean. Remove from pan; cool on a wire rack.
To make syrup, combine sugar and water in a small saucepan; bring to a boil, stirring constantly. Boil rapidly 6 to 8 minutes or until syrupy. Cool 5 minutes; stir in sherry or rum. Prick top and bottom of cake with a fork. Place cake on a dish with a rim; pour syrup over cake. Let stand 3 hours, occasionally spooning syrup over top.
To make glaze, press jam through a sieve into a small saucepan. Bring to a boil over low heat. Cool to room temperature; stir in rum. Brush glaze over cake, covering completely.
To serve, fill center of Savarin with sweetened whipped cream and sliced strawberries or other fresh fruit. Makes 1 savarin.

Christmas Wreath

1/3 Holiday Sweet Bread dough, page 118
4 to 6 red candied cherries, halved
1/3 cup candied lemon peel or mixed candied fruits, if desired
1/4 cup sugar
2 or 3 drops red or green food coloring
2 tablespoons butter or margarine, melted

Snowy Frosting:
1/2 cup powdered sugar
2 to 2-1/2 teaspoons milk

Grease a large baking sheet or 12-inch pizza pan. Using 1/2 of dough, pinch off 4 or 5 (1-inch) pieces of dough. Repeat with remaining 1/2 of dough. Shape small pieces of dough into balls, pinching and tucking sides under. Arrange balls in a circle, seam-side down, about 2-1/2 inches apart, on greased baking sheet or pan. Roll remaining dough into 2 ropes 3/4 to 1 inch thick and 30 to 36 inches long. Weave ropes around balls of dough, crossing ropes between balls of dough, placing first one, then the other rope on top as they cross. Adjust number of balls and length of ropes, if necessary. Pinch rope ends to seal. Press your finger into top of each ball of dough. Insert 1 cherry half, rounded-side up, in each ball. Place pieces of candied peel or fruit on each side of balls of dough, if desired. In a small bowl, combine sugar and red or green food coloring. Brush dough with butter or margarine. Sprinkle with colored sugar. Cover; let rise until doubled in bulk. Preheat oven to 375F (190C). Bake wreath 25 to 30 minutes until golden brown and ropes sound hollow when bottoms are tapped. Cool on pan on a wire rack.
To make frosting, in a small bowl, combine powdered sugar and enough milk to make a smooth frosting of drizzling consistency. Drizzle frosting over cooled wreath. Makes 1 loaf.

Marzipan-Raisin Ring

Marzipan-Raisin Ring

1 (1/4-oz.) pkg. active dry yeast (1 tablespoon)
1 teaspoon sugar
1/4 cup warm water (110F, 45C)
1/4 cup butter or margarine
1/4 cup sugar
1 teaspoon salt
1/3 cup milk, scalded
2 eggs, beaten
About 3-1/2 cups all-purpose flour

Marzipan-Fruit Filling:
1/4 cup butter or margarine
1 (7-oz.) pkg. marzipan or Marzipan, page 232, crumbled
1 teaspoon rum extract
1/2 cup raisins
1/4 cup chopped almonds
3 tablespoons currants or chopped raisins
Milk

Topping:
3/4 cup powdered sugar
2 to 3 teaspoons milk
2 tablespoons sliced almonds

In a large bowl, combine yeast, 1 teaspoon sugar and water. Let stand until foamy, 5 to 10 minutes. In a small bowl, combine butter or margarine, 1/4 cup sugar, salt and milk; cool to room temperature. Stir milk mixture into yeast mixture. Add eggs and 2-1/2 cups flour; beat vigorously. Stir in enough remaining flour to make a stiff dough. Turn out dough onto a lightly floured surface; knead until smooth and elastic, 8 to 10 minutes. Clean and grease bowl; place dough in greased bowl, turning to coat all sides. Cover; let rise in a warm place, free from drafts, until doubled in bulk. Grease a large baking sheet. Punch down dough. On a lightly floured surface, roll out dough to a 20" x 16" rectangle.
To make filling, in a small bowl, beat 1/4 cup butter or margarine, marzipan and rum extract until blended. In another small bowl, combine raisins, almonds and currants or chopped raisins. Spread marzipan mixture over dough. Cut dough in half lengthwise. Sprinkle each half with raisin mixture. Starting on a long side, roll up each piece of dough jelly-roll fashion; pinch seams to seal. Twist each roll; pinch ends to seal. Place on greased baking sheet, letting each twisted roll form half of a ring. Pinch ends together to seal. Cover; let rise until doubled in bulk. Preheat oven to 375F (190C). Brush raised ring with milk. Bake 30 to 35 minutes or until golden brown. Remove from baking sheet; cool on a wire rack.
To make topping, in a small bowl, blend powdered sugar and milk until smooth. Spoon over top of cooled ring. Sprinkle with almonds. Let stand until icing sets. Makes 1 coffeecake.

Braided Raisin Bread

1 (1/4-oz.) pkg. active dry yeast (1 tablespoon)
1 teaspoon sugar
1/4 cup warm water (110F, 45C)
3 tablespoons butter or margarine, room temperature
1/4 cup sugar
1 teaspoon salt
1 cup milk, scalded
2 eggs, beaten
About 4-1/4 cups all-purpose flour
1 cup raisins
1 egg yolk blended with 1 tablespoon milk for glaze

In a large bowl, combine yeast, 1 teaspoon sugar and water. Let stand until foamy, 5 to 10 minutes. In a small bowl, combine butter or margarine, 1/4 cup sugar, salt and milk; cool to room temperature. Stir milk mixture into yeast mixture. Add eggs, 3 cups flour and raisins; beat vigorously. Stir in enough remaining flour to make a soft dough. Turn out dough onto a lightly floured surface; knead in enough remaining flour to make a stiff dough. Knead until dough is smooth and elastic, 8 to 10 minutes. Clean and grease bowl; place dough in greased bowl, turning to coat all sides. Cover; let rise in a warm place, free from drafts, until doubled in bulk. Grease a large baking sheet. Punch down dough.

To complete, cut 2/3 of dough into 3 equal pieces. Shape each piece into a 16-inch rope. On greased baking sheet, braid ropes, pinching ends to seal; brush with egg-yolk glaze. Cut remaining dough into 3 equal pieces. Shape each piece into a 14-inch rope. Braid ropes, pinching ends to seal. Place small braid on top of large braid. Cover; let rise until doubled in bulk. Preheat oven to 375F (190C). Brush egg-yolk glaze over raised loaf. Bake 30 to 35 minutes or until bread sounds hollow when tapped on bottom. Remove from baking sheet; cool on a wire rack. Makes 1 large loaf.

Braided Raisin Bread

Cheese-Filled Coffeecake

1 (1/4-oz.) pkg. active dry yeast (1 tablespoon)
1 teaspoon sugar
1/4 cup warm water (110F, 45C)
1/4 cup butter or margarine, room temperature
1/4 cup sugar
1/2 teaspoon salt
1/2 cup milk, scalded
1 egg, beaten
About 2-1/4 cups all-purpose flour
1 egg white blended with 1 tablespoon water for glaze

Cheese Filling:
1 cup ricotta cheese (8 oz.)
1 egg yolk
1 (3-oz.) pkg. egg-custard mix
1/2 teaspoon almond extract

Chocolate Topping:
4 oz. semisweet chocolate, broken into pieces
4 teaspoons vegetable shortening

In a large bowl, combine yeast, 1 teaspoon sugar and water. Let stand until foamy, 5 to 10 minutes. In a small bowl, combine butter or margarine, 1/4 cup sugar, salt and milk; cool to room temperature. Stir milk mixture into yeast mixture. Add egg and 1-1/2 cups flour; beat vigorously. Stir in enough remaining flour to make a soft

Sweet Lemon Rolls

dough. Turn out dough onto a lightly floured surface; knead in enough remaining flour to make a stiff dough. Clean and grease bowl; place dough in greased bowl, turning to coat all sides. Cover; let rise in a warm place, free from drafts, until doubled in bulk. Grease a 9-inch, 6-cup ring mold. Punch down dough. Roll out dough on a lightly floured surface to a 15-inch circle. Carefully fit dough in bottom and up side of greased mold. Center of mold will be covered with dough. Edge of dough should come slightly above rim of mold.

To make cheese filling, in a small bowl, combine all ingredients. Spoon filling into bottom of dough-lined mold. Fold outside edge of dough over filling, pressing edge to inside ring of dough. Cut an **X** in dough that covers center of ring. Fold each triangle of dough over ring; pinch to seal. Brush top with egg-white glaze. Cover; let rise in a warm place, free from drafts, until almost doubled in bulk. Preheat oven to 350F (175C). Bake 30 to 35 minutes or until top is golden brown and a wooden pick inserted in center comes out clean. Remove from pan; cool on a wire rack.

To make chocolate topping, melt chocolate and shortening in a small saucepan over low heat. Cool to room temperature. Place cooled coffeecake on a platter; spoon topping over coffeecake. Let stand until chocolate sets. Makes 1 coffeecake.

Sweet Lemon Rolls

1 (1/4-oz.) pkg. active dry yeast (1 tablespoon)
1 teaspoon granulated sugar
1/4 cup warm water (110F, 45C)
1/2 cup butter or margarine, room temperature
3 tablespoons granulated sugar
1 teaspoon salt
1/2 cup milk, scalded
1 egg, beaten
About 3 cups all-purpose or bread flour
2 tablespoons grated lemon peel
3 tablespoons butter or margarine, melted
Powdered sugar, sifted

In a large bowl, combine yeast, 1 teaspoon granulated sugar and water. Let stand until foamy, 5 to 10 minutes. In a small bowl, combine 1/2 cup butter or margarine, 3 tablespoons granulated sugar, salt and milk; cool to room temperature. Stir milk mixture into yeast mixture. Add egg, 2 cups flour and lemon peel; beat vigorously. Stir in enough remaining flour to make a stiff dough. Turn out dough onto a lightly floured surface; knead until dough is smooth and elastic, 8 to 10 minutes. Clean and grease bowl; place dough in greased bowl, turning to coat all sides. Cover; let rise in a warm place, free from drafts, until doubled in bulk. Grease a 12'' x 8'' baking pan. Punch down dough.

To complete, divide dough into 12 equal pieces. Shape each piece into a ball, pinching and tucking sides under. Place balls, seam-side down and 1-1/2 inches apart, in greased pan. Cover; let rise until doubled. Preheat oven to 400F (205C). Brush rolls with 3 tablespoons butter or margarine. Bake 18 to 22 minutes or until tops are golden brown. Dust tops of baked rolls with powdered sugar; serve warm. Makes 12 rolls.

Vienna Bread

1 (1/4-oz.) pkg. active dry yeast (1 tablespoon)
1 teaspoon sugar
1 cup warm water (110F, 45C)
About 3 cups all-purpose or bread flour
2 teaspoons sugar
2 teaspoons salt
Cornmeal
1 egg white blended with 1 tablespoon water for glaze
Sesame seeds

In a large bowl, combine yeast, 1 teaspoon sugar and 1 cup water. Let stand until foamy, 5 to 10 minutes. Stir in 2 cups flour, 2 teaspoons sugar and salt; beat vigorously. Stir in enough remaining flour to make a stiff dough. Turn out dough onto a lightly floured surface; knead until dough is smooth and elastic, 8 to 10 minutes. Clean and grease bowl; place dough in greased bowl, turning to coat all sides. Cover; let rise in a warm place, free from drafts, until doubled in bulk. Sprinkle a large baking sheet with cornmeal. Punch down dough.

To complete, shape dough into a 14-inch-long loaf; place seam-side down on prepared baking sheet. Cover; let rise until doubled. Preheat oven to 400F (205C). Use a razor blade to cut 3 or 4 diagonal slashes in top of raised loaf. Brush with egg-white glaze; sprinkle with sesame seeds. Bake 20 to 25 minutes or until loaf sounds hollow when tapped on bottom. Cool on a wire rack. Makes 1 loaf.

Refrigerated Rolls

4-1/2 to 5 cups all-purpose flour
2 (1/4-oz.) pkgs. active dry yeast (2 tablespoons)
2 teaspoons salt
1/4 cup sugar
2/3 cup instant or non-instant milk powder
2 cups warm water
1/4 cup vegetable shortening, melted
2 eggs, beaten
Poppy seeds or sesame seeds, if desired

In a large bowl, blend 2-1/2 cups flour, yeast, salt, sugar and milk powder. Stir in warm water, shortening and eggs. Let stand 10 minutes. Beat 100 strokes by hand or about 2 minutes with an electric mixer. Stir in 1-1/2 cups flour. Stir in enough of remaining flour to make a medium-stiff dough. On a lightly floured surface, knead 8 to 10 minutes until smooth with small bubbles under surface. Add more flour to surface as needed. **To bake in 2 to 24 hours,** cover and let dough stand about 20 minutes. Grease 2 large baking sheets. Punch down dough. Shape into rolls according to variations below. Place rolls, 2 to 3 inches apart, on greased baking sheets. Sprinkle rolls with poppy seeds or sesame seeds, if desired. Cover rolls loosely with plastic wrap or foil. Refrigerate 2 to 24 hours. Carefully uncover rolls. Let stand at room temperature 20 to 30 minutes. Preheat oven to 375F (190C). Bake rolls 20 to 23 minutes or until evenly browned. Remove from pans; cool on wire racks. **To bake in 2 to 5 days,** grease a 2-quart container with a tight-fitting lid. Place kneaded dough in container, turning to grease all sides. Refrigerate 2 to 5 days. When ready to use, turn dough out onto a lightly floured surface. Let rest 30 minutes. Shape into rolls according to variations below. Let rolls rise 30 minutes. Bake 23 to 25 minutes according to directions above. Makes about 48 rolls.

Variations

Pan Rolls: Pinch off pieces of dough about the size of medium eggs. Shape into balls, pinching and tucking sides under. Dip smooth top of each roll in melted butter or margarine. Arrange rounded-side up in greased round 9-inch baking pans.

Rosettes: Roll out 1/2 of dough to a 1/4-inch-thick rectangle. Cut rolled dough into 12'' x 1'' strips. Place 1 end of a strip around your index finger. Holding other end of dough in your other hand, wind dough around your finger. Dough will twist. Pull your finger out of center. Tuck end of dough under roll. Arrange rolls, tucked-end down, in greased muffin cups.

Crescents: Roll out 1/2 of dough to a 1/4-inch-thick circle. Cut dough into wedges, about 3 inches wide on outer edge. Roll each wedge, jelly-roll fashion, from outer edge to point. Arrange on a greased baking sheet, with point under roll. Curve ends of roll to make crescents.

Pull Throughs: Roll out dough until 1/4 inch thick. Cut in 3- to 4-inch circles. Make a 2-inch slash on 1 side of each dough circle following curve of circle. Firmly pull opposite side of circle through slash. Arrange on a greased baking sheet.

Double Twists: Roll out 1/2 of dough to a 12'' x 8'' rectangle. Brush with melted butter or margarine. Use a sharp knife or scissors to cut dough in 1/2- to 1-inch crosswise strips. Fold strips in half; starting at fold, twist strips. Pinch ends to seal. Arrange as sticks or shape into circles on a greased baking sheet.

Parker House Rolls: Roll out 1/2 of dough until 1/4 inch thick. Cut into circles with a biscuit cutter or top of a small drinking glass. Cut almost through center of circles with blunt side of a knive blade. Brush top of each scored circle with melted butter or margarine. Fold circle in half with buttered surface inside. Arrange on a greased baking sheet.

Polka-Dot Bread

1/2 cup whole-wheat kernels (berries)
1 cup boiling water
2 cups warm water
1/4 cup honey
1 (1/4-oz.) pkg. active dry yeast (1 tablespoon)
2 teaspoons salt
1/3 cup instant or non-instant milk powder
1/4 cup vegetable shortening, melted
4-1/2 to 5-1/2 cups whole-wheat flour

Heat a 2-cup thermos bottle with a narrow neck. Pour wheat kernels into hot thermos. Add boiling water. Attach lid. Set aside 6 hours or overnight. Pour warm water into a medium bowl. Stir in honey. Sprinkle yeast over surface. Let stand 5 minutes or until foamy. Stir in salt, milk powder, shortening and 3 cups flour. Beat until smooth. Drain off water not absorbed by wheat. Stir soaked wheat into batter. Stir in enough remaining flour to make a stiff dough. Turn out onto a lightly floured surface. Cover; let rest 3 to 5 minutes. Clean and grease bowl; set aside. Knead dough 8 to 10 minutes, adding flour to surface as needed. Place kneaded dough in greased bowl, turning to grease all sides. Cover; let rise in a warm place, free from drafts, until doubled in bulk. Grease 2 (9'' x 5'') loaf pans. Punch down dough. On a lightly floured surface, roll out 1/2 of dough to a 14'' x 7'' rectangle. Beginning at a short end, roll tightly jelly-roll fashion. Pinch edges to seal. Place rolled dough, seam-side down, in greased pans; grease top. Repeat with remaining dough. Cover; let rise until dough rises above top of pan. Preheat oven to 375F (190C). Bake loaves about 25 minutes or until browned and loaves sound hollow when tapped on bottom. Remove from pans; cool on a wire rack. Makes 2 loaves.

Half & Half Bread

4 cups hot water
1/3 cup vegetable shortening
1-1/2 teaspoons salt
1/3 cup sugar, honey or molasses
2 (1/4-oz.) pkgs. active dry yeast (2 tablespoons)
4 to 5 cups whole-wheat flour
4 to 5 cups all-purpose flour

In a large bowl, combine water, shortening, salt and sugar, honey or molasses. Stir until shortening melts and water is warm. Sprinkle yeast over surface. Let stand 5 minutes or until foamy. Add whole-wheat flour. Stir to combine, then beat thoroughly. Stir in enough all-purpose flour to make a medium-firm dough that is not sticky. Turn out onto a lightly floured surface. Cover; let rest 3 to 5 minutes. Clean and grease bowl. Knead dough until smooth and elastic, about 10 minutes. Place in greased bowl, turning to grease all sides. Cover; let rise until doubled in bulk. Grease 3 (9" x 5") loaf pans. Punch down dough. Divide into 3 equal portions. Shape into loaves. Place seam-side down in greased pans. Cover; let rise until rounded above pans, about 45 minutes. Preheat oven to 350F (175C). Bake 30 minutes or until golden brown and loaves sound hollow when tapped on bottom. Remove from pans; cool on wire racks. Makes 3 loaves.

Almond Bread

Almond Bread

1 (1/4-oz.) pkg. active dry yeast (1 tablespoon)
1 teaspoon granulated sugar
1/4 cup warm water (110F, 45C)
1/2 cup butter or margarine, room temperature
1/3 cup granulated sugar
1 teaspoon salt
1/2 cup milk, scalded
2 eggs, beaten
About 3-1/2 cups all-purpose or bread flour
1/2 cup raisins
1/3 cup currants or chopped raisins
1/2 cup chopped almonds
1 egg white blended with 1 tablespoon water for glaze
1 tablespoon crystal sugar or crushed sugar cubes
1 tablespoon chopped almonds

In a large bowl, combine yeast, 1 teaspoon granulated sugar and 1/4 cup water. Let stand until foamy, 5 to 10 minutes. In a small bowl, combine butter or margarine, 1/3 cup sugar, salt and milk; cool to room temperature. Stir milk mixture into yeast mixture. Add eggs, 2-1/2 cups flour, raisins, currants or chopped raisins and 1/2 cup almonds; beat vigorously. Stir in enough remaining flour to make a soft dough. Turn out dough onto a lightly floured surface; knead in enough remaining flour to make a stiff dough. Knead until dough is smooth and elastic, 8 to 10 minutes. Clean and grease bowl; place dough in greased bowl, turning to coat all sides. Cover; let rise in a warm place, free from drafts, until doubled in bulk. Grease a large baking sheet. Punch down dough.

To complete, shape dough into a flat ball; place on greased baking sheet. Cover; let rise until almost double. Preheat oven to 375F (190C). Brush raised loaf with egg-white glaze; sprinkle with crystal sugar or crushed sugar cubes and 1 tablespoon almonds. Bake 35 to 40 minutes or until bread sounds hollow when tapped on bottom. Remove from baking sheet; cool on a wire rack. Makes 1 loaf.

Honey Crescent Rolls

Honey Crescent Rolls

1 (1/4-oz.) pkg. active dry yeast (1 tablespoon)
1 teaspoon sugar
1/4 cup warm water (110F, 45C)
1/4 cup butter or margarine, room temperature
1/4 cup honey
1 teaspoon salt
2/3 cup milk, scalded
1 egg, beaten
About 3 cups all-purpose flour
1 egg yolk blended with 1 tablespoon milk for glaze

In a large bowl, combine yeast, 1 teaspoon sugar and water. Let stand until foamy, 5 to 10 minutes. In a small bowl, combine butter or margarine, honey, salt and milk; cool to room temperature. Stir milk mixture into yeast mixture. Add egg and 2 cups flour; beat vigorously. Stir in enough remaining flour to make a soft dough. Turn out dough onto a lightly floured surface; knead in enough remaining flour to make a stiff dough. Knead until dough is smooth and elastic, 8 to 10 minutes. Clean and grease bowl; place dough in greased bowl, turning to coat all sides. Cover; let rise in a warm place, free from drafts, until doubled in bulk. Grease baking sheets; set aside. Punch down dough.
To complete, divide dough into 4 equal pieces. Roll out each piece to a 10-inch circle; cut each circle into quarters. Starting at wide end, roll up each quarter, making crescents. Place crescents on greased baking sheets; curve ends in slightly. Cover; let rise until doubled in bulk. Preheat oven to 375F (190C). Brush egg-yolk glaze over crescents. Bake 18 to 20 minutes or until golden brown. Remove from baking sheets; cool on wire racks. Makes 16 crescents.

Marzipan Coffeecake

Basic Sweet Dough:
1 (1/4-oz.) pkg. active dry yeast (1 tablespoon)
1 teaspoon sugar
1/4 cup warm water (110F, 45C)
1/4 cup butter or margarine, room temperature
1/4 cup sugar
1/2 teaspoon salt
1/2 cup milk, scalded
1 egg, beaten
About 2-3/4 cups all-purpose flour
1 egg white blended with 1 tablespoon water for glaze

Marzipan Filling:
1/2 cup butter or margarine, room temperature
1 (7-oz.) pkg. marzipan or Marzipan, page 232, crumbled
1/2 cup ground almonds
1/4 cup packed light-brown sugar
1/2 teaspoon almond extract
1/2 teaspoon ground cinnamon

Topping:
1/2 cup powdered sugar, sifted
2 to 3 teaspoons milk
2 tablespoons sliced almonds

To make basic sweet dough, in a large bowl, combine yeast, 1 teaspoon sugar and water. Let stand until foamy, 5 to 10 minutes. In a small bowl, combine butter or margarine, 1/4 cup sugar, salt and milk; cool to room temperature. Stir milk mixture into yeast mixture. Add egg and 2 cups flour; beat vigorously. Stir in enough remaining flour to make a stiff dough. Turn out dough onto a lightly floured surface; knead until smooth and elastic, 8 to 10 minutes. Clean and grease bowl; place dough in greased bowl, turning to coat all sides. Cover; let rise in a warm place, free from drafts, until doubled in bulk. Grease a large baking sheet. Punch down dough. On a lightly floured surface, roll out dough to a 16'' x 10'' rectangle.
To make filling, in a medium bowl, beat butter or margarine and marzipan until creamy. Stir in almonds, brown sugar, almond extract and cinnamon. Spread filling over dough to within 1/2 inch of edges. Starting on a long side, roll up dough jelly-roll fashion. Pinch seam to seal. Place dough, seam-side down, on greased baking sheet; shape like a horseshoe. Cover; let rise until doubled. Preheat oven to 350F (175C). Brush horseshoe with egg-white glaze. Bake 30 to 35 minutes or until browned. Cool on a wire rack.
To make topping, in a small bowl, blend powdered sugar and milk until smooth. Drizzle over baked loaf; sprinkle with almonds. Makes 1 coffeecake.

Fried Prune Treats

1 (1/4-oz.) pkg. active dry yeast (1 tablespoon)
1 teaspoon sugar
1/4 cup warm water (110F, 45C)
6 tablespoons butter or margarine, room temperature
3 tablespoons sugar
1/2 cup milk, scalded
3 eggs, beaten
About 3 cups all-purpose flour
1/2 teaspoon ground cinnamon
36 pitted prunes
Vegetable oil for deep-frying
1/2 cup sugar
1 teaspoon ground cinnamon

In a large bowl, combine yeast, 1 teaspoon sugar and water. Let stand until foamy, 5 to 10 minutes. In a small bowl, combine butter or margarine, 3 tablespoons sugar and milk; cool to room temperature. Stir milk mixture into yeast mixture. Add eggs, 2 cups flour and 1/2 teaspoon cinnamon; beat vigorously. Stir in enough remaining flour to make a soft dough. Turn out dough onto a lightly floured surface; knead in enough remaining flour to make a stiff dough. Knead until dough is smooth and elastic, 8 to 10 minutes. Clean and grease bowl; place dough in greased bowl, turning to coat all sides. Cover; let rise in a warm place, free from drafts, until doubled in bulk. Grease 2 large baking sheets. Punch down dough.
To complete, divide dough in half. Cut each half into 18 equal pieces. Press 1 prune into center of each piece of dough, covering completely. Place 1 inch apart on greased baking sheets. Cover; let rise until almost doubled in bulk. Heat oil in a deep-fryer to 350F (175C) or until a 1-inch cube of bread turns golden brown in 65 seconds. Lower 4 or 5 balls at a time into hot oil. Fry 1 to 2 minutes on each side or until deep golden brown. Use a slotted spoon to lift cooked prune treats from oil; drain on paper towels. Repeat with remaining balls. In a small bowl, combine 1/2 cup sugar and 1 teaspoon cinnamon. Roll prune balls in sugar-cinnamon mixture to coat. Makes about 36 prune treats.

Jelly Doughnuts

1 (1/4-oz.) pkg. active dry yeast (1 tablespoon)
1 teaspoon sugar
1/4 cup warm water (110F, 45C)
1/3 cup butter or margarine, room temperature
3 tablespoons sugar
1 teaspoon salt
1/2 cup milk, scalded
2 eggs, beaten
About 2-1/2 cups all-purpose flour
Vegetable oil for deep-frying
Jelly or jam, any flavor desired
Sugar

In a large bowl, combine yeast, 1 teaspoon sugar and water. Let stand until foamy, 5 to 10 minutes. In a small bowl, combine butter or margarine, 3 tablespoons sugar,

Jelly Doughnuts

salt and milk; cool to room temperature. Stir milk mixture into yeast mixture. Add eggs and 1-3/4 cups flour; beat vigorously. Stir in enough remaining flour to make a stiff dough. Turn out dough onto a lightly floured surface; knead until smooth and elastic, 8 to 10 minutes. Clean and grease bowl; place dough in greased bowl, turning to coat all sides. Cover; let rise in a warm place, free from drafts, until doubled in bulk. Grease and flour baking sheets. Punch down dough.
To complete, on a lightly floured surface, roll out dough until 1/2 inch thick. Flour a round 2-1/2-inch biscuit cutter; use to cut dough. Place dough circles on greased baking sheets. Cover; let rise until doubled in bulk. Heat oil in a deep-fryer to 350F (175C) or until a 1-inch cube of bread turns golden brown in 65 seconds. Gently lower 4 or 5 dough circles into hot oil. Fry about 1 minute on each side or until browned. Use a slotted spoon to remove from oil; drain on paper towels. Repeat with remaining dough. Pierce doughnuts on one side with a sharp knife, almost through to other side. Spoon 2 teaspoons jelly into center of each doughnut. Or, spoon jelly into a pastry bag fitted with a plain tip. Pipe about 2 teaspoons jelly into each doughnut. Roll doughnuts in sugar. Makes 14 to 18 doughnuts

Marzipan & Raisin Pastry

Marzipan & Raisin Pastry

Photo on pages 128-129.

Filling:
1 (7-oz.) pkg. marzipan or Marzipan, page 232, crumbled
1/2 cup butter or margarine, room temperature
3/4 cup raisins
1/2 cup currants or chopped raisins
3/4 cup chopped walnuts, pecans, hazelnuts or almonds
2 tablespoons brown sugar
1 teaspoon ground cinnamon
1/4 cup chopped candied lemon peel or candied citron

Pastry:
1 recipe Sweet Cream-Cheese Pastry, page 133
Milk

Glaze:
1-1/2 cups powdered sugar, sifted
2 to 3 tablespoons orange juice
1/4 cup sliced almonds

To make filling, in a medium bowl, beat marzipan and butter or margarine until blended; set aside. In another medium bowl, combine raisins, currants or chopped raisins, nuts, brown sugar, cinnamon and candied lemon peel or candied citron; set aside.

To make pastry, prepare pastry as directed. Preheat oven to 350F (175C). Grease baking sheets; set aside. On a lightly floured surface, roll out 1/2 of dough to a 12-inch square. Spread 1/2 of marzipan mixture over pastry square. Top with 1/2 of raisin-nut mixture. Loosely roll up dough and filling, jelly-roll fashion. Pinch seams to seal. Repeat with remaining dough and filling. Place filled rolls, seam-side down, on greased baking sheets. Flatten rolls until 4 inches wide. Make 2 slashes down length of each roll, about 1 inch apart; brush rolls with milk. Bake 30 to 35 minutes or until golden brown. Cool on baking sheets on wire racks 10 minutes.

To make glaze, in a small bowl, beat powdered sugar and orange juice until smooth. Drizzle glaze over rolls; sprinkle each roll with 2 tablespoons sliced almonds. Let stand until glaze sets. Remove from baking sheets; cool on wire racks. Makes 2 filled pastries.

On preceding pages: Marzipan & Raisin Pastry.

Cream Ring

Pastry:
1 recipe Cream-Puff Pastry dough, opposite

Filling:
2 teaspoons unflavored gelatin powder
2 tablespoons warm water
2 cups whipping cream (1 pint)
2 tablespoons brandy, kirsch or other cherry-flavored liqueur
1/3 cup powdered sugar

To make pastry, grease and flour a baking sheet. Draw an 8-inch circle in flour on baking sheet, using bottom of a round 8-inch cake pan as a guide. Prepare pastry as directed; do not bake. Preheat oven to 400F (205C). Spoon dough into a pastry bag fitted with a 1/2-inch star tip. Pipe dough in a circle following guide on baking sheet. Pipe second circle inside, touching first circle of dough. Pipe a third circle, centering it on top of other circles. Bake 35 to 40 minutes or until golden brown. Remove from baking sheet; cut ring in half horizontally. Cool on a wire rack.

To make filling, in a small saucepan, combine gelatin and water. Stir well; let stand 3 minutes. Stir over low heat until gelatin dissolves; set aside to cool. In a medium bowl, whip cream until soft peaks form. Add cooled gelatin mixture, brandy or liqueur and 1/4 cup powdered sugar. Beat until stiff peaks form. Spoon whipped-cream mixture into a pastry bag fitted with a plain or star tip. Pipe whipped-cream mixture into bottom of ring. Replace top; sprinkle with remaining powdered sugar. Refrigerate until ready to serve. Makes 1 filled ring.

Cream Ring

Cream Puffs

Photo on pages 2-3.

Cream-Puff Pastry:
1 cup water or 1/2 cup water and 1/2 cup half and half
1 tablespoon sugar
1/2 teaspoon salt
1/2 cup unsalted butter
1 cup all-purpose or bread flour
5 eggs

Filling:
Sliced strawberries, fresh or canned raspberries,
 pitted cherries or other fruit, drained
Powdered sugar
2 cups whipping cream (1 pint)
2 teaspoons vanilla extract or 1 teaspoon almond extract

To make pastry, grease 2 baking sheets; set aside. In a medium saucepan, combine water or water and half and half, sugar, salt and butter. Stirring constantly over low heat, slowly bring to a rolling boil. Remove pan from heat; add flour all at once, beating vigorously with a wooden spoon until dough comes away from side of pan and forms a ball, about 1 minute. Let cool 3 minutes. Add eggs, 1 at a time, beating well after each addition. Preheat oven to 375F (190C). Spoon dough into a large pastry bag fitted with a 1/2-inch star tip. *To make large puffs,* pipe 12 large mounds with 3-inch diameters, 2-1/2 inches apart, on greased baking sheets. *To make miniature puffs,* pipe 24 small mounds with 1-1/2-inch diameters, 2 inches apart, on greased baking sheets. Bake cream puffs 45 minutes. Cut a slit in side of each cream puff. Return to oven; bake 10 minutes or until golden brown. Remove from baking sheets; cool on wire racks. When cool, slice tops from puffs; set tops aside.
To make filling, sprinkle fruit with powdered sugar; let stand 20 minutes. In a medium bowl, whip cream until soft peaks form. Add 1/4 cup powdered sugar and vanilla or almond extract. Beat until stiff peaks form. Spoon whipped-cream mixture into a pastry bag fitted with a star tip. Spoon 1 or 2 teaspoons sweetened fruit into bottom of each cream puff. Pipe whipped-cream mixture over fruit, filling bottom of puff and mounding high in center. Replace tops; sprinkle with powdered sugar. Refrigerate until ready to serve. Makes 12 large puffs or 24 miniature puffs.

Tea-Time Treats

1/2 (17-1/4-oz.) pkg. frozen puff pastry (1 sheet), thawed,
 or 1/2 recipe Puff Pastry, page 232
Strawberry preserves or raspberry preserves
Powdered sugar

Preheat oven to 425F (220C). On a lightly floured surface, unfold pastry; roll out to a 12-inch square. Cut into 4 (3-inch-wide) strips. Cut each strip into 4 (3-inch) squares. Spoon 1 to 2 teaspoons preserves onto center of each square. Moisten edges of pastry with water; fold over filling so opposite corners come together, making triangles. Press edges together with tines of a fork to seal. Place on an ungreased baking sheet. Bake 8 to 10 minutes or until puffed and golden brown. Remove from baking sheet; cool on a wire rack. Dust cooled pastries with powdered sugar. Makes 16 pastries.

Cream Puff

Mandarin & Cream Ring

Little Swans

Mandarin & Cream Ring

Pastry:
1 recipe Cream-Puff Pastry dough, page 131

Filling:
1 (11-oz.) can mandarin oranges
1 cup whipping cream (1/2 pint)
1 teaspoon vanilla extract
Powdered sugar

To make pastry, grease and flour a baking sheet. Draw an 8-inch circle in flour on baking sheet, using bottom of a round 8-inch cake pan as a guide. Prepare pastry as directed; do not bake. Preheat oven to 400F (205C). Spoon dough into a pastry bag fitted with a 1/2-inch plain tip. Pipe dough in a circle following guide on baking sheet. Pipe second circle inside, touching first circle of dough. Pipe a third circle, centering it on top of other circles. Bake 35 to 40 minutes or until golden brown. Remove from baking sheet; cut ring in half horizontally. Cool on a wire rack.

To make filling, drain oranges, reserving 3 tablespoons liquid. In a medium bowl, whip cream until soft peaks form. Beat in reserved mandarin liquid, vanilla and 2 tablespoons powdered sugar until stiff peaks form. Spoon whipped-cream mixture into a pastry bag fitted with a star tip; set aside. Reserve 12 orange sections for decoration. Scatter remaining orange sections in bottom of pastry ring. Pipe whipped-cream mixture into bottom ring. Replace top; arrange reserved orange sections around outside of ring, as shown. Dust with powdered sugar, if desired. Refrigerate until ready to serve. Makes 1 filled ring.

Little Swans

Pastry:
1 recipe Cream-Puff Pastry dough, page 131

Filling:
2 teaspoons unflavored gelatin powder
2 tablespoons warm water
2 cups whipping cream (1 pint)
2 teaspoons vanilla extract or 1 teaspoon almond extract
About 1/3 cup powdered sugar

To make pastry, grease 2 baking sheets; set aside. Prepare pastry as directed; do not bake. Preheat oven to 375F (190C). Spoon 3/4 of dough into a pastry bag fitted with a 1/2-inch plain tip. Pipe 36 mounds with 1-1/2-inch diameters for swan bodies, 1 inch apart, onto 1 greased baking sheet. Spoon remaining dough into pastry bag fitted with a 1/8-inch plain tip. On remaining greased baking sheet, pipe 36 figure **2**s for swan necks and heads, making small dollops at beginning of each for swan heads. Bake swan necks and heads about 10 minutes or until golden. Remove from baking sheets; cool on wire racks. Bake swan bodies 25 to 30 minutes or until golden. Cut off top third of swan bodies; set aside. Cool on wire racks.

To make filling, in a small saucepan, combine gelatin and water; let stand 3 minutes. Stir over low heat until gelatin dissolves; set aside to cool. In a medium bowl, whip cream until soft peaks form. Add cooled gelatin mixture, vanilla or almond extract and 1/4 cup powdered sugar. Beat until stiff peaks form. Spoon whipped-cream mixture into a pastry bag fitted with a 1/2-inch star tip. Pipe whipped-cream mixture into bottom of swan bodies. Cut reserved tops of swan bodies in half lengthwise; press into whipped cream for wings. Or, cut 2 wings and a small tail from reserved body tops, as shown. Position swan necks forward of wings. Dust with powdered sugar. Refrigerate until ready to serve. Makes 36 swans.

Jam-Filled Pastries

Sweet Cream-Cheese Pastry:
2 (3-oz.) pkgs. cream cheese, room temperature
6 tablespoons butter or margarine, room temperature
1/3 cup sugar
6 tablespoons milk or half and half
2-1/4 cups all-purpose flour
1 teaspoon baking powder
1/2 teaspoon salt

Filling:
1/2 cup cherry preserves or 1/2 cup strawberry jam
Milk

To make pastry, in a large bowl, beat cream cheese, butter or margarine, sugar and milk or half and half until smooth. Blend flour, baking powder and salt; stir into cream-cheese mixture until dough begins to bind together. Knead dough in bowl 10 strokes or until smooth. On a lightly floured surface, roll out 1/2 of dough to a 12" x 9" rectangle. Cut into 12 (3-inch) squares. Repeat with remaining dough. Preheat oven to 350F (175C). Grease baking sheets.

To make pinwheels, place 1/2 teaspoon preserves or jam in center of each square. Make a 1-inch slash from each corner toward center of square. Fold 2 opposite points of pastry toward center, over filling; pinch points together to seal. Do not fold in remaining points.

To make triangles, place 1/2 teaspoon preserves or jam in center of each square. Fold pastry squares diagonally in half over filling; press edges together with tines of a fork to seal.

To complete, place filled pastries on greased baking sheets; brush with milk. Bake 12 to 15 minutes or until golden brown. Remove from baking sheets; cool on wire racks. Makes 24 pastries.

Strawberry-Custard Pie

Single Pastry for 9- or 10-inch Pie, page 142

Filling:
4 eggs
2 cups milk
1/2 cup half and half
2/3 cup sugar
1 teaspoon vanilla extract
1/4 teaspoon salt
1/8 teaspoon ground nutmeg
4 cups strawberries (1 qt.)
1/2 cup red-currant jelly, melted

Prepare pastry as directed. Fit pastry into a 9- or 10-inch pie plate; do not bake. Preheat oven to 350F (175C).
To make filling, in a large bowl, beat eggs; stir in milk, half and half, sugar, vanilla, salt and nutmeg. Pull out center rack of oven; place pastry-lined pie plate on rack. Pour custard into pastry; carefully return rack to original position. Bake 35 to 40 minutes or until custard is set. Cool on a wire rack; refrigerate until ready to serve. Wash and hull strawberries. Arrange in a circular pattern on top of chilled pie. Brush with jelly; let stand until jelly sets. Serve chilled. Makes 1 pie or 6 to 8 servings.

Jam-Filled Pastries

Nut Crescents

1 (17-1/4-oz.) pkg. frozen puff pastry (2 sheets), thawed,
   or 1 recipe Puff Pastry, page 232
1/2 cup finely chopped walnuts, pecans, almonds or hazelnuts
2 tablespoons brown sugar
1 teaspoon ground cinnamon
1/2 teaspoon ground nutmeg
1 egg yolk blended with 1 tablespoon water for glaze

Preheat oven to 400F (205C). On a lightly floured surface, unfold pastry. Cut each pastry sheet in half lengthwise, then crosswise, making 8 (5-inch) squares. Cut each square diagonally in half, making triangles. In a small bowl, combine nuts, brown sugar, cinnamon and nutmeg. Spoon about 1 tablespoon nut mixture along longest edge of each triangle. Brush pastry edges with water. Starting at longest triangle edge, roll up toward point to make crescents. Place crescents with points down, 3 inches apart, on ungreased baking sheets; brush with egg-yolk glaze. Bake 12 to 15 minutes or until puffed and golden brown. Remove from baking sheets; cool on wire racks. Makes 16 crescents.

Apple Strudel

Filling:
1/4 cup butter or margarine
2 cups fresh breadcrumbs
1/2 cup sugar
1/2 teaspoon ground cinnamon
1/4 teaspoon ground nutmeg
2 teaspoons grated lemon peel
1/2 cup raisins
1/2 cup chopped slivered almonds or chopped walnuts
1 tablespoon rum
1 teaspoon vanilla extract
6 medium, tart apples (about 2 lbs.)

Pastry:
1/2 lb. filo leaves (about 12 leaves), thawed if frozen
1/2 cup butter or margarine, melted
Powdered sugar
Sweetened whipped cream or ice cream, if desired

To make filling, melt butter or margarine in a large skillet. Add breadcrumbs; stir over medium heat until browned. In a large bowl, combine sugar, cinnamon, nutmeg, lemon peel, raisins, nuts, rum, vanilla and 1/3 cup browned breadcrumbs; set aside. Peel, core and thinly slice apples; set aside.

To make pastry, carefully unfold filo leaves; place between damp towels. Remove 1 leaf; place on a dry towel. Brush with butter or margarine. Top with another pastry leaf; brush with butter or margarine. Repeat with remaining leaves. Sprinkle remaining 1-2/3 cups browned breadcrumbs over top of buttered pastry leaves. Preheat oven to 375F (190C). Lightly grease a large baking sheet or 15" x 10" jelly-roll pan.

To complete, arrange apple slices over breadcrumbs to within 2 inches of long sides and 1 inch of short sides of stacked pastry leaves. Sprinkle raisin mixture over apples. Using towel to lift pastry and filling, gently roll up strudel from a long side, jelly-roll fashion. Brush seam with water; gently press seam to seal. Tuck ends into roll. Lift strudel in towel; carefully roll from towel onto greased baking sheet or jelly-roll pan. Turn seam-side down. Generously brush top and sides of roll with remaining butter or margarine. Bake 35 to 40 minutes or until golden brown. Cool slightly on baking sheet on a wire rack. Place on a long serving dish; dust warm roll with powdered sugar. Serve warm with whipped cream or ice cream, if desired. Makes 1 strudel or 8 to 10 servings.

Viennese Poppy Strudel

Viennese Poppy Strudel

Poppy-Seed Filling:
3 cups poppy seeds
3/4 cup sugar
1 cup milk
2 tablespoons grated lemon peel
1/3 cup raisins

Pastry:
1/2 lb. filo leaves (about 12 leaves), thawed if frozen
1/2 cup butter or margarine, melted
Powdered sugar
Poppy seeds, if desired

To make filling, in a medium saucepan, combine poppy seeds, sugar, milk, lemon peel and raisins. Stirring constantly, cook over low heat until thickened; set aside.

To make pastry, carefully unfold filo leaves; place between damp towels. Remove 1 leaf; place on a dry towel. Brush with butter or margarine. Top with another leaf; brush with butter or margarine. Repeat with remaining leaves. Preheat oven to 375F (190C). Lightly grease a large baking sheet or 15" x 10" jelly-roll pan.

To complete, spoon poppy-seed mixture over filo leaves to within 2 inches of long sides of leaves; smooth surface. Using towel to lift pastry and filling, gently roll up from a long side, jelly-roll fashion. Brush seam with water; gently press seam to seal. Lift strudel in towel; carefully roll from towel onto greased baking sheet. Turn seam-side down. Generously brush top and sides with remaining butter or margarine. Bake 35 to 40 minutes or until golden brown. Cool slightly on baking sheet on a

Cheese Strudel

Filling:
3 eggs, separated
1/2 cup sugar
2 teaspoons grated lemon peel
3 cups cottage cheese (24 oz.)
1/2 cup golden raisins

Pastry:
1/2 lb. filo leaves (about 12 leaves), thawed if frozen
1/2 cup butter or margarine, melted
Powdered sugar

To make filling, in a medium bowl, beat egg yolks and sugar until thick and pale; stir in lemon peel. In a blender or food processor, puree cottage cheese. Stir pureed cottage cheese and raisins into egg-yolk mixture. In another medium bowl, beat egg whites until stiff but not dry. Fold into cheese mixture; set aside.

To make pastry, unfold filo leaves; place between damp towels. Remove 1 leaf; place on a dry towel. Brush with butter or margarine. Top with another leaf; brush with butter or margarine. Repeat with remaining leaves. Preheat oven to 375F (190C). Lightly grease a large baking sheet or 15'' x 10'' jelly-roll pan; set aside.

To complete, spoon cheese filling onto stacked filo leaves to within 2 inches of long sides and to within 1 inch of short ends. Using towel to lift filo and filling, gently roll up from a long side, jelly-roll fashion. Brush seam with water; gently press seam to seal. Tuck ends in. Lift strudel in towel; carefully roll from towel onto greased baking sheet. Turn seam-side down. Generously brush top and sides with remaining butter or margarine. Bake 35 to 40 minutes or until golden brown. Cool slightly on baking sheet on a wire rack. Place on a long serving dish; dust with powdered sugar. Serve warm or refrigerate until chilled. Makes 1 strudel or 8 to 10 servings.

wire rack. Place on a long serving dish; dust with powdered sugar. Sprinkle with poppy seeds, if desired. Serve warm. Makes 1 strudel or 8 to 10 servings.

Apricot Pinwheels

1/2 (17-1/4-oz.) pkg. frozen puff pastry (1 sheet), thawed, or 1/2 recipe Puff Pastry, page 232
12 canned apricot halves, drained
3 tablespoons powdered sugar
1 to 2 teaspoons lemon juice

Preheat oven to 400F (205C). On a lightly floured surface, unfold pastry. Roll out pastry to a 14'' x 10-1/2'' rectangle. Cut into 3 equal lengthwise strips. Cut each strip into 4 (3-1/2-inch) squares. Make a 1-1/2-inch slash from each corner toward center of each square. Place an apricot half in center of each square. Fold 2 opposite points of pastry toward center, over apricot half; pinch points together to seal. Do not fold in remaining points. Place on ungreased baking sheets. Bake 10 to 15 minutes or until puffed and golden brown. Remove from baking sheets; cool on wire racks. In a small bowl, beat powdered sugar and 1 teaspoon lemon juice until smooth. Add more lemon juice, if necessary. Spoon over warm pastries. Makes 12 pinwheels.

Apricot Pinwheels

Cherry Envelopes

Filling:
1 (16-oz.) can pitted tart red cherries
1 tablespoon sugar
4 teaspoons cornstarch
1 teaspoon lemon juice
1 teaspoon grated lemon peel, if desired

Pastry:
1 recipe Sweet Cream-Cheese Pastry, page 133
Milk
1/2 teaspoon ground cinnamon
2 tablespoons sugar
1/4 cup slivered almonds

To make filling, drain cherry juice into a small saucepan; set drained cherries aside. Add sugar, cornstarch and lemon juice to saucepan; stir until blended. Stirring constantly, cook over low heat until mixture comes to a boil and thickens. Cool slightly. Stir in lemon peel, if desired, and reserved cherries; set aside.

To make pastry, prepare as directed. On a lightly floured surface, roll out 1/2 of dough to a 15" x 10" rectangle. Cut dough into 6 (5-inch) squares. Repeat with remaining dough. Preheat oven to 350F (175C). Grease baking sheets.

To complete, spoon 1 heaping tablespoon cherry filling onto center of each pastry square. Bring 4 corners of pastry to center, enclosing filling, envelope-style. Pinch corners together; pinch sides together to seal. Place filled pastries on greased baking sheets; brush with milk. In a small bowl, combine cinnamon and sugar; sprinkle over filled pastries. Sprinkle with almonds. Bake 18 to 22 minutes or until golden brown. Remove from baking sheets; cool on wire racks. Makes 12 pastries.

Cherry Envelopes

Southern Pecan Pie

Single Pastry for 9- or 10-inch Pie, page 142

Filling:
1-1/4 cups pecan halves
1 cup dark corn syrup
3/4 cup sugar
3 tablespoons butter or margarine
3 eggs
1 teaspoon vanilla extract or brandy extract
1/4 teaspoon salt
Flavored whipped cream, if desired

Prepare pastry as directed. Fit pastry into a 9- or 10-inch pie plate; do not bake. Preheat oven to 375F (190C).

To make filling, arrange pecan halves, rounded-sides up, in pastry-lined pie plate. In a medium saucepan, combine corn syrup and sugar. Stirring constantly over low heat, cook until sugar dissolves. Remove from heat; stir in butter or margarine. In a medium bowl, beat eggs; stir in vanilla or brandy extract and salt. Stir in 1/4 cup corn-syrup mixture. Stirring constantly, pour egg mixture into remaining syrup mixture. Slowly pour combined mixture over pecans. Pecans will rise to top of liquid. Bake 40 to 45 minutes or until center is set. Cool pie on a wire rack. Serve warm or cold with whipped cream, if desired. Makes 1 pie or 6 to 8 servings.

Old-Fashioned Apple Pie

Double Pastry for 9- or 10-inch Pie, page 142

Filling:
8 cups sliced, peeled tart apples (about 3 lbs.)
1 tablespoon lemon juice
1/2 to 3/4 cup sugar
2 tablespoons cornstarch
1 teaspoon grated lemon peel
1 teaspoon ground cinnamon
1/4 teaspoon ground cloves
1/4 teaspoon ground nutmeg
2 tablespoons butter or margarine
Milk
Sugar
Sharp Cheddar cheese or ice cream, if desired

Prepare pastry as directed. Fit bottom pastry into a 9- or 10-inch pie plate; set aside.

To make filling, place apples in a large bowl. Sprinkle with lemon juice; toss lightly. In a small bowl, blend 1/2 to 3/4 cup sugar, cornstarch, lemon peel, cinnamon, cloves and nutmeg. Sprinkle over apples; toss gently to coat. Spoon into pastry-lined pie plate; dot with butter or margarine. Preheat oven to 425F (220C).

To complete, place top pastry over apple filling. Trim pastry to 1 inch beyond rim of pie plate. Fold edges under; flute. Cut vents in top pastry. Brush with milk; sprinkle with sugar. Cover pastry edge with foil. Place on a baking sheet; bake 15 minutes. Reduce oven temperature to 375F (190C). Bake 25 to 30 minutes longer or until pastry is golden and juices are bubbly. Remove foil during final 20 minutes of baking. Cool pie on a wire rack. Serve warm or cold with cheese or ice cream, if desired. Makes 1 pie or 6 to 8 servings.

Raspberry-Filled Shells

1 (10-oz.) pkg. frozen patty shells, thawed,
  or 1/2 recipe Puff Pastry, page 232

Filling:
1 pint fresh raspberries
1 cup whipping cream (1/2 pint)
2 tablespoons powdered sugar
1 teaspoon vanilla extract or brandy extract

Preheat oven to 450F (230C). Place pastry shells on an ungreased baking sheet. Place in center of oven; reduce oven heat to 400F (205C). Bake 20 to 25 minutes or until pastry shells are golden brown. Cut off tops of cooked pastry shells; cool on a wire rack. Reserve 6 to 12 raspberries for decoration.

To make filling, press remaining raspberries through a sieve into a small bowl; set aside. In a medium bowl, whip cream until soft peaks form. Beat in powdered sugar and vanilla or brandy extract until stiff peaks form. Stir 3 or 4 tablespoons whipped-cream mixture into pureed raspberries. Spoon raspberry mixture evenly into bottoms of cooked pastry shells. Spoon remaining whipped-cream mixture over raspberry mixture. Add pastry tops, placing off-center; decorate with reserved raspberries. Refrigerate until ready to serve. Makes 6 servings.

Blueberry-Patch Pie

Double Pastry for 9- or 10-inch Pie, page 142

Filling:
4 cups fresh or frozen blueberries (1 qt.)
1-1/2 tablespoons lemon juice
1/2 to 3/4 cup sugar
3 tablespoons cornstarch
1 teaspoon grated lemon peel
1/2 teaspoon ground cinnamon
2 tablespoons butter or margarine
Milk
Sugar
Flavored whipped cream or ice cream, if desired.

Prepare pastry as directed. Fit bottom pastry into a 9- or 10-inch pie plate; set aside.

To make filling, place blueberries in a large bowl. Sprinkle with lemon juice; toss lightly. In a small bowl, blend 1/2 to 3/4 cup sugar, cornstarch, lemon peel and cinnamon. Sprinkle over blueberries; toss gently to coat. Spoon into pastry-lined pie plate; dot with butter or margarine. Preheat oven to 425F (220C).

To complete, roll out top pastry to an 11-inch circle. Cut into 12 (1/2-inch-wide) strips using center of circle. Use remaining dough for another purpose. Arrange 6 strips over blueberry filling, spacing about 1 inch apart. At each end, press strips to seal. Place remaining 6 pastry strips diagonally across first strips. At each end, press strips to seal. Trim strips even with edge of pie plate. Fold bottom pastry up and over strips to seal and build up edge; flute edge. Brush strips with milk; sprinkle with sugar. Cover pastry edge with foil. Place on a baking sheet; bake 40 to 45 minutes or until pastry is golden and juices are bubbly. Remove foil during final 20 minutes of baking. Cool pie on a wire rack. Serve warm or cold with whipped cream or ice cream, if desired. Makes 1 pie or 6 to 8 servings.

Raspberry-Filled Shells

Apple Pockets

Apple Pockets

Filling:
2 medium, tart cooking apples (about 1 lb.)
1/3 cup raisins
1/4 to 1/2 cup sugar
1 tablespoon lemon juice
1 teaspoon grated lemon peel
1/2 teaspoon ground cinnamon

Pastry:
1 recipe Sweet Cream-Cheese Pastry, page 133
Milk

Glaze:
1 cup powdered sugar
1 to 2 tablespoons hot water

To make filling, peel, core and coarsely chop apples. In a medium saucepan, combine chopped apples, raisins, sugar, lemon juice, lemon peel and cinnamon. Bring to a boil over low heat. Reduce heat; cover and simmer until apples are tender. Set aside to cool.
To make pastry, preheat oven to 350F (175C). Grease baking sheets; set aside. Prepare pastry as directed. Roll out 1/2 of pastry to a 10-inch square. Cut pastry square into 4 (5-inch) circles. Repeat with remaining pastry. Spoon about 2 tablespoons apple filling off center on each pastry circle; brush edge with milk. Fold pastry over filling, placing edges together. Press edges together with tines of a fork to seal. Place filled pastries on greased baking sheets; brush tops with milk. Bake 15 to 20 minutes or until golden brown. Remove from baking sheets; cool on wire racks.
To make glaze, in a small bowl, combine powdered sugar and enough hot water to make a smooth, medium glaze. Brush glaze over tops of warm pastries. Let stand until glaze sets. Makes 8 pastries.

On preceding pages: Apple Dumpling, opposite.

Deep-Dish Peach Pie

Single Pastry for 9- or 10-inch Pie, page 142

Filling:
8 cups peeled, sliced peaches (about 4 lbs.)
1 cup sugar
1/4 cup cornstarch
1/2 teaspoon ground cinnamon
1/2 teaspoon ground nutmeg
1/2 cup coarsely chopped almonds, pecans or walnuts
2 tablespoons butter or margarine
Milk
Sugar
Flavored whipped cream or ice cream, if desired

Prepare pastry as directed; do not bake. Cover; set aside. Preheat oven to 425F (220C).
To make filling, place peaches in a large bowl. In a small bowl, blend 1 cup sugar, cornstarch, cinnamon and nutmeg. Sprinkle over peaches; toss gently to coat. Spoon peaches into a deep 9-inch pie plate. Sprinkle nuts over peaches; dot with butter or margarine.
To complete, roll out dough to an 11-inch circle; place over peaches. Trim pastry edge to 1 inch beyond rim of pie plate. Fold edge under; flute. Cut vents in pastry. Brush with milk; sprinkle with sugar. Place on a baking sheet; cover edge with foil. Bake 40 to 45 minutes or until pastry is golden and juices are bubbly. Remove foil during final 20 minutes of baking. Cool pie on a wire rack. Serve warm or cold with whipped cream or ice cream, if desired. Makes 1 pie or 8 to 10 servings.

Strawberry-Rhubarb Pie

Double Pastry for 9- or 10-inch Pie, page 142

Filling:
3 cups sliced rhubarb (about 1 lb.)
2 cups sliced strawberries (1 pint)
1 to 1-1/4 cups sugar
2 tablespoons cornstarch
2 teaspoons ground cinnamon
1/2 teaspoon ground nutmeg
1 tablespoon grated orange peel
1/4 teaspoon salt
2 tablespoons butter or margarine
Milk
Sugar

Prepare pastry as directed, fitting bottom pastry into a 9- or 10-inch pie plate. Preheat oven to 425F (220C).
To make filling, in a large bowl, combine rhubarb and strawberries; set aside. In a small bowl, blend 1 to 1-1/4 cups sugar, cornstarch, cinnamon, nutmeg, orange peel and salt. Sprinkle over fruit; toss gently to coat. Spoon fruit mixture into pastry-lined pie plate; dot with butter or margarine.
To complete, roll out remaining pastry; place over filling. Trim pastry to 1 inch beyond rim of pie plate. Fold edges under; flute edge. Cut vents in top pastry. Brush with milk; sprinkle with sugar. Cover pastry edge with foil. Place on a baking sheet; bake 40 to 45 minutes or until pastry is golden and juices are bubbly. Remove foil during final 20 minutes of baking. Cool pie on a wire rack. Serve warm or cold. Makes 1 pie or 6 to 8 servings.

Apple Dumpling

Apple Dumplings

Photos on pages 138-139; 230-231.

1/2 cup chopped mixed candied fruit
1-1/2 tablespoons rum
8 cooking apples with 3-inch diameters
1 (17-1/4-oz.) pkg. frozen puff pastry (2 sheets), thawed,
   or 1 recipe Puff Pastry, page 232
1 egg yolk blended with 1 tablespoon water for glaze
Half and half, if desired

Preheat oven to 400F (205C). In a small bowl, combine candied fruit and rum; set aside to soak. Peel and core apples. On a lightly floured surface, unfold pastry; roll out each sheet to a 14-inch square. Cut each pastry sheet in half lengthwise, then crosswise, making 8 (7-inch) squares. Place 1 apple in center of each square. Fill apples with fruit-rum mixture. Moisten edges of pastry with water; bring opposite corners of pastry together over apples. Pinch seams and corners to seal. Place wrapped apples, 1/2 inch apart, on an ungreased baking sheet. Brush with egg-yolk glaze. Bake 20 to 25 minutes or until pastry is puffed and golden brown. Remove from baking sheet; arrange on serving dishes. Serve warm with half and half, if desired. Makes 8 servings.

Variation
Substitute 1/4 cup raisins, 1/4 cup chopped walnuts, 1/4 cup brown sugar, 1/2 teaspoon ground cinnamon and 1/2 teaspoon ground nutmeg for fruit-rum mixture. Combine and spoon into cored apples. Proceed as above.

Cherry-Filled Rolls

Cherry Filling:
2 (16-oz.) cans pitted tart red cherries
2 tablespoons sugar
2 tablespoons cornstarch
1 tablespoon lemon juice
1 tablespoon grated lemon peel, if desired

Pastry:
1 recipe Sweet Cream-Cheese Pastry, page 133
Milk
Crystal sugar or crushed sugar cubes

To make filling, drain cherry juice into a small saucepan; set drained cherries aside. Blend sugar and cornstarch; stir sugar mixture and lemon juice into cherry juice. Stirring constantly, cook over low heat until mixture comes to a boil and thickens. Remove from heat; cool slightly. Stir in reserved cherries and lemon peel, if desired; set aside.
To complete, preheat oven to 350F (175C). Grease a large baking sheet; set aside. Prepare pastry as directed. On a lightly floured surface, roll out 1/2 of pastry to a 12-inch square. Spoon 1/2 of cherry filling down center of pastry in a 2-1/2-inch-wide strip. Fold sides of pastry over filling, pressing edges together to seal. Tuck ends under. Repeat with remaining pastry and filling. Place on greased baking sheet; brush with milk. Sprinkle with crystal sugar or crushed sugar cubes. Bake 30 to 35 minutes or until golden brown. Let stand on baking sheet on a wire rack 5 minutes. Carefully remove from baking sheet; cool on wire rack. Makes 2 filled rolls.

Cherry-Filled Rolls

Palmiers

Palmiers

Sugar
1 (17-1/4-oz.) pkg. frozen puff pastry (2 sheets), thawed,
  or 1 recipe Puff Pastry, page 232

Generously sprinkle sugar over a work surface. On sugared surface, unfold 1 pastry sheet; roll out to a 12'' x 10'' rectangle. Sprinkle with sugar. Starting on a short end, roll up pastry toward center. Brush inside edge of roll with water. Roll opposite end toward center; gently press rolls together. Repeat with remaining pastry sheet, sprinkling with sugar and rolling short sides to center. Sprinkle outside of each roll with sugar. Cover; refrigerate 1 hour. Preheat oven to 400F (205C). Cut refrigerated rolls into 1/2-inch slices. Dip cut sides in sugar; place coated slices, cut-side up and 1-1/2 inches apart, on ungreased baking sheets. Slightly flatten each slice, pressing with back of a spoon. Place baking sheets on top rack in oven. Bake about 6 minutes or until lightly browned on bottom. Turn palmiers over; bake about 6 minutes or until deep golden brown. Remove from baking sheets immediately; cool on wire racks. Makes about 40 pastries.

Single Pastry for 9- or 10-inch Pie

1-1/2 cups all-purpose flour
1/2 teaspoon salt
6 tablespoons vegetable shortening, chilled,
  or 3 tablespoons unsalted butter or margarine and
  3 tablespoons vegetable shortening, chilled
4 to 5 tablespoons ice water

In a medium bowl, blend flour and salt. Use a pastry blender or 2 knives to cut in shortening or butter or margarine and shortening until mixture resembles coarse crumbs. Sprinkle with ice water, 1 tablespoon at a time; toss lightly with a fork until mixture begins to bind together. Gather dough into a slightly flat ball. Cover; refrigerate about 30 minutes. On a lightly floured surface, roll out refrigerated dough to a 12-inch circle. Fold dough over rolling pin; unroll over pie plate. Ease dough into pie plate without stretching; trim with a sharp knife or scissors to 1 inch beyond rim of pie plate. Fold edge under; flute edge. Bake or fill as recipe directs. If pie is filled before baking, cover edge with foil. Remove foil during final 20 minutes of baking.

Double Pastry for 9- or 10-inch Pie

2-1/4 cups all-purpose flour
1 teaspoon salt
3/4 cup vegetable shortening, chilled,
  or 6 tablespoons unsalted butter or margarine and
  6 tablespoons vegetable shortening, chilled
5 to 6 tablespoons ice water
Milk
Sugar

In a medium bowl, blend flour and salt. Use a pastry blender or 2 knives to cut in shortening or butter or margarine and shortening until mixture resembles coarse crumbs. Sprinkle with ice water, 1 tablespoon at a time; toss lightly with a fork until mixture begins to bind together. Gather dough into a ball. Divide dough into 2 pieces, making 1 piece slightly larger than the other. Shape each piece into a slightly flat ball. Wrap balls separately; refrigerate about 30 minutes. On a lightly floured surface; roll out larger piece of refrigerated dough to a 12-inch circle. Fold dough over rolling pin; unroll over pie plate. Ease dough into pie plate without stretching. Do not trim pastry edge. Fill as desired. Roll out smaller piece of refrigerated dough to a 12-inch circle. Fold dough over rolling pin; place over filling. Trim pastry edges to 1 inch beyond rim of pie plate. Fold edges under. Press edges together to seal; flute edge. Cut several slits in center of top pastry to let steam escape. Brush surface of pie with milk; sprinkle with sugar. Cover edge with foil; bake as recipe directs. Remove foil during final 20 minutes of baking.

Banana-Rum Pie

Single Pastry for 9- or 10-inch Pie, opposite

Filling:
1/2 cup sugar
1/3 cup all-purpose flour
1/4 teaspoon salt
2 cups half and half (1 pint)
3 egg yolks
2 tablespoons butter or margarine
2 tablespoons dark rum
3 ripe bananas

Topping:
1 cup whipping cream (1/2 pint)
2 tablespoons powdered sugar
1 teaspoon vanilla extract

Preheat oven to 425F (220C). Prepare pastry as directed. Fit pastry into a 9- or 10-inch quiche pan. Line pastry with foil. Cover foil with rice, dry beans or pie weights. Bake in center of oven 8 minutes. Reduce oven temperature to 375F (190C). Remove foil and rice, dry beans or pie weights from pastry; bake 5 to 7 minutes longer. Cool on a wire rack.
To make filling, in a medium saucepan, combine sugar, flour and salt; slowly stir in half and half. Stirring constantly, cook over low heat until mixture thickens. Boil 1 minute longer. Remove from heat. In a small bowl, beat egg yolks until blended. Stir in 1/4 cup cooked mixture. Stir egg mixture into remaining cooked mixture. Stirring constantly, cook over low heat until very thick. Remove from heat; stir in butter or margarine and rum. Pour 1/2 of custard into baked pie pastry. Slice bananas; arrange over custard. Pour remaining custard over bananas. Cover surface of pie with waxed paper or plastic wrap; refrigerate until chilled.
To make topping, in a medium bowl, whip cream until soft peaks form. Beat in powdered sugar and vanilla until stiff peaks form. Remove paper or plastic from top of pie. Spoon whipped-cream mixture over top, covering as desired. Refrigerate until ready to serve. Makes 1 pie or 6 to 8 servings.

Chocolate Chiffon Pie

Single Pastry for 9- or 10-inch Pie, opposite

Filling:
1 cup milk
2 eggs, separated
1/2 cup granulated sugar
1/4 teaspoon salt
1 (1/4-oz.) envelope unflavored gelatin powder
8 oz. semisweet chocolate, broken into small pieces
2 tablespoons brandy, if desired
1 cup whipping cream (1/2 pint)
2 tablespoons powdered sugar

Prepare pastry as directed. Fit pastry into a 9- or 10-inch pie plate. Preheat oven to 425F (220C). Line pastry with foil; cover foil with rice, dry beans or pie weights. Bake in center of oven 8 minutes. Reduce oven temperature to 375F (190C). Remove foil and rice, dry beans or pie weights from pastry; bake 5 to 7 minutes longer. Cool on a wire rack.
To make filling, in a medium, heavy saucepan, combine milk, egg yolks, granulated sugar and salt; beat until blended. Sprinkle gelatin over top; stir in. Add chocolate. Stirring constantly, cook over low heat until chocolate melts and gelatin dissolves. Stir in brandy, if desired. Pour into a large bowl; beat about 2 minutes or until smooth and thick. Press waxed paper onto surface of chocolate mixture. Refrigerate about 30 minutes or until almost set. Beat refrigerated mixture until fluffy. In a medium bowl, whip cream until soft peaks form. Beat in powdered sugar until stiff peaks form. Reserve 1/2 cup whipped-cream mixture in refrigerator. Fold remaining whipped-cream mixture into chocolate mixture. In a medium bowl, beat egg whites until stiff but not dry; fold into chocolate mixture. Spoon into cooled pastry; smooth top. Refrigerate 3 hours or until set. Spoon reserved whipped-cream mixture into a small pastry bag fitted with a star tip. Pipe small rosettes on top of pie. Makes 1 pie or 6 to 8 servings.

Raisin Beignets

Photo on pages 144-145.

1 recipe Cream-Puff Pastry dough, page 131
1/2 cup raisins
Vegetable oil for deep-frying
Powdered sugar

Prepare pastry as directed. After addition of last egg, beat raisins into dough. Heat oil in a wok, deep-fat fryer or deep saucepan to 370F (190C) or until a 1-inch cube of bread turns golden brown in 50 seconds. Drop dough by heaping teaspoons into hot oil. Do not crowd. Fry until golden on all sides. Use a slotted spoon to remove from hot oil; drain on paper towels. Sprinkle with powdered sugar; serve warm. Makes about 24 beignets.

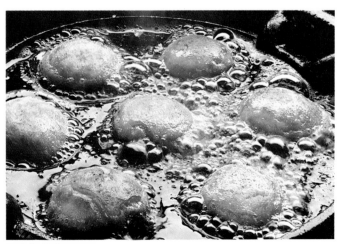

Raisin Beignets

Almond-Flavored Treats

Butterscotch Pie

Single Pastry for 9- or 10-inch Pie, page 142

Filling:
1-1/2 cups packed light-brown sugar
1/3 cup all-purpose flour
1/4 teaspoon salt
1 (13-oz.) can evaporated milk
4 egg yolks
2 tablespoons butter or margarine
1/2 teaspoon vanilla extract

Meringue Topping:
4 egg whites
1/4 teaspoon cream of tartar
1/2 cup superfine or powdered sugar

Preheat oven to 425F (220C). Prepare pastry as directed. Fit pastry into a 9- or 10-inch pie plate. Line pastry with foil; cover foil with rice, dry beans or pie weights. Bake in center of oven 8 minutes. Reduce oven temperature to 375F (190C). Remove foil and rice, dry beans or pie weights from pastry; bake 5 to 7 minutes longer. Cool on a wire rack.
To make filling, in a medium saucepan, combine brown sugar, flour and salt. Stir in evaporated milk. Stirring constantly, cook over low heat until thick and bubbly. Boil gently 1 minute longer. Remove from heat. In a small bowl, beat egg yolks until blended. Stir in 1/4 cup cooked mixture. Stir egg mixture into remaining cooked mixture. Stirring constantly, cook over low heat until very thick. Do not boil. Remove saucepan from heat; stir in butter or margarine and vanilla. Pour into cooled pastry. Increase oven temperature to 400F (205C).
To make meringue topping, in a medium bowl, beat egg whites with cream of tartar until soft peaks form. Beat in sugar, 2 tablespoons at a time, until stiff peaks form. Spoon onto pie filling, spreading to edge of pastry to seal completely. Swirl top of egg whites with back of a large spoon. Bake 8 to 10 minutes or until meringue is lightly browned. Cool on a wire rack. Refrigerate until ready to serve. Makes 1 pie or 6 to 8 servings.

On preceding pages: Raisin Beignets, page 143.

Almond-Flavored Treats

1-3/4 cups all-purpose flour
1/2 cup sugar
1 teaspoon baking powder
1/2 teaspoon baking soda
1/4 teaspoon salt
1 tablespoon vegetable shortening, room temperature
1 egg, slightly beaten
6 tablespoons milk or buttermilk
1 teaspoon almond extract
Vegetable oil for deep-frying
Sugar

In a medium bowl, blend 1 cup flour, 1/2 cup sugar, baking powder, baking soda and salt. Add shortening, egg, milk or buttermilk and almond extract; beat until smooth. Stir in remaining 3/4 cup flour; beat until smooth. Cover dough; refrigerate 30 minutes. On a lightly floured surface, roll out refrigerated dough until 1/2 inch thick. Cut dough into small 1-inch-wide almond shapes, or lightly flour a 1-inch cookie cutter; use to cut dough. In a wok, deep-fat-fryer or deep saucepan, heat oil to 360F (180C) or until a 1-inch cube of bread turns golden brown in 60 seconds. Deep-fry pastries until golden on all sides, about 1 minute. Use a slotted spoon to remove from hot oil; drain on paper towels. Roll in sugar. Makes 36 to 42 pastries.

Ham & Mushroom Pasties

1 recipe Cream-Cheese Pastry, page 151

Filling:
2 tablespoons butter or margarine
1/4 lb. mushrooms, finely chopped
1/4 lb. boiled ham, finely chopped
1 tablespoon finely chopped parsley
  or 1 teaspoon dried leaf parsley
1 tablespoon snipped chives
Salt and freshly ground pepper
1 egg yolk blended with 1 tablespoon milk for glaze

Prepare pastry as directed; do not bake. Refrigerate until chilled.
To make filling, melt butter or margarine in a medium skillet. Add mushrooms; stirring occasionally, sauté until liquid has evaporated. Remove skillet from heat; stir in ham, parsley and chives. Season with salt and pepper to taste; set aside.
To complete, on a lightly floured surface, roll out 1/2 of refrigerated dough to an 18" x 9" rectangle. Cut in half lengthwise. Cut each strip into 4 (4-1/2-inch) squares. Repeat with remaining dough. Preheat oven to 350F (175C). Place 1 tablespoon filling off center on each dough square. Brush pastry edges with egg-yolk glaze; fold pastry over filling, making triangles. Press edges together with tines of a fork to seal. Place on ungreased baking sheets. Brush tops with egg-yolk glaze; gently pierce tops with tines of a fork. Bake 20 to 25 minutes or until golden brown; serve immediately. Makes 16 pasties.

Beef Wellington

Beef Filling:
1 (5-lb.) beef-loin tenderloin roast
2 tablespoons butter or margarine
1 onion, finely chopped
1 garlic clove, minced
3/4 lb. chicken livers, trimmed, halved
1/4 cup Madeira or sweet sherry
Salt and freshly ground pepper

Pastry:
1/2 (17-1/4-oz.) pkg. frozen puff pastry (1 sheet), thawed,
  or 1/2 recipe Puff Pastry, page 232
1 egg yolk blended with 1 tablespoon milk for glaze

Sauce Bearnaise:
1/4 cup tarragon vinegar
1/4 cup dry white wine or water
1 tablespoon finely chopped shallots
1/4 cup finely chopped fresh tarragon or 1-1/2 tablespoons
  dried leaf tarragon
3 egg yolks
1/2 cup butter, cut in 6 pieces
Salt and white pepper

To make filling, preheat oven to 425F (220C). Fold thin end of roast under; tie with kitchen string. Place roast on a rack in a roasting pan; roast 25 minutes. Set aside to cool. Melt butter or margarine in a large skillet. Add onion, garlic and chicken livers. Sauté until onion is transparent and chicken livers are no longer pink. Process onion mixture in a food processor or blender until smooth. With machine running, add Madeira or sherry. Add salt and pepper to taste. Process until blended.

To wrap roast, on a lightly floured surface, unfold pastry; roll out to a rectangle large enough to wrap around meat. Spread pureed mixture over rolled-out pastry. Remove string from cooked roast; place roast, flat-side up, on center of pastry. Fold a long pastry side over meat. Brush pastry edge with egg-yolk glaze. Fold other long side of pastry over meat, covering completely. Trim ends of pastry; brush ends with glaze. Fold and pinch ends to seal. Reduce oven temperature to 400F (205C). Place pastry-wrapped meat, seam-side down, on an ungreased baking sheet. Brush top and sides with glaze. Cut pastry trimmings into decorative shapes; brush glaze on bottom of decorative pieces. Arrange pieces over top of pastry; brush with glaze. Bake 20 to 25 minutes or until golden brown. Place baked pastry-wrapped roast on a platter; let stand 10 minutes.

To make sauce, in a small saucepan, combine vinegar, wine or water, shallots and tarragon. Bring to a boil over medium heat; boil rapidly until liquid is reduced to 1/4 cup. Strain liquid into a small bowl; set aside. Place egg yolks in top of a double boiler; beat well. Place over, not in, simmering water. Slowly add reduced liquid, beating constantly. Cook until mixture thickens. Remove from heat; stir in butter, 1 piece at a time. Season with salt and white pepper to taste. Pour into a small serving bowl or sauce boat; serve immediately with Beef Wellington. Makes 10 servings.

French Cruellers

French Cruellers

1 recipe Cream-Puff Pastry, page 131
Vegetable oil for deep-frying

Icing:
2 cups powdered sugar, sifted
2 tablespoons lemon juice
1 to 2 tablespoons hot water

Cut 18 (4-inch) squares of parchment paper. Lightly brush each square with vegetable oil. Prepare pastry as directed. Spoon dough into a large pastry bag fitted with a 5/8-inch star tip. Pipe a 2-1/4- to 2-1/2-inch circle on each piece of parchment paper. Heat oil in a wok, deep-fryer or large saucepan to 370F (190C) or until a 1-inch cube of bread turns golden brown in 50 seconds. Leaving paper attached, invert 3 or 4 circles of dough into hot oil, paper-side up. Deep-fry until paper releases from pastry. Use tongs to remove and discard paper. Deep-fry pastry until golden on both sides, 1 to 2 minutes. Use a slotted spoon to remove cruellers from hot oil; drain on paper towels. Repeat with remaining pastry.

To make icing, in a small bowl, beat powdered sugar, lemon juice and hot water until smooth. Spoon icing over cruellers; let stand until set. Makes about 18 cruellers.

Chicken Puffs

8 boneless chicken-breast halves
2 teaspoons dried leaf thyme
Salt and freshly ground pepper
5 tablespoons butter or margarine
1 large onion, finely chopped
1 lb. mushrooms, sliced
3 tomatoes, peeled, chopped
2 tablespoons freshly chopped parsley
   or 2 teaspoons dried leaf parsley
1 (17-1/4-oz.) pkg. frozen puff pastry (2 sheets), thawed,
   or 1 recipe Puff Pastry, page 232
8 slices boiled ham
1 egg white blended with 1 tablespoon water for glaze

Place chicken-breast halves between pieces of waxed paper or plastic wrap. Using a meat mallet or cleaver, flatten each until about 1/4 inch thick. Sprinkle flattened chicken breasts with thyme. Season with salt and pepper to taste. Melt 3 tablespoons butter or margarine in a medium skillet. Brown seasoned chicken breasts 2 minutes on each side; set browned chicken aside. Add remaining butter or margarine to skillet. Add onion; sauté until transparent. Add mushrooms and tomatoes; stirring occasionally, cook until liquid has evaporated. Add parsley. Stir in salt and pepper to taste; remove from heat. On a lightly floured surface, unfold pastry. Cut each pastry sheet in half lengthwise, then crosswise, making 8 (5-inch) squares. Roll out each square until large enough to enclose a chicken breast. Preheat oven to 375F (190C). Place 1 ham slice on each pastry square; spread with 2 tablespoons mushroom mixture. Place a browned chicken breast over mushroom mixture. Brush edges of pastry with water; wrap pastry around chicken, pressing edges to seal. Place wrapped chicken breasts, seam-side down, on ungreased baking sheets. Brush tops with egg-white glaze. Bake 25 to 30 minutes or until puffed and golden brown. Serve immediately or cool on wire racks until ready to serve. Makes 8 servings.

Chicken Puffs

Creamed Chicken in Patty Shells

1 (10-oz.) pkg. frozen patty shells, thawed,
    or 1/2 recipe Puff Pastry, page 232

Filling:
2 tablespoons butter or margarine
2 tablespoons all-purpose flour
1-1/2 cups half and half
1 teaspoon Dijon-style mustard
1/2 cup dry vermouth, dry white wine or water
Salt and freshly ground pepper
2-1/2 cups finely chopped cooked chicken
1 cup sliced mushrooms
1/2 cup sliced green onions
1 (2-oz.) jar sliced pimiento, drained
3 tablespoons slivered almonds
Chopped parsley for garnish

Preheat oven to 450F (230C). Place pastry shells on an ungreased baking sheet. Place in center of oven; reduce temperature to 400F (205C). Bake 20 to 25 minutes or until golden brown. Remove from oven; cut off pastry-shell tops. Set aside in a warm place.
To make filling, in a medium saucepan, melt butter or margarine. Stir in flour; stirring constantly, cook 1 minute. Slowly stir in half and half. Stirring constantly, cook until sauce is smooth and slightly thickened. Stir in mustard and vermouth, wine or water. Season with salt and pepper to taste. Stirring constantly, cook over low heat 4 minutes or until smooth and thick. Stir in chicken, mushrooms, green onions, pimiento and almonds. Simmer over low heat about 12 minutes. Adjust seasonings, if desired. Reheat pastry shells, if necessary. Spoon creamed-chicken mixture into warm pastry shells. Sprinkle with parsley; cover with pastry-shell tops, if desired. Makes 6 servings.

Variation
Reduce chopped cooked chicken to 1-1/2 cups. Add 1 cup finely chopped cooked ham.

Cocktail Cheese Crackers

Cocktail Cheese Crackers

1-3/4 cups all-purpose flour
1 teaspoon baking powder
1 teaspoon salt
1 teaspoon paprika
Pinch of red (cayenne) pepper, if desired
1 cup freshly grated Parmesan cheese (3 oz.)
1 cup shredded Swiss cheese (4 oz.)
1/2 cup butter or margarine, chilled
1 egg
1/2 cup whipping cream
1 egg yolk beaten with 1 tablespoon milk for glaze
Poppy, sesame or caraway seeds
Finely chopped pistachios, walnuts, almonds or hazelnuts
Coarse salt

Preheat oven to 375F (190C). In a large bowl, blend flour, baking powder, salt, paprika and red pepper, if desired. Stir in cheeses. Use a pastry blender or 2 knives to cut in butter or margarine until mixture resembles fine crumbs. In a small bowl, beat egg; stir in whipping cream. Add egg mixture to flour mixture; toss with a fork until mixture binds together. Knead dough in bowl 10 strokes or until smooth. On a lightly floured surface, roll out 1/2 of dough to a 10-inch square. Cut dough into 2-inch squares. Place squares, 2 inches apart, on ungreased baking sheets. Brush each square with egg-yolk glaze; sprinkle with poppy, sesame or caraway seeds; chopped nuts; or coarse salt. Repeat with remaining dough. Bake 10 to 12 minutes or until edges are golden. Remove from baking sheets; cool on wire racks. Makes 50 crackers.

Little Beef Appetizers

Cream-Cheese Pastry:
1 (8-oz.) pkg. cream cheese, room temperature
1 cup butter or margarine, room temperature
1/4 cup whipping cream
2-1/2 cups all-purpose flour
1/2 teaspoon salt

Filling:
1 tablespoon butter or margarine
1 large onion, finely chopped
3/4 lb. lean ground beef
2 hard-cooked eggs, finely chopped
1/2 cup cooked white rice
2 tablespoons dairy sour cream
2 tablespoons chopped dill or 2 teaspoons dill weed
1/2 teaspoon Worcestershire sauce
Salt and freshly ground pepper
1 egg yolk blended with 1 tablespoon milk for glaze

To make pastry, in a medium bowl, beat cream cheese and butter or margarine until blended. Slowly beat in whipping cream until blended. Gradually stir in flour and salt. Shape into a slightly flat ball. Cover; refrigerate 1 hour or until chilled.

To make filling, melt butter or margarine in a medium skillet. Add onion; sauté until transparent. Add ground beef; stirring occasionally, cook over medium heat until meat is browned. Drain off pan drippings; spoon meat into a medium bowl. Stir in hard-cooked eggs, rice, sour cream, dill and Worcestershire sauce. Season with salt and pepper to taste; set aside.

To complete, on a lightly floured surface, roll out 1/2 of refrigerated dough until 1/8 inch thick. Using a 3-inch biscuit cutter, cut about 20 rounds. Repeat with remaining dough. Preheat oven to 375F (190C). Place 1 teaspoon meat filling off center on each pastry round. Brush pastry edge with egg-yolk glaze. Fold pastry over filling; press edges together with tines of a fork to seal. Place on ungreased baking sheets. Brush tops with egg-yolk glaze; pierce tops with tines of fork. Bake 20 to 25 minutes or until golden brown. Serve immediately. Makes about 40 appetizers.

Cocktail Cheese Bits

1 cup finely shredded sharp Cheddar cheese (4 oz.),
  room temperature
1/2 cup butter or margarine, room temperature
4 drops hot-pepper sauce
1 cup all-purpose flour
1/4 teaspoon salt
Sesame seeds, if desired

In a medium bowl, beat cheese, butter or margarine and hot-pepper sauce until blended. Gradually beat in flour and salt until blended. Shape into a slightly flat ball. Cover; refrigerate 1 hour or until chilled. On a lightly floured surface, roll out refrigerated dough until 1/2 inch thick. Preheat oven to 375F (190C). Lightly grease 2 baking sheets. Using lightly floured canapé cutters, cut dough into a variety of shapes. Or, cut into thin strips. Brush with water; sprinkle with sesame seeds. Place on greased baking sheets. Bake 10 to 12 minutes or until golden. Remove from baking sheets; cool on wire racks. Place in containers with tight-fitting lids. Store in refrigerator or freezer. Makes 36 to 48 appetizers.

Variation
Substitute 1/2 cup (1-1/2-oz.) grated Parmesan cheese for 1/2 cup (2 oz.) Cheddar cheese. Omit salt.

Ham Snails

Ham Snails

1/2 lb. boiled ham, finely chopped
1/2 cup finely chopped parsley
1 egg, beaten
Salt and freshly ground pepper
1/2 (17-1/4-oz.) pkg. frozen puff pastry (1 sheet), thawed, or 1/2 recipe Puff Pastry, page 232

Preheat oven to 400F (205C). In a medium bowl, combine ham, parsley and egg. Stir in salt and pepper to taste; set aside. On a lightly floured surface, unfold pastry; roll out to a 16'' x 12'' rectangle. Spread filling over pastry to within 1/4 inch of edges. Starting on a long end, roll up pastry toward center. Brush inside edge of roll with water. Roll opposite end toward center; gently press rolls together. Cut into 1/2-inch slices; arrange slices, cut-side up, on ungreased baking sheets. Bake 15 to 20 minutes or until puffed and golden brown. Remove from baking sheets; cool on wire racks. Makes about 30 appetizer servings.

Quiche Lorraine

Single Pastry for 9- or 10-inch Pie, page 142

Filling:
8 bacon slices
1 cup finely shredded Swiss or Gruyère cheese (4 oz.)
3 eggs
1-1/2 cups half and half
1/4 teaspoon ground nutmeg
Salt and freshly ground pepper

Preheat oven to 425F (220C). Prepare pastry as directed. Fit pastry into a 9- or 10-inch quiche pan. Line pastry with foil; cover foil with rice, dry beans or pie weights. Bake in center of oven 8 minutes. Reduce oven temperature to 375F (190C). Remove foil and rice, dry beans or pie weights from pastry; bake 5 to 7 minutes longer. Cool on a wire rack.
To make filling, in a medium skillet, cook bacon until slightly crisp; drain on paper towels. Cut each cooked bacon strip into 4 pieces. Place bacon pieces in bottom of baked pie shell; sprinkle 1/2 cup cheese over bacon. In a medium bowl, beat eggs; stir in half and half and nutmeg. Season with salt and pepper to taste. Pour over cheese in pie shell. Sprinkle with remaining 1/2 cup cheese. Cover pastry edge with foil. Bake in center of oven 30 to 35 minutes or until top is golden and center is set. Remove foil during final 20 minutes of cooking. Cool on a wire rack 10 minutes. Serve warm. Makes 1 quiche or 6 to 8 servings.

Spinach Appetizers

Filling:
1/4 cup butter or margarine
1 bunch green onions, (10 to 12 onions), thinly sliced
2 (10-oz.) pkgs. frozen chopped spinach, thawed, well drained
1/2 lb. feta cheese, crumbled
3/4 cup ricotta cheese (6 oz.)
3 eggs
1/4 cup dry breadcrumbs
1/4 teaspoon ground nutmeg
Salt and freshly ground pepper

Pastry:
1/2 lb. filo leaves (about 12 leaves), thawed if frozen
1/2 cup butter or margarine, melted

To make filling, melt butter or margarine in a large skillet. Add green onions; sauté until soft. Stir in spinach, feta cheese and ricotta cheese. In a small bowl, beat eggs; stir in breadcrumbs and nutmeg. Season with salt and pepper to taste. Stir into spinach mixture. Stirring occasionally, cook over low heat 2 minutes; set aside. Preheat oven to 375F (190C). Lightly grease baking sheets.
To complete, unfold filo leaves; place between damp towels. Remove 1 leaf; place on a dry work surface. Brush gently with butter or margarine; cut lengthwise into 2-inch strips. Place 1 to 2 teaspoons spinach mixture on a corner of 1 strip. Pick up corner and fold over to opposite edge to make a filled triangle. Continue to fold filled strip as you would fold a flag, keeping triangle shape. Brush seam with water; gently press to seal. Repeat with remaining pastry and filling, brushing each pastry leaf with butter or margarine. Place triangles, seam-side down, on greased baking sheets. Brush with remaining butter or margarine. Bake about 16 minutes or until golden brown. Cool slightly on baking sheets; serve warm. Makes about 48 appetizers.

Ham Crescents

Ham Crescents

**1 (17-1/4-oz.) pkg. frozen puff pastry (2 sheets), thawed,
or 1 recipe Puff Pastry, page 232**
Mustard
8 thin slices boiled ham, halved diagonally
1 egg white blended with 1 tablespoon water for glaze

Preheat oven to 425F (220C). On a lightly floured
surface, unfold pastry. Cut pastry sheets in half
lengthwise, then crosswise, making 8 (5-inch) squares.
Cut each square diagonally in half. Lightly spread each
triangle with mustard; top each with a half-slice of ham.
Brush pastry edges with water. Starting at longest edge of
pastry, roll up each triangle toward point. Press points to
seal. Place crescents on ungreased baking sheets. Brush
with egg-white glaze. Bake 12 to 15 minutes or until
puffed and golden brown. Remove from baking sheets;
cool on wire racks. Makes 16 crescents.

Cocktail Sausages

1 (3-oz.) pkg. cream cheese, room temperature
1/2 cup butter or margarine, room temperature
1 cup all-purpose flour
1/4 teaspoon salt
16 cocktail sausages (about 1/2 lb.)
1 egg yolk blended with 1 tablespoon milk for glaze

In a medium bowl, beat cream cheese and butter or
margarine until blended. Blend flour and salt; gradually
stir into cream-cheese mixture. Shape into a slightly flat
ball. Cover; refrigerate 1 hour or until chilled. On a
lightly floured surface, roll out refrigerated dough to a
10-inch square. Cut into 4 (2-1/2-inch-wide) strips. Cut
each strip into 4 (2-1/2-inch) squares. Preheat oven to
375F (190C). Wrap each sausage in a pastry square; press
seams to seal. Place wrapped sausages, seam-side down,
on an ungreased baking sheet. Brush with egg-yolk glaze.
Bake 15 to 20 minutes or until lightly browned. Serve
immediately. Makes 16 appetizers.

Crabmeat Appetizers

Filling:
1/4 cup butter or margarine
1 small onion, finely chopped
1/4 lb. mushrooms, finely chopped
2 teaspoons lemon juice
2 teaspoons all-purpose flour
1/4 cup half and half
1 (7-oz.) can crabmeat, drained, flaked, cartilage removed
1 (2-oz.) jar chopped pimiento, drained
2 tablespoons snipped chives
Salt and freshly ground pepper

Pastry:
1/2 lb. filo leaves (about 12 leaves), thawed if frozen
1/2 cup butter or margarine, melted

To make filling, melt butter or margarine in a large
skillet. Add onion and mushrooms; sauté until onion is
transparent. Add lemon juice; sprinkle with flour. Stir
until flour is blended; cook 1 minute. Stir in half and half;
stirring gently, cook only until slightly thickened. Stir in
crabmeat, pimiento and chives. Season with salt and
pepper to taste; set aside. Preheat oven to 375F (190C).
Lightly grease 2 large baking sheets.
To complete, unfold filo leaves; place between damp
towels. Remove 1 leaf; place on a dry work surface. Brush
gently with butter or margarine; cut lengthwise into 3
equal strips. Place 1 to 2 teaspoons crab filling at short
end of 1 pastry strip; fold edge of pastry over filling. Fold
in both long sides of pastry, 1/4 inch toward center. Roll
up strip from filling end. Brush seam with water; press
gently against roll to seal. Repeat with remaining pastry
and filling, brushing each pastry leaf with butter or
margarine. Place appetizers, seam-side down, on greased
baking sheets. Brush with remaining butter or margarine.
Bake about 16 minutes or until golden brown. Cool
slightly on baking sheets; serve warm. Makes about 30
appetizers.

Franks in Pastry

Cheese & Ham Appetizers

Franks in Pastry

1/2 (17-1/4-oz.) pkg. frozen puff pastry (1 sheet), thawed,
 or 1/2 recipe Puff Pastry, page 232
8 frankfurters
1 egg white blended with 1 tablespoon water for glaze

Preheat oven to 400F (205C). On a lightly floured
surface, unfold pastry; roll out to a 14'' x 10'' rectangle.
Cut into 2 lengthwise strips. Cut each strip into 4 (5'' x
3-1/2'') rectangles. Wrap 1 frankfurter in each pastry
rectangle, covering completely. Brush pastry edges with
water; pinch seams to seal. Place wrapped frankfurters,
seam-side down, on an ungreased baking sheet. Brush
with egg-white glaze. Bake 10 to 12 minutes or until
puffed and golden brown. Serve immediately. Makes 8
servings.

Cheese & Ham Appetizers

1 recipe Cream-Cheese Pastry, page 151
8 slices boiled ham
8 slices Swiss cheese (about 1 lb.)
1 egg yolk blended with 1 tablespoon milk for glaze

Prepare pastry as directed. Refrigerate until chilled. On a
lightly floured surface, roll out 1/2 of refrigerated dough
to a 16'' x 8'' rectangle. Cut rectangle into 8 (4-inch)
squares. Repeat with remaining dough. Preheat oven to
375F (190C). Cut ham and cheese slices in half
diagonally. Place 1 half-slice of ham and 1 half-slice of
cheese on each pastry square with diagonal cuts
overlapping, if necessary. Starting at cheese-covered
corner, roll up each square to make a crescent. Place
crescents on an ungreased baking sheet; brush with
egg-yolk glaze. Bake 20 to 25 minutes or until lightly
browned. Serve immediately. Makes 16 appetizers.

Pork Pasties

Filling:
1/4 cup butter or margarine
1 tablespoon vegetable oil
8 (3/4-inch-thick) slices pork-loin tenderloin
Salt and freshly ground pepper
1 large onion, finely chopped
4 medium tomatoes, peeled, chopped
3/4 lb. mushrooms, sliced
8 bacon slices, cooked crisp, crumbled
1 tablespoon chopped parsley or 1 teaspoon dried leaf parsley

Pastry:
1 (17-1/4-oz.) pkg. frozen puff pastry (2 sheets), thawed,
  or 1 recipe Puff Pastry, page 232
1 egg white blended with 1 tablespoon water for glaze

Herb Sauce:
1 tablespoon butter or margarine
1 small onion, finely chopped
1 large tomato, peeled, finely chopped
1 cup whipping cream (1/2 pint)
1 tablespoon chopped parsley or 1 teaspoon dried leaf parsley
1 tablespoon snipped chives
1 teaspoon chopped basil or 1/3 teaspoon dried leaf basil
Salt and freshly ground pepper

To make filling, melt 2 tablespoons butter or margarine
in a medium skillet; add oil. Sauté pork slices, a few at a
time, until lightly browned on both sides. Remove from
skillet. Season with salt and pepper to taste; set aside.
Melt remaining 2 tablespoons butter or margarine in
skillet. Add onion; sauté until transparent. Add tomatoes
and mushrooms; stirring occasionally, cook until liquid
has evaporated. Stir in bacon and parsley; set aside.
To make pastry, on a lightly floured surface, unfold
pastry sheets. Roll out each sheet to a 12-inch square. Cut
each pastry square in half lengthwise, then crosswise,
making 8 (6-inch) squares. Preheat oven to 375F
(190C). Place 1 browned pork slice in center of each
pastry square; spoon mushroom mixture equally over
pork slices. Moisten edges of pastry with water; fold
corners toward center, envelope-style. Pinch seams and
corners together to seal. Place on ungreased baking
sheets. Brush with egg-white glaze. Bake 25 to 30
minutes or until puffed and golden brown.
To make sauce, melt butter or margarine in a medium
saucepan. Add onion; sauté until transparent. Add
tomato; stirring occasionally, cook 5 minutes or until
tomato is soft. Stir in whipping cream; stirring
occasionally, bring to a boil. Reduce heat; stir in parsley,
chives and basil. Season with salt and pepper to taste.
Simmer gently 2 to 3 minutes; pour into a serving dish or
sauce boat. Arrange cooked pasties on a platter. Serve
with Herb Sauce. Makes 8 servings.

Spinach-Cheese Quiche

Single Pastry for 9- or 10-inch Pie, page 142

Filling:
3 tablespoons butter or margarine
1 bunch green onions (10 to 12 onions), thinly sliced
1 (10-oz.) pkg. frozen chopped spinach, thawed, well drained
1/2 cup finely chopped cooked ham
1 cup finely shredded Monterey Jack cheese (4 oz.)
3 eggs
1-3/4 cups half and half
1/2 teaspoon ground nutmeg
Salt and freshly ground pepper

Prepare pastry as directed. Fit pastry into a 9- or 10-inch
quiche pan. Preheat oven to 425F (220C). Line pastry
with foil. Cover foil with rice, dry beans or pie weights.
Bake in center of oven 8 minutes. Reduce oven
temperature to 375F (190C). Remove foil and rice, dry
beans or pie weights from pastry; bake 5 to 7 minutes
longer. Cool on a wire rack.
To make filling, melt butter or margarine in a medium
skillet. Add green onions; sauté 5 minutes. Stir in
spinach; cook 1 minute. Sprinkle ham and 1/2 cup cheese
in cooled pie shell. Spoon spinach mixture over top. In a
medium bowl, beat eggs; stir in half and half and nutmeg.
Season with salt and pepper to taste. Carefully pour into
pie shell. Sprinkle with remaining 1/2 cup cheese. Bake in
center of oven 30 to 35 minutes or until top is golden and
center is set. Cool on a wire rack 10 minutes. Serve warm.
Makes 1 quiche or 6 to 8 servings.

Pork Pasties

Convenience
Baking

Smoked-Pork Roll

Sicilian-Style Pizza

Smoked-Pork Roll

1 (1-lb.) loaf frozen white-bread dough, thawed
1 (2-lb.) pkg. Canadian-style bacon or smoked pork tenderloin

Grease a large bowl. Place dough in greased bowl, turning to coat all sides. Cover; let rise in a warm place, free from drafts, until doubled in bulk. Grease a baking sheet; set aside. Punch down dough. On a lightly floured surface, roll out dough to a rectangle twice the size of meat. Cut off about 1/4 of dough; set aside for decoration. Place meat in center of rolled-out dough; fold dough over meat, pinching seams to seal. Place wrapped meat, seam-side down, on greased baking sheet; tuck ends of dough under. Cut decorations from reserved dough, or shape into a braid. Brush undersides of decorations with water; place on top of dough. Cover; let rise 15 minutes. Preheat oven to 350F (175C). Cut several slits in dough to let steam escape. Brush dough with water. Bake 70 minutes or until a thermometer inserted in meat registers 160F (70C) and crust is golden brown. Remove from baking sheet; cool slightly on a wire rack. Slice to serve. Makes 6 to 8 servings.

Sicilian-Style Pizza

1 (1-lb.) loaf frozen white-bread dough or 1 lb. pizza dough, homemade or frozen, thawed
2 tablespoons vegetable oil or olive oil
1 large onion, finely chopped
1 (8-oz.) can tomato sauce
1/4 cup tomato paste
1 teaspoon dried leaf oregano
Salt and freshly ground pepper
3 medium tomatoes, peeled, thinly sliced
1/4 lb. thinly sliced Genoa salami, ham or pepperoni
3/4 lb. mozzarella cheese, thinly sliced
3 to 4 pickled Italian peppers, if desired

Grease a medium bowl. Place dough in a greased bowl, turning to coat all sides. Cover; let rise in a warm place, free from drafts, until doubled in bulk. Heat oil in a medium saucepan. Add onion; sauté until transparent. Stir in tomato sauce, tomato paste and oregano. Over medium heat, bring to a boil. Reduce heat to low; simmer 10 minutes, stirring occasionally. Season with salt and pepper; set aside. Preheat oven to 425F (220C). Grease a 15" x 10" jelly-roll pan. Punch down dough. Pat or roll out dough to fit greased pan. Spread onion mixture over dough. Arrange tomatoes and salami, ham or pepperoni over sauce. Top with cheese and Italian peppers, if desired. Cover; let rise 15 minutes. Bake 18 to 22 minutes or until crust is golden brown and cheese is bubbly. Serve hot. Makes 8 servings.

On previous pages: Royal Apple Cake, page 174.

Ham & Mushroom Pizza

Salami & Broccoli Pizza

Ham & Mushroom Pizza

1 (1-lb.) pkg. frozen pizza dough or white-bread dough, thawed
1 cup canned tomatoes, drained, coarsely chopped
1 cup tomato sauce
1 teaspoon dried leaf oregano
Salt and freshly ground pepper
1/2 red bell pepper, cut in strips
1/2 green bell pepper, cut in strips
1/4 lb. ham or mortadella, cubed
1 (3-oz.) can sliced mushrooms, drained
1/2 lb. mozzarella, Edam, Swiss or provolone cheese, grated or
  thinly sliced
1 tablespoon freshly chopped parsley

Preheat oven to 425F (220C). Roll or pat out dough until
1/2 inch thick; place in a 12- or 14-inch pizza pan. Pinch
edge of dough to make a rim. Let dough stand 15
minutes. In a small saucepan, combine tomatoes, tomato
sauce and oregano. Add salt and pepper to taste. Over
medium heat, bring to a boil. Reduce heat; simmer 3 to 5
minutes, stirring occasionally. Spread sauce over dough.
Arrange red- and green-pepper strips over sauce. Scatter
ham or mortadella and mushrooms over sauce and
peppers. Top with cheese and parsley. Bake 20 to 25
minutes or until crust is golden brown and cheese is
bubbly. Makes 1 pizza.

Salami & Broccoli Pizza

1 (1-lb.) pkg. frozen pizza dough or white-bread dough, thawed
1-1/4 cups thick spaghetti sauce
1 cup chopped broccoli, cooked crisp-tender
1/2 cup chopped red or green bell pepper
1/2 lb. mozzarella cheese, grated or thinly sliced
1/4 lb. sliced salami

Preheat oven to 425F (220C). Roll or pat out dough until
1/2 inch thick; place in a 12- or 14-inch pizza pan. Pinch
edge of dough to make a rim. Let dough stand 15
minutes. Spread sauce over dough. Scatter broccoli and
bell pepper over sauce. Arrange cheese over pizza; top
with salami. Bake 20 to 25 minutes or until crust is golden
brown and cheese is bubbly. Makes 1 pizza.

Bolognese Pizza

Bolognese Pizza

1/2 lb. lean ground beef
1 garlic clove, minced
1 (8-oz.) can tomato sauce
1 (6-oz.) can tomato paste
1 teaspoon dried leaf oregano
Salt and freshly ground pepper
1 (1-lb.) pkg. frozen pizza dough or white-bread dough, thawed
1/2 red bell pepper, cut in strips
1/2 green bell pepper, cut in strips
1 small zucchini, diced
3 or 4 canned artichoke hearts, quartered
1/2 lb. mozzarella cheese, grated or thinly sliced
Pitted ripe olives

Brown meat in a medium skillet. Drain off excess fat. Add garlic; cook 1 minute. Add tomato sauce, tomato paste and oregano. Add salt and pepper to taste. Over medium heat, bring to a boil. Reduce heat; simmer 5 to 8 minutes, stirring occasionally. Preheat oven to 425F (220C). Roll or pat out dough until 1/2 inch thick; place in a 12- or 14-inch pizza pan. Pinch edge of dough to make a rim. Let dough stand 15 minutes. Spread sauce over dough. Arrange red- and green-pepper strips, zucchini and artichoke hearts over sauce. Top with cheese and olives. Bake 20 to 25 minutes or until crust is golden brown and cheese is bubbly. Makes 1 pizza.

Vegetable Pizza

1 (1-lb.) pkg. frozen pizza dough or white-bread dough, thawed
1 (10-1/2-oz.) can pizza sauce or 1-1/4 cups spaghetti sauce

Toppings:
Canned artichoke hearts, drained, quartered
Red or green bell-pepper strips
Sautéed sliced mushrooms
Roasted peppers
Pitted green or ripe olives, sliced
Sautéed onion rings
Thinly sliced tomatoes
Thinly sliced zucchini
1 teaspoon dried Italian seasoning
8 oz. mozzarella cheese, grated or thinly sliced

Preheat oven to 425F (220C). Roll or pat out dough until 1/2-inch thick; place in a 12- or 14-inch pizza pan. Pinch edge of dough to make a rim. Let stand 15 minutes. Spread sauce over dough. Arrange vegetables over sauce; sprinkle with Italian seasoning. Top with cheese. Bake 20 to 25 minutes or until crust is golden brown and cheese is bubbly. Makes 1 pizza.

Shrimp & Tuna Pizza

1 (1-lb.) pkg. frozen pizza dough or white-bread dough, thawed
1 (10-1/2-oz.) can pizza sauce or 1-1/4 cups spaghetti sauce
1 (3-1/4-oz.) can chunk-style tuna, drained
1/2 lb. cooked, shelled small shrimp
1 teaspoon drained capers
1 teaspoon dried Italian seasoning
8 oz. mozzarella cheese, grated or thinly sliced

Preheat oven to 425F (220C). Roll or pat out dough until 1/2 inch thick; place in a 12- or 14-inch pizza pan. Pinch edge of dough to make a rim. Let dough stand 15 minutes. Spread sauce over dough. Scatter tuna and shrimp over sauce. Sprinkle capers and Italian seasoning over fish. Top with cheese. Bake 20 to 25 minutes or until crust is golden brown and cheese is bubbly. Makes 1 pizza.

Clockwise from top: Shrimp & Tuna Pizza; Italian-Sausage Pizza; Vegetable Pizza; Ham & Onion Pizza

Italian-Sausage Pizza

1 (1-lb.) pkg. frozen pizza dough or white-bread dough, thawed
1 (10-1/2-oz.) can pizza sauce or 1-1/4 cups spaghetti sauce
1/4 lb. dried salami, pepperoni or garlic salami, sliced
1 to 2 teaspoons dried Italian seasoning
1/2 lb. mozzarella cheese, grated or thinly sliced

Preheat oven to 425F (220C). Roll or pat out dough until 1/2 inch thick; place in a 12- or 14-inch pizza pan. Pinch edge of dough to make a rim. Let dough stand 15 minutes. Spread sauce over dough. Arrange sausage slices over sauce. Sprinkle with Italian seasoning; top with cheese. Bake 20 to 25 minutes or until crust is golden brown and cheese is bubbly. Makes 1 pizza.

Ham & Onion Pizza

1 (1-lb.) pkg. frozen pizza dough or white-bread dough, thawed
1 (10-1/2-oz.) can pizza sauce or 1-1/4 cups spaghetti sauce
1/4 lb. boiled ham or Italian cappacola, thinly sliced
Cocktail onions, drained, or onion rings
1/2 teaspoon dried leaf oregano
1/2 teaspoon dried leaf thyme
1/2 lb. mozzarella cheese, grated or thinly sliced

Preheat oven to 425F (220C). Roll or pat out dough until 1/2 inch thick; place in 12- or 14-inch pizza pan. Pinch edge of dough to make a rim. Let stand 15 minutes. Spread sauce over dough. Arrange ham or cappacola over sauce. Scatter onions, oregano and thyme over ham. Top with cheese. Bake 20 to 25 minutes or until crust is golden brown and cheese is bubbly. Makes 1 pizza.

Crusty Dinner Rolls

Easter Breakfast Ring

1 (16-oz.) pkg. white yeast-bread mix
1/4 cup all-purpose flour
1/2 teaspoon ground cinnamon
1/2 teaspoon ground cardamom
1/2 teaspoon ground mace
1 egg, beaten
1-1/4 cups water
1/4 cup granulated sugar
1/2 cup raisins
1/3 cup currants
2 tablespoons chopped candied lemon peel, if desired
2 tablespoons butter or margarine, room temperature
1/2 (7-oz.) pkg. marzipan or 1/2 recipe Marzipan,
  page 232, crumbled
Milk
1 cup powdered sugar, sifted
3 to 4 teaspoons lemon juice
Dyed eggs

In a medium bowl, blend bread mix, flour, cinnamon, cardamom and mace. Stir in egg and water until dough comes away from side of bowl. On a lightly floured surface, knead until smooth and elastic, 6 to 8 minutes. Cover dough with bowl; let rest 5 minutes. Meanwhile, blend granulated sugar, raisins, currants and lemon peel; set aside. Roll out dough to an 18'' x 14'' rectangle. Beat butter or margarine and marzipan until smooth. Spread over rolled-out dough. Cut dough and marzipan mixture in half lengthwise. Sprinkle raisin mixture evenly over both pieces of dough. Starting at a long side, tightly roll up dough pieces, jelly-roll fashion. Pinch seams to seal. Grease a baking sheet. Place rolls, seam-side down, on greased baking sheet. Twist rolls together; pinch ends to seal. Shape twisted rolls into a ring. Slash with a sharp razor blade at 1-inch intervals. Cover; let rise 10 to 15 minutes. Preheat oven to 375F (190C). Brush ring with milk. Bake 35 to 40 minutes or until golden brown. Remove from baking sheet; cool on a wire rack. Combine powdered sugar and lemon juice; drizzle over warm ring. Place on a platter; fill center with dyed eggs. Makes 1 ring.

Crusty Dinner Rolls

1 (1-lb.) loaf frozen white-bread dough, thawed
Milk
All-purpose flour

Grease a medium bowl. Place dough in a greased bowl, turning to coat all sides. Cover; let rise in a warm place, free from drafts, until doubled in bulk. Grease baking sheets; set aside. Punch down dough. Cut dough into 8 equal pieces. Shape each piece into a flat ball, pinching and tucking ends under. Place balls, 4 inches apart, on greased baking sheets. Using a sharp razor blade, cut a deep slash across top of each roll. Cover; let rise until doubled. Preheat oven to 375F (190C). Brush rolls with milk; dust with flour. Bake 20 to 25 minutes or until rolls are browned and sound hollow when tapped on bottom. Remove from baking sheets; cool on wire racks. Makes 8 rolls.

Easter Breakfast Ring

Orange-Berry Cornbread

1 (8-1/2-oz.) pkg. corn-muffin mix
1 egg, slightly beaten
1/3 cup orange juice
2 teaspoons grated orange peel, if desired
1 cup coarsely chopped cranberries
1/2 cup coarsely chopped walnuts

Preheat oven to 350F (175C). Grease an 8-inch-square baking pan. In a medium bowl, combine muffin mix, egg, orange juice and orange peel, if desired; gently stir until blended. Fold in cranberries and walnuts. Pour batter into greased pan; smooth top. Bake 20 to 25 minutes or until a wooden pick inserted in center comes out clean. Cool in pan on a wire rack 10 to 15 minutes. Serve warm. Makes 6 to 8 servings.

Parmesan Rolls

1 (16-oz.) pkg. white yeast-bread mix
1 cup grated Parmesan cheese (3 oz.)
1-1/3 cups water
2 tablespoons vegetable oil
All-purpose flour

In a medium bowl, blend bread mix and cheese. Add water and oil; stir with a wooden spoon until dough comes away from side of bowl. On a lightly floured surface, knead dough until smooth and elastic, 6 to 8 minutes. Cover dough with bowl; let stand 5 minutes. Grease baking sheets; set aside. Cut dough into 8 equal pieces. Roll out or pat each piece of dough into a 6" x 4" rectangle. Fold each rectangle in thirds, letter style. Pinch seams to seal. Place rolls, folded-side up, on greased baking sheets. Cover; let rise 15 minutes. Preheat oven to 375F (190C). Brush tops of rolls with water; dust with flour. Bake 20 to 25 minutes or until rolls are golden brown and sound hollow when tapped on bottom. Remove from baking sheets; cool on wire racks. Makes 8 rolls.

Caraway Breadsticks

Caraway Breadsticks

1 (1-lb.) loaf frozen white- or whole-wheat-bread dough,
  thawed
1 egg white beaten with 1 tablespoon water for glaze
Caraway seeds

Grease a medium bowl. Place dough in a greased bowl, turning to coat all sides. Cover; let rise in a warm place, free from drafts, until doubled in bulk. Grease baking sheets; set aside. Punch down dough. On a lightly floured surface, roll out dough to a 12" x 6" rectangle. Cut dough lengthwise into 1/2-inch-wide strips. Twist ends of each strip in opposite directions. Place strips, 2 inches apart, on greased baking sheets. Cover; let rise until almost doubled in bulk, 20 to 25 minutes. Preheat oven to 375F (190C). Brush breadsticks with egg-white glaze; sprinkle with caraway seeds. Bake 20 to 25 minutes or until golden brown. Remove from baking sheets; cool on wire racks. Makes 12 breadsticks.

Parmesan Rolls

Raisin Loaf Cake

Almond Loaf

Raisin Loaf Cake

1 (16- or 17-oz.) pkg. pound-cake mix
2 eggs
1/4 cup milk
1/2 cup dairy sour cream
1 cup golden raisins or currants
Powdered sugar, if desired

Preheat oven to 350F (175C). Grease and flour a 9" x 5" loaf pan. In a large bowl, combine cake mix, eggs, milk and sour cream; beat until blended. Beat with electric mixer 3 minutes on high speed. Fold in raisins or currants. Pour batter into prepared pan. Bake 70 to 75 minutes or until deep golden brown and a wooden pick inserted in center comes out clean. Cool in pan on a wire rack 15 minutes. Remove from pan; cool on wire rack. Before serving, dust top of cake with powdered sugar, if desired. Makes 1 loaf cake.

Almond Loaf

1 (16- or 17-oz.) pkg. pound-cake mix
3 eggs
1/2 cup butter or margarine, room temperature
1 teaspoon almond extract
3/4 cup finely ground blanched almonds
4 oz. semisweet chocolate
1 tablespoon vegetable shortening

Preheat oven to 325F (165C). Grease and flour a 9" x 5" loaf pan. In a large bowl, combine cake mix, eggs, butter or margarine and almond extract; beat until blended. Beat with electric mixer 3 minutes on high speed. Fold in ground almonds. Pour into prepared pan; smooth top. Bake 65 to 70 minutes or until a wooden pick inserted in center comes out clean. Cool in pan on a wire rack 15 minutes. Remove from pan; cool on wire rack. In a small heavy saucepan, melt chocolate and shortening over low heat; stir until smooth. Set aside to cool. Place cooled cake on a platter or cake plate; spread chocolate mixture over top and sides of cake, covering completely. Let stand until chocolate sets. Makes 1 loaf cake.

Nut Loaf Cake

Marbled Pear Cake

Nut Loaf Cake

1 cup ground toasted hazelnuts or walnuts
1/4 cup packed dark-brown sugar
1 (16- or 17-oz.) pkg. pound-cake mix
4 oz. semisweet chocolate
1 tablespoon vegetable shortening

Preheat oven to 325F (165C). Grease 2 (12" x 4" or 9" x 5") loaf pans. In a small bowl, combine nuts and brown sugar; set aside. Prepare cake mix according to package directions. Spoon 1/2 cup batter into bottom of each greased pan. Sprinkle 2 to 3 tablespoons nut mixture over batter. Top each with 1 cup batter. Sprinkle remaining nut mixture evenly into pans. Divide remaining batter between pans. Bake 50 to 55 minutes or until tops are golden brown and a wooden pick inserted in center comes out clean. Cool in pans on wire racks 10 minutes. Remove from pans; cool on wire racks. In a small heavy saucepan, melt chocolate and shortening over low heat; stir until smooth. Set aside to cool. Place cakes, bottom-side up, on separate platters or cake plates. Spoon 1/2 of chocolate mixture down center of each cake. Let chocolate run down sides of cakes. Let stand until chocolate sets. Makes 2 loaf cakes.

Marbled Pear Cake

1 (18-1/4-oz.) pkg. marble-cake mix
3 eggs
1 cup water
1/3 cup vegetable oil
1 teaspoon almond extract
1/2 cup ground almonds, if desired
1 (16-oz.) can sliced pears, well drained
Powdered sugar

Preheat oven to 350F (175C). Grease and flour a 10-inch springform pan with a center tube and fluted bottom, or a 12-cup Bundt pan. In a large bowl, combine cake mix, eggs, water, oil and almond extract; beat until blended. Beat with electric mixer 2 minutes on medium speed. Fold in almonds, if desired. Pour 2/3 of batter into prepared pan; smooth top. Arrange pear slices over batter. To reserved batter, add contents of small packet from cake mix; beat until blended. Spoon chocolate batter over pears; spread evenly with back of a spoon. Bake 45 to 50 minutes or until a wooden pick inserted in center comes out clean. Cool in pan on a wire rack 15 to 20 minutes. Remove from pan; cool on wire rack. Place cake on a platter or cake plate; dust with powdered sugar. Makes 1 cake.

Variations

Marinate pear slices 3 to 6 hours in orange-flavored liqueur. Drain well on paper towels before using.

Use any well-drained cooked or canned fruit.

Currant-Nut Coffeecake

Currant-Nut Coffeecake

1 (16-oz.) loaf frozen white-bread dough, thawed
1 tablespoon butter or margarine, melted
1 egg
2/3 cup currants or chopped raisins
1/3 cup crystal sugar or crushed sugar cubes
1/4 cup sliced or slivered almonds
1/2 teaspoon ground cinnamon

Grease a large bowl. Place thawed dough in greased bowl, turning to coat all sides. Cover; let rise in a warm place, free from drafts, until doubled in bulk. Grease a 13" x 9" baking pan. Punch down dough. Press or pat dough evenly into prepared pan. In a small bowl, beat butter or margarine and egg until blended; generously brush over dough. Sprinkle currants or raisins over dough; press down lightly. In another small bowl, combine sugar, almonds and cinnamon; sprinkle over dough. Cover; let rise 20 minutes. Preheat oven to 375F (190C). Bake 20 to 25 minutes or until top is golden brown. Cool in pan on a wire rack. Serve warm. Makes 1 coffeecake.

Apple "Pizzazz"

Apple "Pizzazz"

1 (1-lb.) loaf frozen white-bread dough, thawed
1 tablespoon butter or margarine, melted
6 medium, tart apples, peeled, cored, quartered
1/4 cup apple jelly
1 tablespoon water
1/4 cup crystal sugar or crushed sugar cubes
1/2 teaspoon ground cinnamon
3 tablespoons sliced or slivered almonds

Grease a medium bowl; place dough in greased bowl, turning to coat all sides. Cover; let rise in a warm place, free from drafts, until doubled in bulk. Grease a 13" x 9" baking pan. Punch down dough. Press or pat dough evenly in greased pan. Brush dough with butter or margarine. Cut several slashes lengthwise on top of each apple quarter. Arrange apples in even rows, about 1 inch apart, on dough. Cover; let rise 10 minutes. Preheat oven to 375F (190C). Bake 20 to 25 minutes or until top is golden brown. In a small saucepan, combine apple jelly and water. Stir over low heat until mixture comes to a boil. Brush hot jelly mixture over apples. Combine sugar, cinnamon and almonds; sprinkle over cake. Cool in pan on a wire rack. Makes 12 servings.

Blueberry Coffeecake

1 (1-lb.) loaf frozen white-bread dough, thawed
1/2 teaspoon ground cinnamon
1 (21-oz.) can blueberry-pie filling
Milk

Glaze:
1 cup powdered sugar, sifted
1 tablespoon butter or margarine, melted
1 to 2 tablespoons milk

Grease a medium bowl. Place dough in greased bowl, turning to coat all sides. Cover; let rise in a warm place, free from drafts, until doubled in bulk. Grease a large baking sheet. Punch down dough. On a lightly floured surface, roll out dough to a 15" x 12" rectangle. Place rolled-out dough on greased baking sheet. Stir cinnamon into pie filling. Spoon filling lengthwise down center of dough in a 4-inch-wide strip. At 1-inch intervals, cut diagonal slashes from filling to edge of dough. Alternately fold dough strips over filling; tuck ends under to seal. Cover; let rise until almost doubled. Preheat oven to 375F (190C). Brush with milk. Bake 20 to 25 minutes or until golden brown. Carefully remove coffeecake from baking sheet; cool on a wire rack.

To make glaze, in small bowl, combine powdered sugar, butter or margarine and milk. Stir until smooth. Spoon over coffeecake; let stand until glaze sets. Makes 1 coffeecake.

Almond Pound Cake

Almond-Pear Cake

2 cups buttermilk baking mix
1/4 cup sugar
1 teaspoon ground cinnamon
1 egg, slightly beaten
1/2 cup milk
1/2 teaspoon almond extract
1 (16-oz.) can sliced pears, drained

Almond-Crumb Topping:
1/4 cup all-purpose flour
1/4 cup packed light-brown sugar
2 tablespoons butter or margarine, chilled
1/4 cup sliced or slivered almonds

Preheat oven to 375F (190C). Grease a 9-inch-square baking pan. In a medium bowl, combine baking mix, sugar, cinnamon, egg, milk and almond extract. Beat with a wooden spoon until blended. Spread batter evenly in greased pan. Arrange pear slices in even rows on top of batter.

To make topping, in a small bowl, combine flour and brown sugar. Use a pastry blender or 2 knives to cut in butter or margarine until mixture resembles coarse crumbs. Stir in almonds. Sprinkle over pears. Bake 30 to 35 minutes or until a wooden pick inserted in center comes out clean. Cool in pan on a wire rack. Makes 8 servings.

Almond Pound Cake

1/2 cup chopped or slivered blanched almonds
1 (16- or 17-oz.) pkg. pound-cake mix
2 eggs
1 tablespoon grated lemon peel
2 tablespoons lemon juice
2/3 cup milk

Preheat oven to 325F (165C). Generously grease a 9" x 5" loaf pan. Sprinkle 1/2 of almonds on sides of pan. In a medium bowl, combine cake mix, eggs, lemon peel, lemon juice and milk; beat until blended. Beat with electric mixer 3 minutes on high speed. Carefully pour batter into prepared pan. Sprinkle remaining almonds over top of batter. Bake 65 to 70 minutes or until a wooden pick inserted in center comes out clean. Cool in pan on a wire rack 10 minutes. Remove from pan; cool on wire rack. Makes 1 loaf cake.

Cinnamon-Prune Muffins

2 cups buttermilk baking mix
1/4 cup sugar
1 teaspoon ground cinnamon
1 egg, slightly beaten
2/3 cup milk
2 tablespoons vegetable oil
1 cup chopped pitted prunes

Preheat oven to 400F (205C). Line a 12-cup muffin pan with paper baking cups. In a medium bowl, combine baking mix, sugar, cinnamon, egg, milk and oil. Beat with a wooden spoon until blended. Fold in prunes. Spoon batter into lined muffin cups, filling cups 2/3 full. Bake 15 to 18 minutes or until golden brown on top. Remove from muffin cups; cool on a wire rack. Makes 12 muffins.

Coffee-Time Cake

1 (18-1/4-oz.) pkg. white-, yellow- or lemon-cake mix
1/2 cup butter or margarine, room temperature
1/3 cup water
2 eggs
1/2 cup currants or chopped raisins
2 tablespoons sliced or slivered almonds
1/4 cup crystal sugar or crushed sugar cubes

Preheat oven to 350F (175C). Grease and flour a 15" x 10" jelly-roll pan. In a large bowl, combine cake mix, butter or margarine, water and eggs; beat until blended. Beat with electric mixer 2 minutes on high speed. Spread batter evenly in prepared pan. In a small bowl, combine currants or raisins, almonds and crystal sugar or crushed sugar cubes; sprinkle over batter. Bake 25 to 30 minutes or until cake springs back when pressed lightly. Cool in pan on a wire rack. Cut cooled cake into 3" x 2" bars. Makes 25 servings.

Farmer Brown

Farmer Brown

1 (16-oz.) pkg. white yeast-bread mix
1 egg white beaten with 1 tablespoon water for glaze

Prepare bread mix according to package directions. Cover with bowl; let stand 5 minutes. Grease baking sheets; set aside. On a lightly floured surface, roll out dough to a 20" x 12" rectangle. Arrange pattern on dough; use a sharp knife to cut around pattern. Use a wide, flat spatula to lift pieces of dough. Place farmer's body in center of greased baking sheet; brush with egg-white glaze. Brush underside of apron, shoes, arms, pipe, mustache, nose and eyes with egg-white glaze; place on farmer. Generously brush egg-white glaze over farmer. Bake as soon as farmer is assembled; do not let dough rise. Bake 25 to 30 minutes or until golden brown. Place basket on a separate greased baking sheet. Cut small thin strips of dough; weave, if desired, and arrange on top of basket. Twist other strips of dough to make a handle and rim for basket. Brush with glaze. Bake 25 to 30 minutes or until golden brown. Carefully remove farmer and basket from baking sheets; cool on wire racks. Place basket on farmer's apron. Give a raised appearance by inserting short pieces of wooden picks between basket and farmer. Arrange herbs or small flowers in basket, if desired.
To use leftover dough, gather scraps together; knead until smooth. Cut into 8 equal pieces. Shape into balls; arrange balls on a greased baking sheet. Cover; let rise 15 minutes. Brush with melted butter. Bake 20 to 25 minutes or until browned. Remove from baking sheet; cool on a wire rack. Makes 1 farmer and about 8 rolls.

Coffee-Time Cake

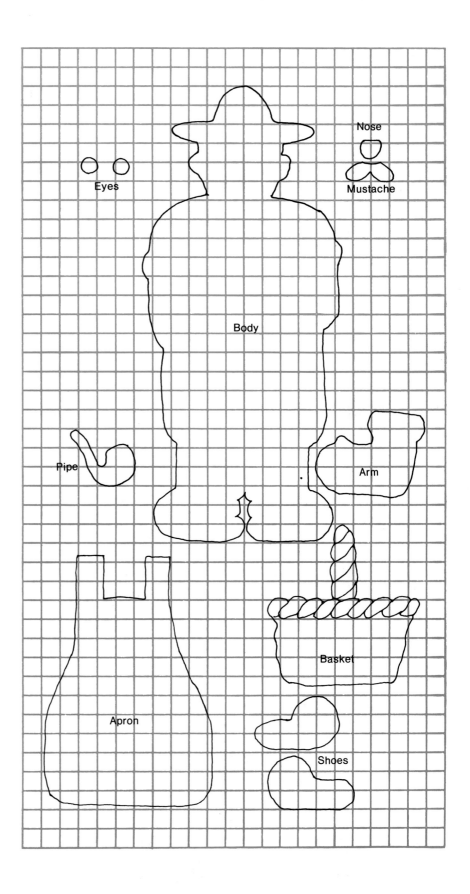

Draw pattern for farmer on cardboard. One square equals 1/2 inch; enlarge pattern as desired.

Lemon-Apricot Cheesecake

Cake:
1 (18-1/4-oz.) pkg. lemon-cake mix
1 egg, slightly beaten
1 tablespoon vegetable oil

Apricot-Cheese Filling:
2 (8-oz.) pkgs. cream cheese, room temperature
1/3 cup sugar
3 eggs
1 teaspoon lemon extract
1 (29-oz.) can apricot halves, drained

Glaze:
1/4 cup apricot jam or apricot preserves
1 tablespoon water

To make cake, preheat oven to 325F (165C). Grease a 10-inch springform pan; set aside. Reserve 1 cup cake mix. In a medium bowl, combine remaining cake mix, egg and oil; beat with a fork until mixture resembles coarse crumbs. Press mixture over bottom and halfway up side of greased pan.

To make filling, in a large bowl, beat cream cheese and sugar until fluffy. Add eggs and lemon extract; beat until blended. Add reserved cake mix; beat until blended. Beat with electric mixer 1 minute on high speed. Pour into crust-lined pan. Bake 25 minutes. Arrange apricots, cut-side down, over filling. Bake 30 to 35 minutes longer or until top is golden and center is set. Cool in pan on a wire rack.

To make glaze, press jam or preserves through a sieve into a small saucepan. Add water; stir over low heat until mixture comes to a boil. Brush warm glaze over top of cheesecake; cool completely. Remove side of pan; place cake on a platter or cake plate. Serve chilled or at room temperature. Makes 1 cheesecake.

Lemon-Apricot Cheesecake

Miniature Fantasy Cakes

1 (9-oz.) pkg. devil's food cake mix

Chocolate Glaze:
1 (7-1/2-oz.) pkg. fudge-frosting mix
1/4 cup boiling water
Sweetened whipped cream
Small candies
Candy flowers and leaves

Cut 12 (6-inch) foil circles; grease foil. Place a small juice glass or jar with a 2-inch base in center of 1 foil circle. Press foil up around side of glass. Remove glass and place foil mold in a muffin cup. Repeat with remaining foil circles. Preheat oven to 350F (175C). Prepare cake mix according to package directions. Spoon batter evenly among foil molds. Bake 25 to 30 minutes or until centers spring back when pressed lightly. Cool in muffin cups on a wire rack. Remove from cups; peel off foil.

To make glaze, pour frosting mix into a small bowl; stir in water. Continue stirring until smooth and creamy.

To complete, dip each cake in glaze; tilt cakes from side to side to distribute glaze evenly. Place a wire rack over a baking sheet. Place cakes, glazed-side up, on wire rack; refrigerate 1 hour or until glaze sets. Decorate with whipped cream, small candies or candy flowers. Makes 12 miniature cakes.

Miniature Fantasy Cakes

Apricot-Chocolate Loaf

3 cups buttermilk baking mix
3/4 cup granulated sugar
3 eggs
1/2 cup orange juice
1 tablespoon grated orange peel
1/2 cup chopped almonds or hazelnuts
3 oz. semisweet chocolate, chopped
1/2 cup chopped dried apricots (3 oz.)
1 cup powdered sugar, sifted
1 to 2 tablespoons almond-flavored liqueur

Preheat oven to 350F (175C). Grease and flour a 9'' x 5'' loaf pan. In a medium bowl, combine baking mix, granulated sugar, eggs and orange juice; beat until blended. Beat with electric mixer 3 minutes on high speed. Fold in orange peel, nuts, chocolate and apricots. Pour batter into prepared pan; smooth top. Bake 55 to 60 minutes or until a wooden pick inserted in center comes out clean. Cool in pan on a wire rack 10 minutes. Remove from pan; cool on wire rack. In a small bowl, combine powdered sugar and liqueur; stir until smooth. Spread glaze over sides and top of warm cake. Let stand until set. Makes 1 loaf cake.

Chocolate-Coated Macaroons

1 (15-oz.) pkg. sugar-cookie mix
1 egg, slightly beaten
2 tablespoons orange juice
1 teaspoon almond extract
1-1/2 cups flaked or shredded coconut
6 oz. semisweet chocolate
2 tablespoons vegetable shortening

Preheat oven to 375F (190C). In a medium bowl, combine contents of both cookie-mix packets, egg, orange juice and almond extract. Stir with a wooden spoon until blended. Fold in coconut. Drop by rounded teaspoons, 1-1/2 inches apart, on ungreased baking sheets. Bake 10 to 12 minutes or until golden brown. Cool on baking sheets 1 minute. Remove from baking sheets; cool on wire racks. Line baking sheets with foil; set aside. In a small heavy saucepan, melt chocolate and shortening over low heat; stir until smooth; cool slightly. Dip half of each cookie into chocolate mixture. Place dipped cookies on foil; let stand until chocolate sets. Makes 40 cookies.

Top: Apricot-Chocolate Loaf; bottom: Chocolate-Coated Macaroons

Cherry-Crumb Cake

Cherry-Crumb Cake

Cake:
1 (9-oz.) pkg. yellow-cake mix
1/4 cup butter or margarine, chilled
1 tablespoon milk
1 (21-oz.) can cherry-pie filling

Crumb Topping:
1 cup rolled oats
1/2 cup all-purpose flour
1/4 cup packed light-brown sugar
5 tablespoons butter or margarine

To make cake, preheat oven to 350F (175C). Grease a 10-inch springform pan; set aside. Pour cake mix into a medium bowl. Use a pastry blender or 2 knives to cut in butter or margarine until mixture resembles coarse crumbs. Sprinkle milk over mixture; toss with a fork until mixture binds together. Dough will be slightly sticky. Pat dough over bottom and 1 inch up side of greased pan. Spoon cherry filling into crust.
To make crumb mixture, in a medium bowl, blend oats, flour and brown sugar. Use a pastry blender or 2 knives to cut in butter or margarine until mixture resembles coarse crumbs. Sprinkle crumbs over cherry filling, covering completely.
To complete, bake 45 to 50 minutes or until top is golden brown. Cool in pan on a wire rack. When cool, remove side of pan. Makes 1 cake.

Breakfast Coffeecake

Topping:
1/2 cup rolled oats
1/4 cup all-purpose flour
2/3 cup packed light-brown sugar
1 teaspoon ground cinnamon
1/4 cup butter or margarine, chilled
1/2 cup chopped almonds or hazelnuts

Cake:
2 cups buttermilk baking mix
1/2 cup rolled oats
1/3 cup sugar
1 egg, slightly beaten
2 tablespoons vegetable oil
2/3 cup milk

To make topping, in a medium bowl, combine oats, flour, brown sugar and cinnamon. Use a pastry blender or 2 knives to cut in butter or margarine until mixture resembles coarse crumbs. Stir in nuts; set aside.
To make cake, preheat oven to 375F (190C). Grease a 9-inch-square baking pan. In a medium bowl, combine baking mix, oats, sugar, egg, oil and milk; beat until blended. Spread 1/2 of batter in prepared pan. Sprinkle 1/2 of topping over batter in pan. Top with remaining batter, then with remaining topping. Bake 30 to 35 minutes or until a wooden pick inserted in center comes out clean. Cool in pan on a wire rack. Serve warm or cool completely. Makes 8 servings.

Peach-Crumb Cake

Peach-Crumb Cake

1 (18-1/4-oz.) pkg. banana-cake mix or yellow-cake mix
1 egg, slightly beaten
1/3 cup butter or margarine, chilled

Cheese Filling:
1 cup ricotta cheese (8 oz.)
2 eggs
1/4 cup sugar
2 tablespoons cornstarch
1 teaspoon vanilla extract
1 (29-oz.) can peach halves, well drained
2 tablespoons all-purpose flour
1/4 teaspoon ground cinnamon

Preheat oven to 350F (175C). Grease and flour a 10-inch springform pan. In a medium bowl, combine cake mix and egg; stir until blended. Use a pastry blender or 2 knives to cut in butter or margarine until mixture resembles coarse crumbs. Reserve 1/3 of crumbs in a small bowl. Press remaining crumbs onto bottom and 1 inch up side of prepared pan.
To make filling, in a medium bowl, combine cheese, eggs, sugar, cornstarch and vanilla; beat until blended.
To complete, pour filling into crust-lined pan. Arrange peaches, rounded-side up, over filling. To reserved crumbs, add flour and cinnamon; toss with a fork until blended. Sprinkle crumb mixture over filling and peaches. Bake 60 to 65 minutes or until a wooden pick inserted in center comes out clean and top is golden brown. Cool in pan on a wire rack. Remove side of pan; place cake on a platter or cake plate. Makes 1 cake.

Lemon Tea Cake

1 (16- or 17-oz.) pkg. pound-cake mix
2 eggs
1/4 cup butter or margarine, room temperature
1/2 cup milk
2 tablespoons lemon juice
2 tablespoons grated lemon peel

Lemon Glaze:
1 cup powdered sugar, sifted
1 tablespoon lemon juice
1 teaspoon grated lemon peel, if desired

Preheat oven to 325F (165C). Grease and flour a 9" x 5" loaf pan. In a medium bowl, combine cake mix, eggs, butter or margarine, milk and lemon juice; beat until blended. Beat with electric mixer 3 minutes on high speed. Fold in lemon peel. Pour batter into prepared pan; smooth top. Bake 65 to 70 minutes or until a wooden pick inserted in center comes out clean. Cool in pan on a wire rack 15 minutes. Remove from pan; cool on wire rack.
To make glaze, in a small bowl, blend powdered sugar and lemon juice until smooth. Stir in lemon peel, if desired. Place cake on a platter or cake plate; spoon glaze over top of cake, letting glaze run down sides. Makes 1 cake.

Spicy Pumpkin Cake

1 (18-1/4-oz.) pkg. spice-cake mix
3 eggs
1/3 cup vegetable oil
1 cup canned pumpkin
1/2 cup water
Cream-Cheese Frosting, page 48

Preheat oven to 350F (175C). Grease and flour a 13" x 9" baking pan. In a large bowl, combine cake mix, eggs, oil, pumpkin and water; beat until blended. Beat with electric mixer 3 minutes on high speed. Pour batter into prepared pan; smooth top. Bake 30 to 35 minutes or until a wooden pick inserted in center comes out clean. Cool in pan on a wire rack 15 minutes. Remove from pan; cool on wire rack, bottom-side up. Prepare Cream-Cheese Frosting as directed. Place cake, bottom-side up, on a large platter; spread with frosting. Makes 1 cake.

Royal Apple Cake

Royal Apple Cake

Photo on pages 156-157.

Cake:
1 (27-1/4-oz.) pkg. streusel-cake mix
5 tablespoons butter or margarine
1/3 cup red-currant or seedless raspberry jelly
2 eggs
1/4 cup water
3 to 4 medium, tart apples, peeled, quartered
3 tablespoons all-purpose flour
1 tablespoon butter or margarine

Apricot Glaze:
3 tablespoons apricot jam
1 tablespoon water

To make cake, preheat oven to 350F (175C). Grease bottom of a 10-inch springform pan. Pour 2 cups cake mix into a medium bowl. Use a pastry cutter or 2 knives to cut in 5 tablespoons butter or margarine until mixture resembles coarse crumbs. Press crumbs evenly onto bottom of greased pan. Bake 20 to 25 minutes or until golden brown. Cool in pan on a wire rack. Run tip of a sharp knife around outside edge of crust. Remove side of pan. Using a wide, flat spatula, remove crust from pan. Place crust on a platter or cake plate. Spread jelly over crust; set aside. Wash and dry springform pan. Grease and flour pan. In a medium bowl, combine remaining cake mix, eggs and 1/4 cup water; beat until blended. Beat with electric mixer 2 minutes on high speed. Spread batter evenly in prepared pan. Cut several slashes in top of each apple quarter. Arrange apples, with slashes up, in a circle on top of batter. In a small bowl, combine streusel-mix packet and flour. Use a pastry blender or 2 knives to cut in 1 tablespoon butter or margarine until mixture resembles coarse crumbs. Sprinkle crumbs over batter between apples. Bake 55 to 60 minutes or until a wooden pick inserted in center comes out clean. *Do not remove pan side.*
To make glaze, press jam through a sieve into a small saucepan. Add 1 tablespoon water; stir over low heat until mixture comes to a boil. Spoon glaze over apples in baked cake. Cool in pan on a wire rack. Carefully remove side of pan. Place cake on top of jelly-covered crust. Open glaze-mix packet; dust glaze mix over cake. Makes 1 cake.

Cherry-Currant Cake

1 cup coarsely chopped, pitted, tart red cherries
1 cup red currants, stems removed
1/3 cup sugar
1 (7-oz.) pkg. golden-vanilla-cake mix

Cherry Glaze:
1 (3-oz.) pkg. cherry-flavored gelatin
1/2 cup boiling water
1/2 cup cold water

Preheat oven to 350F (175C). Grease a 10-inch springform pan. Line bottom of pan with foil. In a medium bowl, combine cherries and currants. Sprinkle with sugar; toss gently to coat. Spoon cherry mixture into bottom of prepared pan to within 1/2 inch of edge. Prepare cake mix according to package directions. Slowly pour batter into pan. Bake 40 to 45 minutes or until center of cake springs back when pressed lightly. Cool cake in pan on a wire rack 15 minutes. Remove side of pan; cool cake on wire rack. Invert cooled cake onto a platter or cake plate; remove bottom of pan and foil.
To make glaze, in a small bowl, dissolve gelatin in boiling water. Stir in cold water. Refrigerate until gelatin has consistency of unbeaten egg whites, 30 to 45 minutes. Carefully pour glaze over top of cake; refrigerate until glaze sets. Makes 1 cake.

Spicy Peach Loaf

1 (13-3/4-oz.) pkg. hot-roll mix
1/4 cup peach jam or peach preserves
3 tablespoons light-brown sugar
1 teaspoon ground cinnamon
1/4 teaspoon ground nutmeg
1/8 teaspoon ground cloves
Milk

Prepare hot-roll mix according to package directions. Cover; let rise in a warm place, free from drafts, until doubled in bulk, about 45 minutes. Stir down dough. On a lightly floured surface, knead 4 to 5 minutes, adding flour to surface as necessary, until dough is not sticky. Grease a 9'' x 5'' loaf pan. Roll out dough to a 14'' x 8'' rectangle. In a small saucepan, heat jam or preserves over low heat until melted. Brush over dough to within 1/2 inch of edge. Blend brown sugar, cinnamon, nutmeg and cloves; sprinkle over jam or preserves. Starting at a short end, roll up dough, jelly-roll fashion. Pinch edges to seal; tuck ends under. Place filled roll, seam-side down, in prepared pan. Cover; let rise 30 minutes. Preheat oven to 375F (190C). Brush top of loaf with milk. Bake 30 to 35 minutes or until top is golden brown and loaf sounds hollow when tapped on bottom. Cool in pan on a wire rack 10 minutes. Remove from pan; cool on wire rack before slicing. Makes 1 loaf.

Cherry-Currant Cake

Surprise Strawberry Flan

Surprise Strawberry Flan

1 (18-1/4-oz.) pkg. yellow-cake mix or butter-recipe
   yellow-cake mix
4 oz. semisweet chocolate
1 tablespoon vegetable shortening
2 pints strawberries, hulled
1 cup water
1 cup sugar
3 tablespoons cornstarch
1/4 cup strawberry-flavored gelatin powder

Preheat oven to 350F (175C). Grease and flour a 13'' x 9'' baking pan. Prepare and bake cake mix in prepared pan according to package directions. Remove from pan; cool on a wire rack. In a small heavy saucepan, melt chocolate and shortening over low heat; stir until smooth. Set aside to cool. Place cake, bottom-side up, on a platter; spread with chocolate mixture. Let stand until chocolate sets. Arrange strawberries on top, covering chocolate completely. In a small heavy saucepan, combine water, sugar and cornstarch. Stirring constantly, cook over low heat until mixture thickens and becomes clear. Remove from heat; stir in gelatin until dissolved. Cool slightly. Brush gelatin mixture over strawberries; let stand until glaze sets. Makes 1 cake.

Lemon-Chocolate Cake

Cake:
1 (18-1/4-oz.) pkg. chocolate or devil's food cake mix
2 eggs
1 cup minus 1 tablespoon water
1 tablespoon lemon juice
1/4 cup vegetable oil
1/2 teaspoon grated lemon peel

Whipped-Cream Frosting:
2 teaspoons unflavored gelatin powder
2 tablespoons warm water
2 cups whipping cream (1 pint)
1/4 cup powdered sugar, sifted
2 teaspoons lemon extract
Thin lemon slices
Grated lemon peel

To make cake, preheat oven to 350F (175C). Grease and flour an 11" x 4" or 9" x 5" loaf pan. In a large bowl, combine cake mix, eggs, water, lemon juice, oil and lemon peel; beat until blended. Beat with electric mixer 2 minutes on high speed. Pour batter into prepared pan. Bake 50 to 55 minutes or until a wooden pick inserted in center comes out clean. Cool in pan on a wire rack 15 minutes. Remove from pan; cool on wire rack. Cut cooled cake into 3 horizontal layers.

To make frosting, in a small saucepan, combine gelatin and water. Stir well; let stand 3 minutes. Stir over low heat until gelatin dissolves; set aside to cool. In a large bowl, whip cream until soft peaks form. Add cooled gelatin mixture, powdered sugar and lemon extract; beat until smooth. Refrigerate until ready to use.

To complete, spoon 1 cup frosting into a pastry bag fitted with a star tip; set aside. Place bottom cake layer, cut-side down, on a platter or cake plate. Spread with 1/4 of remaining frosting. Add middle cake layer; spread with 1/4 of frosting. Add top layer, cut-side down. Spread remaining frosting over sides and top of cake, covering completely. Pipe reserved frosting decoratively on top of cake. Decorate with lemon slices and grated lemon peel. Refrigerate until ready to serve. Makes 1 cake.

Glazed Apple Flan

Glazed Apple Flan

1 (16- or 17-oz.) pkg. pound-cake mix
2 eggs
1/4 cup butter or margarine, room temperature
1/4 cup milk
4 medium, tart apples, peeled, cut in thick slices
1/4 cup sugar
2 tablespoons raisins
3 tablespoons apply jelly, melted

Apple-Juice Glaze:
2 teaspoons unflavored gelatin powder
1 cup apple juice

Preheat oven to 325F (165C). Grease a 10-inch springform pan. In a medium bowl, combine cake mix, eggs, butter or margarine and milk; beat until blended. Beat with electric mixer 2 minutes on high speed. Spread batter evenly in prepared pan. In a large bowl, toss apples with sugar. Arrange apple slices in overlapping circles over batter. Scatter raisins over apples. Bake 65 to 70 minutes or until a wooden pick inserted in center comes out clean. Brush top of hot cake with jelly. Cool in pan on a wire rack. Prepare Apple-Juice Glaze, if desired.

To make glaze, in a small saucepan, combine gelatin and 3 tablespoons apple juice. Stir well; let stand 5 minutes. Stir over low heat until gelatin dissolves; stir in remaining apple juice. Set aside to cool. Refrigerate until mixture has consistency of unbeaten egg whites.

To complete, spoon glaze over top of cake. Refrigerate until glaze sets. Remove cake from pan; place on a platter or cake plate. Makes 1 cake.

Lemon-Chocolate Cake

Spicy Slices

1 (18-1/4-oz.) pkg. spice- or apple-cake mix
1 (14-oz.) pkg. creamy white-frosting mix
1-1/2 teaspoons lemon extract

Decoration:
Red candied cherries
Whole blanched almonds
Raisins and currants
Finely chopped nuts
Chocolate sprinkles
Multi-colored sprinkles

Preheat oven to 350F (175C). Grease and flour 2 (13" x 9") baking pans. Prepare cake mix according to package directions. Pour batter evenly into prepared pans. Bake 15 to 20 minutes or until centers spring back when pressed lightly. Cool in pans on wire racks 10 minutes. Remove from pans; cool on wire racks. Prepare frosting mix according to package directions, beating in lemon extract with water. Place 1 cake layer, bottom-side up, on a flat platter; spread with 1/2 of frosting. Top with remaining layer. Spread remaining frosting over top of cake; smooth top with an icing spatula. Do not frost sides of cake. Cut cake into 15 pieces. Decorate each piece as desired. Makes 15 servings.

Note: If desired, bake 1 layer at a time.

Toasted-Nut Torte

Spicy Slices

Toasted-Nut Torte

1 (18-1/4-oz.) pkg. golden-vanilla-cake mix

Whipped-Cream Frosting:
1 (1/4-oz.) envelope unflavored gelatin powder
3 tablespoons warm water
2 cups whipping cream (1 pint)
1/4 cup powdered sugar, sifted
2 teaspoons vanilla extract or 1 teaspoon almond extract
1 cup toasted finely ground hazelnuts or almonds
Whole hazelnuts or almonds

To make cake, preheat oven to 350F (175C). Grease and flour 2 round 9-inch cake pans. Prepare cake mix according to package directions. Pour batter into prepared pans; smooth tops. Bake 30 to 35 minutes or until a wooden pick inserted in center comes out clean. Cool in pans on wire racks 10 minutes. Remove from pans; cool on wire racks.
To make frosting, in a small saucepan, combine gelatin and water. Stir well; let stand 3 minutes. Stir over low

Peanut-Chocolate Ring

Cake:
1 (18-1/4-oz.) pkg. chocolate-cake mix
4 eggs
3/4 cup water
2 tablespoons vegetable oil
1/2 cup chunky or creamy peanut butter

Frosting:
1 (14-oz.) pkg. creamy white-frosting mix
1/2 cup creamy peanut butter
3 oz. semisweet chocolate, melted

To make cake, preheat oven to 350F (175C). Grease and flour an 11-cup ring mold or 12-cup Bundt pan. In a large bowl, combine cake mix, eggs, water, oil and peanut butter; beat until blended. Beat with electric mixer 2 minutes on high speed. Pour batter into prepared pan; smooth top. Bake 35 to 40 minutes or until a wooden pick inserted in center comes out clean. Cool in pan on a wire rack 20 minutes. Remove from pan; cool on wire rack. Cut cake into 2 horizontal layers.

To make frosting, prepare frosting mix according to package directions. Add peanut butter; beat until blended.

To complete, place bottom cake layer, cut-side down, on a platter or cake plate. Spread with 1 cup frosting. Add remaining cake layer, cut-side down. Spread remaining frosting over side and top of cake, covering completely. Smooth frosting with a long icing spatula. Refrigerate cake 1 hour. Drizzle chocolate over cake; let stand until chocolate sets. Makes 1 cake.

Peanut-Chocolate Ring

heat until gelatin dissolves; set aside to cool. In a large bowl, whip cream until soft peaks form. Add cooled gelatin mixture, powdered sugar and vanilla or almond extract; beat until firm peaks form. Refrigerate until ready to use.

To complete, spoon 1 cup frosting into a pastry bag fitted with a star tip; set aside. Fold 1/2 cup ground nuts into 1/2 of remaining frosting. Place 1 cooled cake layer, bottom-side up, on a platter or cake plate. Spread with nut-frosting mixture. Add remaining cake layer. Spread remaining plain frosting over side and top of cake. Reserve 3 tablespoons ground nuts. Lightly press remaining ground nuts around side of cake. Pipe frosting rosettes on top of cake. Top each rosette with a whole nut. Decorate with reserved ground nuts. Makes 1 cake.

Variation

Substitute walnuts or pecans for hazelnuts or almonds.

Zesty Lemon Torte

Zesty Lemon Torte

1 (18-1/4-oz.) pkg. lemon-cake mix
Grated peel of 1 lemon, if desired

Lemon-Cream Frosting:
1 (1/4-oz.) envelope unflavored gelatin powder
3 tablespoons warm water
2 cups whipping cream (1 pint)
1/4 cup powdered sugar, sifted
1 to 2 teaspoons lemon extract
Lemon slices, quartered

Preheat oven to 350F (175C). Grease and flour a deep 10-inch cake pan or springform pan. Prepare cake mix according to package directions. Fold lemon peel into batter, if desired. Pour batter into prepared pan; smooth top. Bake 40 to 45 minutes or until a wooden pick inserted in center comes out clean. Cool in pan on a wire rack 15 minutes. Remove from pan; cool on wire rack. Cut cake into 2 layers.

To make frosting, in a small saucepan, combine gelatin and water. Stir well; let stand 3 minutes. Stir over low heat until gelatin dissolves; set aside to cool. In a large bowl, beat cream until soft peaks form. Add cooled gelatin mixture, powdered sugar and lemon extract; beat until stiff peaks form. Refrigerate until ready to use.

To complete, spoon 1-1/2 cups frosting into a pastry bag fitted with a star tip; set aside. Place 1 cooled cake layer, cut-side down, on a platter or cake plate; spread with 1/3 of remaining frosting. Add remaining cake layer, cut-side down. Spread remaining frosting over side and top of cake. Pipe reserved frosting decoratively on top of cake. Decorate cake with lemon slices. Refrigerate until ready to serve. Makes 1 cake.

Grape-Meringue Flan

1 (3-oz.) pkg. golden egg-custard mix
1 (10-inch) dessert-sponge shell (7.5 oz.)
1-1/2 pounds seedless green grapes, halved
1/4 cup apple jelly, melted
2 egg whites
1/4 cup sugar

Prepare custard mix according to package directions. Refrigerate until mixture mounds when dropped from a spoon, about 30 minutes. Spread custard over sponge shell. Arrange grapes, cut-side down, over custard, covering custard completely. Brush grapes with jelly. Preheat oven to 400F (205C). Place filled sponge shell on an ungreased baking sheet. In a medium bowl, beat egg whites until stiff. Gradually beat in sugar, 1 tablespoon at a time; beat until stiff peaks form. Spoon meringue into a pastry bag fitted with a star tip. Pipe meringue decoratively over grapes. Bake 8 to 10 minutes or until meringue is golden. Remove from baking sheet; cool on a wire rack. Refrigerate until ready to serve. Makes 1 flan.

Grape-Meringue Flan

Apricot Savarin

1 (18-1/4-oz.) pkg. yellow-cake mix
4 eggs
3/4 cup water
1/3 cup vegetable oil

Syrup:
1 (29-oz.) can apricot halves
1 cup water
1/2 cup sugar
1/2 cup dark rum
Sweetened whipped cream
Grated semisweet chocolate

Preheat oven to 350F (175C). Grease and flour an 11-cup ring mold or 12-cup Bundt pan. In a large bowl, combine cake mix, eggs, water and oil; beat until blended. Beat with electric mixer 2 minutes on high speed. Pour batter into prepared pan; smooth top. Bake 35 to 40 minutes or until a wooden pick inserted in center comes out clean. Cool in pan on a wire rack 20 minutes. Remove from pan; cool on wire rack. Wash and dry ring mold.
To make syrup, drain apricots, reserving syrup. Set apricots aside. In a heavy large saucepan, combine water, sugar, and 1/2 cup apricot syrup; bring to a boil, stirring occasionally. Boil rapidly 3 to 5 minutes or until mixture has consistency of a thin syrup. Cool slightly; stir in rum.
To complete, pour 3/4 cup rum syrup into bottom of ring mold. Return cake to pan; prick top of cake with tines of a fork. Slowly pour remaining syrup over top of cake. Let cake stand 2 to 3 hours. To serve, invert cake onto a platter or cake plate. Fill center with drained apricot halves. Pipe whipped cream decoratively on top of cake; sprinkle with grated chocolate. Refrigerate until ready to serve. Makes 1 savarin.

Apricot Savarin; Chocolate-Nut Drops

Chocolate-Nut Drops

1 (18-1/4-oz.) pkg. yellow-cake mix
1 egg
1/4 cup butter or margarine, room temperature
3 tablespoons milk
1 teaspoon almond extract
1/2 cup ground hazelnuts or finely chopped walnuts
6 oz. semisweet chocolate, finely chopped

Preheat oven to 350F (175C). In a medium bowl, combine cake mix, egg, butter or margarine, milk and almond extract. Stir with a wooden spoon until blended. Fold in nuts and chocolate. Drop by rounded teaspoons, 2 inches apart, on ungreased baking sheets. Bake 14 to 16 minutes or until golden. Remove from baking sheets; cool on wire racks. Makes 54 to 58 cookies.

Easy Rocky-Road Cake

1 (13-1/2-oz.) pkg. chocolate-chip snack-cake mix
2 cups miniature marshmallows
1/2 cup coarsely chopped salted peanuts or cashews
3 oz. semisweet chocolate
1 tablespoon butter or margarine

Preheat oven to 350F (175C). Grease a 9-inch-square baking pan. Prepare and bake cake mix according to package directions. Scatter marshmallows on top of baked cake as soon as cake is removed from oven; press down lightly. Sprinkle peanuts or cashews over marshmallows. Cool in pan on a wire rack. In a small saucepan, melt chocolate and butter or margarine over low heat; stir until smooth. Cool slightly; drizzle chocolate mixture over top of cake; let stand until glaze sets. Makes 1 cake.

Chocolate-Custard Cake

1 (18-1/4-oz.) pkg. Swiss-chocolate-cake mix

Chocolate-Custard Filling:
1/3 cup cornstarch
1/2 cup sugar
2 cups milk
4 egg yolks, slightly beaten
2 oz. semisweet chocolate
1 teaspoon vanilla extract
2/3 cup apricot jam
2 cups sliced toasted almonds

Preheat oven to 350F (175C). Grease and flour 3 round 8- or 9-inch cake pans. Prepare cake mix according to package directions. Spoon batter evenly into prepared pans. Bake 25 to 30 minutes or until a wooden pick inserted in center comes out clean. Cool in pans on wire racks 10 minutes. Remove from pans; cool on wire racks.

To make filling, in a medium saucepan, combine cornstarch, sugar and milk; stir until blended. Add egg yolks; beat until blended. Stirring constantly, cook over low heat until mixture thickens. Add chocolate; stir until melted. Stir in vanilla. Pour into a medium bowl; cover surface with waxed paper. Cool to room temperature. Refrigerate 1 to 2 hours or until ready to use.

To complete, place 1 cake layer, bottom-side up, on a platter or cake plate. Spread 1/2 of custard mixture over top. Add a second cake layer, bottom-side up; spread with remaining custard mixture. Add remaining cake layer, top-side up. Refrigerate cake. Press jam through a sieve into a small saucepan. Stir over low heat until jam melts; cool slightly. Brush melted jam over cake. Reserve 1/2 cup sliced almonds. Lightly press remaining almonds around side of cake. Decorate top with reserved almonds. Refrigerate until ready to serve. Makes 1 cake.

Note: If only 2 cake pans are available, bake cake in 2 layers according to package directions. Split 1 layer horizontally, making 3 cake layers. Proceed as directed above, placing thick layer in center of cake.

Chocolate-Custard Cake

Ginger Macaroons

1 (15-oz.) pkg. sugar-cookie mix
1/2 teaspoon ground ginger
1 egg
1 tablespoon water
1-1/2 cups flaked or shredded coconut
1/3 cup finely chopped crystallized ginger

Preheat oven to 375F (190C). In a medium bowl, combine contents of both cookie-mix packets, ground ginger, egg and water. Stir with a wooden spoon until blended. Fold in coconut and 1/2 of crystallized ginger. Drop by rounded teaspoons, 2 inches apart, on ungreased baking sheets. Decorate top of each cookie with a few pieces of reserved crystallized ginger. Bake 8 to 10 minutes or until edges are golden brown. Cool on baking sheets on wire racks 1 minute. Remove from baking sheets; cool on wire racks. Makes 42 to 46 cookies.

Ginger Macaroons

Crumb-Cake Surprise

Crumb-Cake Surprise

1 (18-1/4-oz.) pkg. butter-recipe yellow-cake mix or golden-
  vanilla-cake mix
1 cup all-purpose flour
1 egg, beaten

Cheese Filling:
1 (8-oz.) pkg. cream cheese, room temperature
4 eggs
1/4 cup sugar
1 teaspoon vanilla extract
1 (1.4-oz.) envelope whipped-topping mix
1/2 cup milk

Crumb Topping:
1/2 teaspoon ground cinnamon
5 tablespoons butter or margarine, chilled

Preheat oven to 350F (175C). Grease a 15" x 10"
jelly-roll pan; set aside. Reserve 1 cup cake mix. In a
medium bowl, combine remaining cake mix and 1/2 cup
flour. Stir in egg, making a crumbly mixture. Press dough
over bottom and up sides of greased pan.

To make filling, in a medium bowl, beat cream cheese
until fluffy. Add eggs, sugar and vanilla; beat until
blended. In a small, deep bowl, beat whipped-topping
mix and milk until light and fluffy. Fold into cheese
mixture.

To make topping, in a small bowl, combine 1 cup
reserved cake mix, remaining 1/2 cup flour and
cinnamon. Use a pastry blender or 2 knives to cut in
butter or margarine until mixture resembles coarse
crumbs.

To complete, pour filling into crust-lined pan. Bake 15
minutes. Sprinkle crumbs over filling. Bake 20 to 25
minutes longer or until top is golden. Cool in pan on a
wire rack. Makes 1 cake or 20 servings.

Frosted Cake Roll & Cupcakes

1 (18-1/4-oz.) pkg. yellow-cake mix
4 eggs
1/2 cup water
Powdered sugar
1 (16-oz.) can milk-chocolate frosting

To make cake, preheat oven to 350F (175C). Grease a 15'' x 10'' jelly-roll pan. Line pan with waxed paper; grease paper. In a large bowl, combine cake mix, eggs and water; beat until blended. Beat with electric mixer 2 minutes on high speed. Pour 3 cups batter into prepared pan. Use remaining batter to make cupcakes. Line 8 to 10 muffin cups with paper baking cups; fill lined cups 2/3 full. Bake cake layer 12 to 15 minutes or until center springs back when pressed lightly. Bake cupcakes 15 to 20 minutes. Sprinkle a clean towel with powdered sugar. Immediately invert cake onto sugar-coated towel. Peel off paper; trim edges. Starting on a short end, roll up cake in towel. Cool on a wire rack. Remove cupcakes from muffin pan. Cool on a wire rack.
To complete, unroll cooled cake; spread with 1/2 of frosting. Reroll cake without towel. Place rolled cake, seam-side down, on a flat platter or cake plate. Spread remaining frosting over sides and top of cake. Using tines of a fork, make wavy lines in frosting. Makes 1 cake and 8 to 12 cupcakes.

Banana-Rum Bars

Banana-Rum Bars

1 (11-1/4-oz.) pkg. banana-nut-muffin mix
1/4 cup sugar
1 teaspoon ground cinnamon
1/4 teaspoon ground nutmeg
1/2 cup ground almonds, if desired
2 eggs
1/2 cup milk
1/2 teaspoon rum extract

Chocolate Glaze:
4 oz. semisweet chocolate
1 tablespoon shortening

Preheat oven to 375F (190C). Grease and flour a 13'' x 9'' baking pan. In a medium bowl, blend muffin mix, sugar, cinnamon, nutmeg and almonds, if desired. In a small bowl, combine eggs, milk and rum extract; beat until blended. Stir into dry ingredients. Spread batter evenly in prepared pan. Bake 18 to 20 minutes or until a wooden pick inserted in center comes out clean. Cool in pan on a wire rack 10 to 15 minutes. Remove from pan; cool on wire rack.
To make glaze, in a small heavy saucepan, melt chocolate and shortening over low heat; stir until smooth. Set aside to cool.
To complete, place cake on a platter; spread glaze over top. Let stand until glaze sets. Cut into 15 bars. Makes 15 servings.

Strawberries & Cream Cake

Cake:
1 (18-1/4-oz.) pkg. butter-recipe yellow-cake mix or golden-vanilla-cake mix

Filling & Topping:
1-1/2 pints strawberries, hulled
2 cups whipping cream (1 pint)
1/4 cup powdered sugar, sifted
1-1/2 teaspoons vanilla extract

To make cake, preheat oven to 350F (175C). Grease and flour 2 round 9-inch cake pans. Prepare cake mix according to package directions. Pour batter into prepared pans. Bake 25 to 30 minutes or until a wooden pick inserted in center comes out clean. Cool in pans on wire racks 15 minutes. Remove from pans; cool on wire racks.

To make filling and topping, reserve 10 strawberries for decoration. Slice remaining strawberries. In a large bowl, beat cream until soft peaks form. Add powdered sugar and vanilla; beat until firm peaks form. Fold sliced strawberries into 1/2 of whipped-cream mixture. Place 1 cake layer, bottom-side up, on a platter or cake plate. Spread with sliced-strawberry mixture. Add remaining cake layer. Spread plain whipped-cream mixture over top of cake, swirling decoratively with back of a spoon. Cut reserved strawberries in half; arrange on top of cake. Refrigerate until ready to serve. Makes 1 cake.

Variation

Substitute 3 to 4 cups frozen whipped topping, thawed, for whipped-cream mixture.

Marbled Cookies

Photo on page 189.

1 egg
1/2 cup butter or margarine, room temperature
1/2 teaspoon almond extract
1 (17-1/4-oz.) pkg. golden-vanilla-cake mix
1/4 cup plus 1 tablespoon all-purpose flour
2 tablespoons unsweetened cocoa powder
4 teaspoons very hot water

In a medium bowl, combine egg, butter or margarine and almond extract; beat until creamy. Stir in cake mix and 1/4 cup flour. Place 1/3 of dough in a small bowl. Dissolve cocoa in hot water. Stir cocoa mixture and remaining 1 tablespoon flour into batter in small bowl. Place chocolate dough on top of plain dough in medium bowl. Gently knead 8 to 10 strokes, making a marbled dough. Shape dough into 2 (7-inch-long) logs. Wrap logs separately in plastic wrap or waxed paper; refrigerate 1 hour. Preheat oven to 375F (190C). Remove 1 log from refrigerator; cut into 4 equal pieces. Cut each piece into 9 slices. Or, cut log into 3/8-inch slices. Place cookies, 1-1/2 inches apart, on ungreased baking sheets. Bake 10 to 12 minutes or until edges are golden. Remove from baking sheets; cool on wire racks. Repeat with remaining log. Makes 72 cookies.

Strawberries & Cream Cake

Refreshing Summer Slices

1 (18-1/4-oz.) pkg. white-cake mix
1 cup white-grape juice
3 eggs
Powdered sugar

White Cream Filling:
2 cups white-grape juice, apple juice or sweet white wine
2 (1/4-oz.) envelopes unflavored gelatin powder
1 (2.8-oz.) pkg. whipped-topping mix (2 envelopes)
1 teaspoon vanilla extract
2 egg whites
1/4 cup granulated sugar
Powdered sugar

Preheat oven to 350F (175C). Grease 2 (15'' x 10'') jelly-roll pans. Line pans with waxed paper; grease paper. In a large bowl, combine cake mix, grape juice and eggs; beat until blended. Beat with electric mixer 3 minutes on high speed. Pour batter evenly into prepared pans. Bake 15 minutes or until center of each cake springs back when pressed lightly. Arrange 2 clean towels on wire racks; sprinkle each with powdered sugar. Invert cakes onto sugar-coated towels. Remove paper from cakes; cool cakes on wire racks.

To make filling, pour 1/2 cup grape juice, apple juice or wine into a small saucepan. Sprinkle gelatin over top; let stand 5 minutes. Stir over low heat until gelatin dissolves; pour into a large bowl. Stir in remaining 1-1/2 cups juice or wine. Refrigerate until mixture has consistency of unbeaten egg whites, 30 to 45 minutes. Prepare whipped-topping mix according to package directions, using 1 additional teaspoon vanilla; set aside. Beat egg whites until soft peaks form. Add granulated sugar; beat until stiff peaks form. Fold beaten egg whites into gelatin mixture. Fold in whipped topping. Refrigerate 30 to 45 minutes or until almost set.

To complete, wash and dry 1 jelly-roll pan. Place 1 cake layer, bottom-side up, in clean jelly-roll pan. Spread with partially set filling. Top with remaining cake layer. Without covering, freeze 1 hour. Dust top of cake with powdered sugar before serving. Makes 15 servings.

Variation

Fold 3/4 cup sweetened sliced strawberries into filling mixture.

Refreshing Summer Slices

Chewy Applesauce Bars

1 (14-oz.) pkg. gingerbread mix
3/4 cup applesauce
1 cup raisins
2 teaspoons grated lemon peel

Icing:
1-1/2 cups powdered sugar, sifted
4 to 5 teaspoons milk
1 to 2 teaspoons lemon juice

Preheat oven to 350F (175C). Grease and flour a 13'' x 9'' baking pan. In a medium bowl, combine gingerbread mix and applesauce. Beat with electric mixer 2 minutes on high speed. Fold in raisins and lemon peel. Pour into prepared pan. Bake 25 to 30 minutes or until center springs back when pressed. Cool in pan on a wire rack.

To make icing, in a small bowl, combine powdered sugar and milk; stir until smooth. Stir in lemon juice, 1 teaspoon at a time, until icing is of pouring consistency. Drizzle icing over cake in a zig-zag pattern. Let stand until icing sets. Cut into bars. Makes 36 to 40 bars.

Cheese & Peanut-Butter Swirls

1 (3-oz.) pkg. cream cheese, room temperature
1 egg
1 (16-1/4-oz.) pkg. peanut-butter-cookie mix
1/2 teaspoon ground cinnamon
1 tablespoon water

Icing:
3/4 cup powdered sugar, sifted
4 to 5 teaspoons hot water
Red candied cherries, quartered

Preheat oven to 375F (190C). In a medium bowl, beat cream cheese and egg until fluffy. Add contents of both cookie-mix packets, cinnamon and water. Stir with a wooden spoon until blended. Spoon dough into a pastry bag fitted with large star tip. Pipe 2-inch round swirls of dough, 1-1/2 inches apart, onto ungreased baking sheets. Bake 8 to 10 minutes or until golden. Cool on baking sheets on wire racks 1 minute. Remove from baking sheets; cool on wire racks.

To make icing, in a small bowl, beat powdered sugar and 4 teaspoons water until smooth. Add more water, if needed. Spoon about 1/2 teaspoon icing onto center of each cookie; decorate each with a piece of candied cherry. Let stand until icing is set. Makes 36 cookies.

Cheese & Peanut-Butter Swirls

Rum-Raisin Cookies

1 (15-oz.) pkg. sugar-cookie mix
1 egg, slightly beaten
2 teaspoons water
1 teaspoon rum extract
3/4 cup raisins
6 oz. semisweet chocolate
2 tablespoons vegetable shortening

Preheat oven to 375F (190C). In a medium bowl, combine contents of both cookie-mix packets, egg, water and rum extract. Stir with wooden spoon until blended; stir in raisins. Drop by rounded teaspoons, 1-1/2 inches apart, on ungreased baking sheets. Bake 10 to 12 minutes or until edges are golden brown. Remove from baking sheets; cool on wire racks. In a small heavy saucepan, melt chocolate and shortening over low heat; stir until smooth. Set aside to cool. Dip each cookie halfway into melted chocolate. Place on foil; let stand until chocolate sets. Makes 30 cookies.

Spicy Oat Drops

Colorful Christmas Trees

Spicy Oat Drops

1 (17-1/2-oz.) pkg. oatmeal-raisin-cookie mix
1 teaspoon ground cinnamon
1/4 teaspoon ground nutmeg
1 egg
4 teaspoons milk
1 cup powdered sugar, sifted
1 to 2 tablespoons hot water
Red candied cherries

Preheat oven to 375F (190C). In a medium bowl, combine contents of both cookie-mix packets, cinnamon, nutmeg, egg and milk. Stir with a wooden spoon until blended. Drop by rounded teaspoons, 1-1/2 inches apart, on ungreased baking sheets. Bake 10 to 12 minutes or until edges are golden brown. Cool on baking sheets on wire racks 1 minute. Remove from baking sheets; cool on wire racks. In a small bowl, combine powdered sugar and water; beat until smooth. Drizzle icing over top of each cookie; decorate with candied cherries. Let stand until icing sets. Makes 34 cookies.

Colorful Christmas Trees

1 (14-oz.) pkg. gingerbread mix
5 tablespoons warm milk

Decorator's Icing:
1 egg white
1-1/2 cups powdered sugar, sifted
2 to 3 teaspoons lemon juice
Food coloring
Small silver dragees

In a medium bowl, combine gingerbread mix and milk. Stir with a wooden spoon until blended. Knead dough in bowl until smooth. Shape dough into a slightly flat ball. Wrap in plastic wrap or waxed paper; refrigerate 1 hour. Preheat oven to 375F (190C). On a lightly floured surface, roll out dough until 1/4 inch thick. Flour a 5-inch Christmas-tree cookie cutter; use to cut dough. Place cookies, 1-1/2 inches apart, on ungreased baking sheets. Bake 12 to 15 minutes or until cookies are firm. Remove from baking sheets; cool on wire racks.

To make icing, in a medium bowl, beat egg white until foamy. Gradually beat in powdered sugar; mixture will be very stiff. Beat in lemon juice, 1 teaspoon at a time; continue beating until icing is of good spreading consistency. Place 1/2 of icing in another small bowl. Tint with desired food coloring. Spoon a small amount of colored icing into a pastry bag fitted with a small writing tip; set aside.

To complete, spread plain icing over tops of cookies. Decorate with colored icing or silver dragees. Let stand until icing sets. Makes 28 to 32 cookies.

Left: Marbled Cookies, page 185; right: Easy Iced Cookies

Black & White Treats

Easy Iced Cookies

1 (15-oz.) pkg. sugar-cookie mix
1 egg
1 teaspoon lemon extract

Decorator's Icing:
1 egg white
1-1/2 cups powdered sugar, sifted
2 to 3 teaspoons water

Decorations:
Chocolate sprinkles
Multi-colored sprinkles
Silver dragees
Red candied cherries
Small colored candies

In a medium bowl, combine contents of both cookie-mix packets, egg and lemon extract. Stir with a wooden spoon until blended. Shape dough into a slightly flat ball. Wrap in plastic wrap or waxed paper; refrigerate 30 minutes. Preheat oven to 375F (190C). On a lightly floured surface, roll out refrigerated dough until 1/4 inch thick. Cut dough with a 2-inch rolling cookie cutter or assorted 2-inch cookie cutters. Place cookies, 2 inches apart, on ungreased baking sheets. Bake 10 to 12 minutes or until golden. Remove from baking sheets; cool on wire racks.

To make icing, in a small bowl, beat egg white until foamy. Gradually beat in powdered sugar; beat until icing is smooth. Beat in water, 1 teaspoon at a time, until icing is of good spreading consistency. Keep bowl covered with a damp cloth until ready to use.

To complete, spread icing over top of cookies; decorate as desired. Let stand until icing sets. Makes about 50 cookies.

Black & White Treats

3 oz. semisweet chocolate, melted
20 (3-inch) round chocolate-fudge cookies,
   commercial or homemade
1/4 cup finely chopped almonds
1 cup whipping cream (1/2 pint)
2 tablespoons powdered sugar
1 teaspoon vanilla extract

Line a baking sheet with foil; set aside. Spread melted chocolate over tops of 10 cookies; sprinkle edges with chopped almonds. Place cookies, chocolate-side up, on lined baking sheet; let stand until set. In a medium bowl, whip cream until soft peaks form. Add powdered sugar and vanilla; beat until stiff peaks form. Spoon cream into a pastry bag fitted with a star tip. Pipe whipped cream in spirals on bottoms of remaining 10 cookies. Sandwich cookies together, with whipped-cream mixture between and almond-trimmed cookies on top. Freeze uncovered on a baking sheet 1 hour. Pipe whipped cream rosette on center of each cookie just before serving, if desired. Makes 10 filled cookies.

Variation

Omit whipped-cream mixture. Increase chocolate to 6 ounces. Spread melted chocolate over all cookies. Sandwich cookies, bottoms together. Sprinkle almonds around outside edge of cookies.

Confections

Piped Truffles; Rum-Raisin Balls, opposite

Piped Truffles

4 oz. unsweetened chocolate, coarsely chopped
1/3 cup whipping cream
1/2 cup butter, room temperature
1-1/2 cups powdered sugar, sifted
1 teaspoon vanilla extract
2 egg yolks
48 foil candy cups
Finely chopped pistachios

Heat chocolate and cream in a small, heavy saucepan over low heat, stirring constantly until chocolate is melted. Set aside to cool. In a medium bowl, beat butter, powdered sugar and vanilla until smooth. Beat in egg yolks, 1 at a time, beating well after each addition. Stir in chocolate mixture until blended. Refrigerate 30 minutes or until almost firm. Beat with an electric mixer at high speed until fluffy. Spoon a small amount of fluffy mixture into a pastry bag fitted with a star tip; pipe into candy cups. Repeat with remaining mixture, using a small amount at a time. Sprinkle piped candy mounds with pistachios. Arrange filled candy cups in a single layer on a baking sheet; refrigerate until firm. Store in refrigerator in a container with a tight-fitting lid. Let stand at room temperature 15 minutes before serving. Makes about 48 candies.

French Bonbons

Filling:
1 cup finely chopped or ground dates
1/2 cup finely chopped or ground walnuts
1/2 teaspoon vanilla extract

Meringue:
2 egg whites
Pinch of salt
2/3 cup sugar
1/4 teaspoon vanilla extract
3 to 5 drops red food coloring, if desired
5 to 7 drops green food coloring, if desired

Lightly grease baking sheets or line baking sheets with brown paper.
To make filling, in a small bowl, combine dates, walnuts and vanilla. Shape into 1/2-inch balls; set aside.
To make meringue, in a medium bowl, beat egg whites until frothy. Beat in salt, sugar and vanilla. Beat until stiff peaks form. Divide meringue equally in 2 small bowls. If desired, add red food coloring to 1 bowl and green food coloring to second bowl. Stir gently until coloring is evenly distributed.
To complete, preheat oven to 250F (120C). On prepared baking sheets, spoon meringue mixtures, 1/4 teaspoon at a time, in mounds about 2-1/2 inches apart. Place a date-walnut ball on top of each mound. Spoon about 1 teaspoon of the same color meringue on top of each date-walnut ball. Use a metal spoon to smooth sides, sealing to meringue on bottom. Swirl tops into peaks. Bake about 30 minutes or until set. Remove from baking sheets or brown paper while warm. Cool on wire racks. Makes 50 to 60 bonbons.

Variations
Jim Jams: Omit filling. Use 1/2 teaspoon vanilla extract in meringue. Fold 1/2 cup finely chopped walnuts into meringue. Bake at 225F (105C) 40 to 50 minutes or until dry.
Surprise Balls: Omit filling. Use 1/2 teaspoon vanilla extract in meringue. Fold in 1/2 cup small chocolate pieces and 1/2 cup chopped walnuts. Bake as for French Bonbons.

Fruit Balls

6 tablespoons unsweetened frozen orange-juice concentrate, partially thawed
1/2 teaspoon lemon juice
2 cups powdered sugar
1/4 cup butter or margarine, room temperature
1/2 cup flaked or shredded coconut
About 1 cup instant or non-instant milk powder
About 1/2 cup cornflake crumbs

In a large bowl, combine orange-juice concentrate, lemon juice and powdered sugar. Beat in butter or margarine and coconut. Stir in enough milk powder to make mixture stiff enough to shape into 3/4-inch balls. Roll balls in cornflake crumbs. Refrigerate until ready to serve. Store in refrigerator 1 to 2 weeks or in freezer 3 to 6 months. Makes about 40 fruit balls.

Nut Truffles

5 tablespoons butter, room temperature
1/3 cup sifted powdered sugar
7 oz. semisweet chocolate, coarsely chopped
1/2 cup ground hazelnuts, almonds or walnuts

In a medium bowl, beat butter and powdered sugar until creamy; set aside. Melt chocolate in a small, heavy saucepan over low heat, stirring occasionally. Set aside to cool. Stir cooled chocolate into butter mixture; beat until smooth and creamy. Stir in 1/2 of nuts; refrigerate 30 minutes. Line a baking sheet with waxed paper. Shape refrigerated mixture into small balls; roll in remaining nuts. Place in a single layer on lined baking sheet; refrigerate until firm. Store in a container with a tight-fitting lid. Makes about 30 candies.

Chocolate-Almond Clusters

2 tablespoons butter
1/4 cup sugar
1 cup chopped blanched almonds
4 oz. semisweet chocolate, coarsely chopped
5 tablespoons whipping cream

Grease 1 baking sheet; line a second baking sheet with foil. Melt butter in a medium saucepan over low heat. Add sugar; cook, stirring, until sugar dissolves. Stir in almonds until coated. Pour almond mixture onto greased baking sheet; spread evenly. Let stand until completely cool. Melt chocolate in a small, heavy saucepan over low heat, stirring occasionally. Stir in cream until blended; set aside to cool. Break almond praline into small pieces; stir into cooled chocolate mixture. Spoon by rounded tablespoons onto foil-lined baking sheet. Refrigerate until set. Store in a cool place in a container with a tight-fitting lid. Makes about 24 clusters.

Rum Balls

1 (10-oz.) sponge cake
1/4 cup dark rum
1 cup water
1/3 cup powdered sugar
2 tablespoons unsweetened cocoa powder
1 tablespoon rum extract
1 egg, slightly beaten
1/2 cup butter, melted
Chocolate sprinkles

Crumble cake into a large bowl. Combine rum and water; sprinkle over cake. Set aside. Sift powdered sugar and cocoa powder into a medium bowl. Stir in rum extract, egg and butter until blended. Pour over cake; stir to coat evenly. Line a baking sheet with waxed paper. Shape mixture into walnut-size balls; roll balls in sprinkles to coat. Place in a single layer on lined baking sheet; refrigerate until firm. Store in a container with a tight-fitting lid. Makes about 40 candies.

Nut Truffles

Rum-Raisin Balls

3/4 cup raisins, chopped
3 tablespoons dark rum
1/2 cup butter
10 oz. semisweet chocolate, coarsely chopped
1 cup powdered sugar, sifted
Chocolate sprinkles

In a small bowl, combine raisins and rum; let stand several hours or overnight at room temperature. Melt butter and chocolate in a medium, heavy saucepan over low heat, stirring occasionally. Stir in powdered sugar until smooth. Cool to room temperature. Stir in rum-raisin mixture. Refrigerate 30 minutes. Cover a baking sheet with waxed paper. Shape rounded teaspoons of refrigerated mixture into balls; roll in chocolate sprinkles. Place in a single layer on lined baking sheet. Refrigerate 1 hour or until firm. Store in a container with a tight-fitting lid. Makes about 60 candies.

Stuffed Fruit

1/2 recipe Fondant, page 196
36 dried apricot halves, figs or seeded dates

Prepare fondant as directed. Let ripen 24 hours. With your hands, roll teaspoons of fondant into almond-shaped ovals. Use to stuff fruit. Makes 36 candies.

Apricot-Walnut Creams

Apricot-Walnut Creams

3/4 cup dried apricots, minced
2 tablespoons apricot-flavored liqueur
1 (7-oz.) pkg. marzipan or Marzipan, page 232, crumbled
1/2 cup powdered sugar, sifted
4 oz. semisweet chocolate, coarsely chopped
Walnut halves

In a small bowl, combine apricots and liqueur; cover and let stand 2 hours at room temperature. Add marzipan. Beat with an electric mixer until blended. Spoon onto a sheet of waxed paper. Knead in powdered sugar. Shape mixture into 2 logs, 3/4 inch thick. Cut into 1/2-inch slices. Melt chocolate in a small, heavy saucepan over low heat, stirring occasionally. Dip slices in chocolate to coat. Place in a single layer on waxed paper. Decorate each slice with a walnut half. Let stand until chocolate sets. Store in a container with a tight-fitting lid. Makes about 48 candies.

White-Angel Divinity

2-1/2 cups sugar
1/2 cup water
1/2 cup light corn syrup
Pinch of salt
2 egg whites
1 teaspoon vanilla extract

In a large heavy saucepan, combine sugar, water, corn syrup and salt. Stir over medium heat until sugar dissolves and mixture comes to a boil. Without stirring, cook over medium heat until mixture reaches 250-266F (121-130C) on a candy thermometer or until mixture forms a hard ball that does not flatten when dropped in very cold water. As temperature nears 250F (121C), in a large bowl, beat egg whites until stiff but not dry. Beating constantly, gradually pour a thin stream of hot syrup into beaten egg whites. Beat in vanilla. Beat with electric mixer on high speed until mixture is stiff enough to hold its shape. Drop by teaspoons onto waxed paper; let cool. Or, spoon into a buttered 8-inch-square baking pan. When cool, cut in 1-inch squares.

Marzipan Sweets

Orange-Almond Sticks

Marzipan Sweets

Photo on pages 190-191.

1 (7-oz.) pkg. marzipan or Marzipan, page 232
1 tablespoon kirsch or cherry-flavored brandy
About 1 cup powdered sugar

Icing:
1-1/2 cups powdered sugar
Pinch of cream of tartar
1 egg white
Food coloring

Crumble marzipan into a large bowl; add kirsch or brandy. Dust your hands with powdered sugar. Gradually knead 1/2 to 1 cup powdered sugar into marzipan mixture until firm enough to hold its shape. Dust small plastic candy molds with powdered sugar. Press small amounts of marzipan mixture into prepared molds, wiping off excess. Let stand several hours or until hard. Line a baking sheet with waxed paper. Unmold candies onto lined baking sheet. Let candies air-dry before decorating.
To make icing, sift powdered sugar and cream of tartar into a medium bowl. Add egg white; beat at high speed with an electric mixer until stiff. Tint with food coloring as desired. Spread over candies or spoon into a pastry bag fitted with a small, plain writing tip. Decorate as desired. Let stand until icing sets. Makes about 36 candies.

Orange-Almond Sticks

3/4 cup ground almonds
1/2 cup minced orange peel
1/4 cup powdered sugar
1 egg white
1/4 teaspoon almond extract
Powdered sugar
1 oz. semisweet chocolate
2 teaspoons butter

In a small saucepan, combine almonds, orange peel, 1/4 cup powdered sugar, egg white and almond extract. Stirring constantly, cook over low heat 1 to 2 minutes or until mixture holds together. Set aside to cool. Line a baking sheet with foil. Sprinkle powdered sugar on a work surface and on your hands. Shape rounded teaspoons of almond mixture into small balls. Roll balls in powdered sugar, reshaping balls into 2-1/2-inch sticks. Melt chocolate and butter in a small, heavy saucepan over low heat. Dip ends of sticks in chocolate mixture. Let stand on lined baking sheet until chocolate sets. Store in a container with a tight-fitting lid. Makes 18 candies.

Caramelized Nuts

2 cups sugar
1/4 cup butter
About 1 lb. unblanched almonds,
    walnut halves or pecan halves

In a large heavy skillet, combine sugar and butter. Stir over low heat until sugar is melted and golden brown. Add nuts, stirring quickly until coated. Immediately turn out onto waxed paper; separate while hot. Makes 3 to 4 cups caramelized nuts.

Chocolate Butter Creams

Chocolate Butter Creams

3 tablespoons butter
6 oz. semisweet chocolate, coarsely chopped
1 (3-3/4-oz.) pkg. instant chocolate-pudding mix
1 teaspoon rum extract
3 to 4 tablespoons chocolate sprinkles

Melt butter and chocolate in a medium, heavy saucepan over low heat, stirring occasionally. Stir in pudding mix and rum extract. Stir until pudding is dissolved and mixture is smooth. Set aside until cool enough to handle. Line a baking sheet with waxed paper. Shape mixture into walnut-size balls; roll in chocolate sprinkles. Place in a single layer on lined baking sheet; refrigerate 1 hour or until firm. Store in a container with a tight-fitting lid. Makes about 30 candies.

Fudge Chewies

1 (12-oz.) pkg. semisweet chocolate pieces
1 (14-oz.) can sweetened condensed milk
1/4 cup butter or margarine
1-1/4 cups all-purpose flour
1/2 cup chopped walnuts or pecans

Grease baking sheets. In a medium saucepan, combine chocolate piece, condensed milk and butter or margarine. Stir over very low heat or in a double boiler over simmering water until chocolate pieces are melted. Remove from heat. Preheat oven to 350F (175C). Stir flour and nuts into chocolate mixture. Drop batter by teaspoons onto greased baking sheets. Bake 7 minutes or until firm. Remove candies from baking sheets. Cool on wire racks before storing in airtight containers. Makes 60 to 75 candies.

Christmas Caramels

2 cups sugar
Pinch of salt
1 cup light corn syrup
1 cup evaporated milk
2 tablespoons butter or margarine
1-1/2 teaspoons vanilla extract
1/4 cup chopped walnuts, if desired

Butter a 9'' x 5'' glass loaf dish; set aside. In a large saucepan, combine sugar and salt. Stir in corn syrup and milk. Stirring constantly, bring to a boil over medium heat. Stir occasionally on bottom and sides of pan below surface of mixture. Continue to boil gently until mixture reaches 115F (45C) on a candy thermometer. With a clean spoon, stir in butter or margarine. Over low heat, boil slowly about 1 hour until mixture reaches 240F (115C) or 28F to 30F (15C) above temperature at which water boils at your altitude, or firm-ball stage. Mixture will turn golden brown. Set aside without stirring. Cool to about 150F (65C) or very warm to touch. Stir in vanilla. Stir in walnuts, if desired. Pour candy into prepared dish. **Do not scrape bottom or side of pan.** Cool to room temperature. Turn out on a cutting board. Use a sharp knife to cut candy into 3/4-inch squares. Run a table knife along either side of sharp knife to separate candy from knife. Wrap pieces individually in plastic wrap. Pack wrapped candies in freezer bags or containers with tight-fitting lids. Seal and store in refrigerator up to 2 weeks or in freezer up to 3 months. Makes about 72 candies.

Fondant

2 cups sugar
Pinch of cream of tartar
Pinch of salt
3/4 cup boiling water
1/2 teaspoon vanilla extract

In a large heavy saucepan, blend sugar, cream of tartar and salt. Stir in water. Stir over medium heat until sugar dissolves. When mixture boils, remove spoon. Use a wet cloth to wipe away sugar crystals from side of pan. Without stirring, cook over medium heat until mixture reaches 234-240F (112-116C) on a candy thermometer or until a teaspoon of mixture dropped in very cold water forms a soft ball. Soft ball will flatten slightly when removed from water. Remove from heat. Without stirring, add vanilla. Pour mixture onto a chilled platter to cool quickly. Do not scrape bottom or side of pan. When mixture is cool, begin to knead with a flat wooden spatula; knead until creamy. Knead mixture with your hands until smooth. Place fondant in a glass dish; cover with a damp cloth. After 24 hours, fondant is ready to mold. This is called *ripening*. Keep covered with a damp cloth in a cold place or store in a jar with a tight cover. Use to stuff fruit or make centers for dipped candies. Makes about 1 pound.

Chocolate Fudge

2 oz. unsweetened chocolate, coarsely chopped
3/4 cup milk
2 cups sugar
2 tablespoons light corn syrup
Pinch of salt
2 tablespoons butter or margarine
1 teaspoon vanilla extract
1 cup chopped walnuts or pecans, if desired

Butter an 8-inch-square baking pan or 9'' x 5'' loaf pan; set aside. Butter inside of a heavy large saucepan. In buttered saucepan, combine chocolate, milk, sugar, corn syrup and salt. Stir over medium heat until sugar dissolves and mixture comes to a boil. Without stirring, cook over medium heat until mixture reaches 234-240F (112-116C) on a candy thermometer or until a teaspoon of mixture dropped in very cold water forms a soft ball. Soft ball will flatten slightly when removed from water. Remove from heat. Without stirring, add butter or margarine to surface of mixture. Let cool until just warm (110F, 45C) 30 to 40 minutes. Add vanilla and nuts, if desired. Beat with a wooden spoon, without scraping side of pan, until mixture becomes very thick. Mixture will begin to loose its glossy appearance. Immediately turn into buttered baking pan or loaf pan. Cool; cut into squares. Makes about 1-1/4 pounds fudge.

Variations
White Fudge: Omit chocolate. Increase vanilla extract to 1-1/2 teaspoons.
Marshmallow Fudge: Stir 1 cup miniature marshmallows into fudge before pouring into pan.

Peanut-Butter Fudge

3 cups sugar
1/4 cup cornstarch
1/4 teaspoon salt
1 cup evaporated milk
1/2 cup creamy or chunky peanut butter
2 tablespoons butter or margarine
2 teaspoons vanilla extract
1/2 cup chopped walnuts, if desired
Peanuts for garnish, if desired

Lightly butter a 9-inch-square baking pan. In a medium saucepan, blend sugar, cornstarch and salt. Stir in milk. Bring to a boil over medium heat, stirring constantly to prevent scorching. Stirring constantly, boil gently 4-1/2 minutes; remove from heat. Stir in peanut butter and butter or margarine until both are melted. Stir in vanilla. Add walnuts, if desired. Beat with a wooden spoon until candy mounds when dropped from a spoon onto a plate. Quickly pour or spoon into prepared baking pan, spreading evenly. If desired, garnish with peanuts while fudge is soft. Let cool to room temperature before cutting. This candy freezes well or can be stored at room temperature or in the refrigerator. Makes about 50 pieces.

Chocolate-Butter Sweets

Chocolate-Butter Sweets

2/3 cup butter, room temperature
1 cup powdered sugar
2 egg yolks
7 oz. semisweet chocolate, coarsely chopped
2 tablespoons unsweetened cocoa powder
1 tablespoon powdered sugar, sifted
Chocolate sprinkles

In a medium bowl, beat butter, 1 cup powdered sugar and egg yolks until light and fluffy; set aside. Melt chocolate in a small, heavy saucepan over low heat, stirring occasionally; set aside to cool. Stir melted chocolate into butter mixture; beat until smooth. Refrigerate 30 minutes. Line a baking sheet with waxed paper; set aside. Shape mixture into small balls and rectangles. Blend cocoa powder and 1 tablespoon powdered sugar. Roll half the candies in chocolate sprinkles. Roll remaining candies in cocoa mixture. Place in a single layer on lined baking sheet; refrigerate until firm. Store in refrigerator in a container with a tight-fitting lid. Let stand at room temperature 2 hours before serving. Makes about 60 candies.

Holiday & Special
Occasion Baking

New Year's Eve Torte

To make frosting, in a small saucepan, combine gelatin and water. Stir well; let stand 3 minutes. Stir over low heat until gelatin dissolves; set aside to cool. In a large bowl, whip cream until soft peaks form. Add cooled gelatin mixture, vanilla and powdered sugar; beat until stiff peaks form.

To complete, spread 1/2 of frosting over cake. Reserve 3/4 cup of remaining frosting; set aside. Cut cake lengthwise into 5 (2-inch-wide) strips. Roll up 1 strip in a spiral; stand upright in center of a flat round platter or cake plate. Cut remaining cake strips in half crosswise. Wrap around filled spiral, pressing strips against center of cake. Spread remaining frosting over side and top of cake. Press macaroon crumbs into frosting around side of cake. Using tines of a fork, draw a spiral pattern in frosting on top of cake. Fold chocolate into reserved frosting; spoon into a pastry bag fitted with a plain writing tip. Pipe chocolate frosting decoratively on top edge and in center of cake. Refrigerate until ready to serve. Makes 1 cake.

New Year's Eve Torte

Base:
4 eggs, separated
1/4 cup warm water
1 teaspoon vanilla extract
1/2 cup granulated sugar
3/4 cup cake flour
1/2 teaspoon baking powder
1/4 cup unsweetened cocoa powder
Powdered sugar

Jelly Glaze:
1/2 cup red-currant jelly
3 tablespoons dark rum

Whipped-Cream Frosting:
1 (1/4-oz.) envelope unflavored gelatin powder
3 tablespoons warm water
2-1/2 cups whipping cream
2 teaspoons vanilla extract
6 tablespoons powdered sugar, sifted
16 to 18 Italian macaroons (amaretti biscuits)
1/2 oz. semisweet chocolate, melted

To make base, preheat oven to 400F (205C). Grease a 15" x 10" jelly-roll pan. Line pan with waxed paper; grease paper. In a medium bowl, beat egg yolks and water until foamy. Add vanilla and granulated sugar; beat until thick and pale. In another medium bowl, beat egg whites until stiff but not dry; fold into egg-yolk mixture. In a sifter, combine cake flour, baking powder and cocoa powder. Gradually sift over egg mixture, folding in while sifting. Spread batter in prepared pan. Bake 15 minutes or until center springs back when pressed lightly. Sprinkle a clean towel with powdered sugar. Immediately invert cake onto sugar-coated towel. Peel off paper; trim edges. Let cool.

To make glaze, in small saucepan, melt red-currant jelly over low heat, stirring until smooth. Remove from heat; stir in rum. Remove cooled cake from towel; place cake on a flat surface. Brush with glaze; let stand until glaze sets.

Petits Fours

Cake:
3 eggs, separated
3 tablespoons warm water
1 teaspoon vanilla extract
1/2 cup granulated sugar
3/4 cup all-purpose flour
1 teaspoon baking powder
5 tablespoons butter or margarine, melted
Powdered sugar

Apricot Glaze:
1 (18-oz.) jar apricot jam or preserves
2 to 3 tablespoons water

Marzipan Filling:
1 (7-oz.) pkg. marzipan or Marzipan, page 232
1/2 cup powdered sugar, sifted

Glacé Icing:
4 cups powdered sugar, sifted
1/4 cup light corn syrup
1/4 cup hot water
Food coloring
2 oz. semisweet chocolate, melted
Decorator's Icing, page 57

Decorations:
Small colored candies
Sugar violets
Melted chocolate
Chocolate sprinkles
Red or green candied cherries
Silver or gold dragees

To make cake, preheat oven to 400F (205C). Grease a 15" x 10" jelly-roll pan. Line pan with waxed paper; grease paper. In a medium bowl, combine egg yolks and water; beat until foamy. Add vanilla and granulated sugar; beat until thick and pale. In another medium bowl, beat egg whites until stiff but not dry; fold into egg-yolk mixture. In a sifter, combine flour and baking powder. Gradually sift over egg mixture, folding in while sifting. Fold in butter or margarine until no streaks remain.

On preceding pages: Amaretto-Chocolate Gâteau, page 202.

Petits Fours

Spread batter in prepared pan. Bake 15 minutes or until center springs back when pressed lightly. Place a clean towel on a flat surface; sprinkle with powdered sugar. Immediately invert cake onto sugar-coated towel. Peel off paper; trim edges of cake. Let stand until cool.

To make glaze, press jam or preserves through a fine sieve into a small saucepan; add water. Stirring constantly over low heat, cook until jam or preserves melts and comes to a boil. Set aside to cool slightly. Brush a light coating of Apricot Glaze over top of cooled cake. Set remaining glaze aside. Let cake stand until glaze sets.

To make filling, crumble marzipan into a medium bowl. Knead in powdered sugar until mixture is pliable. Between 2 sheets of waxed paper, roll out Marzipan Filling to a 10" x 7-1/2" rectangle. Peel off top sheet of waxed paper.

To cut shapes, cut glazed cake in half crosswise. Invert marzipan over 1/2 of cake; peel off waxed paper. Place remaining cake layer, jam-side down, over marzipan. Firmly press layers together. Cut out 5 hearts with a 1-inch heart-shaped cutter and 8 rounds with a 1-1/2-inch plain round cutter. Cut remaining cake into 20

(1-1/4-inch) squares. Or, cut cake into small rectangles or diamond shapes. Reheat reserved Apricot Glaze, if necessary. Brush sides and tops of petits fours with glaze. Place wire racks over a clean jelly-roll pan. Place glazed petits fours on wire racks; let stand 1 hour.

To make glacé icing, in top of a double boiler, combine powdered sugar, corn syrup and water; set over pan of simmering water. Cook, stirring constantly, until icing is smooth. Remove 1/2 of icing; tint with a few drops of red food coloring. If icing thickens, thin with a little water. *To make Chocolate Glacé Icing,* stir melted chocolate into 1/2 of icing.

To complete, spoon Glacé Icing over each petit four, covering completely. Scrape up icing that drips into pan; add 1 to 2 teaspoons water while reheating, stirring until smooth. Spoon over petits fours again. Let stand until icing sets. Spoon Decorator's Icing into a pastry bag fitted with a plain writing tip. Pipe Decorator's Icing on petits fours in decorative patterns. Decorate with small colored candies, sugar violets, piped melted chocolate, chocolate sprinkles, cherry halves or dragees. Makes about 30 petits fours.

Wedding Cake

4 (18-1/4-oz.) pkgs. yellow- or white-cake mix

Bridal Frosting:
2 cups vegetable shortening
8 egg whites (1 cup)
4 (16-oz.) pkgs. powdered sugar
2 tablespoons colorless vanilla extract
1 tablespoon almond extract
2 to 4 tablespoons glycerine (for gloss)
Blue food coloring, if desired
Pink candy roses
Green marzipan leaves

To make cake, preheat oven to 350F (175C). Using 2-inch-deep pans, grease and flour 1 (12-inch) cake pan, 1 (9-inch) cake pan and 1 (6-inch) cake pan. Prepare 2 packages cake mix at a time as directed on packages. Pour 6-1/2 cups batter into 12-inch pan, 2-3/4 cups batter into 9-inch pan and remaining 1-3/4 cups batter into 6-inch pan. Bake 6-inch and 9-inch layers 30 to 35 minutes or until a wooden pick inserted in center comes out clean. Bake 12-inch layer 35 to 40 minutes or until a wooden pick inserted in center comes out clean. Cool cakes in pans on wire racks 10 minutes. Remove from pans; cool on wire racks. Repeat layers using remaining 2 boxed mixes. Bake as directed above. When cakes are cool, trim all layers so tops are level. Cut 12-inch, 8-inch and 5-inch circles from heavy cardboard; cover each cardboard circle with foil. Or, use ready-made cardboard cake dividers.

To make frosting, it will be necessary to prepare frosting in 2 batches. Prepare 1 batch at a time. Keep frosting covered with a damp towel until ready to use. In a large bowl, beat 1 cup shortening until fluffy. Add 4 egg whites; beat until blended. Sift 2 packages powdered sugar. Gradually beat into shortening mixture. Beat in 1 tablespoon vanilla, 1-1/2 teaspoons almond extract and 1 to 2 tablespoons glycerine. Continue beating until frosting is of good spreading consistency. Tint with a few drops blue food coloring to make a very white icing. Repeat with remaining frosting ingredients.

To complete, place about 1 tablespoon frosting in center of a large round tray or surface cake will be displayed on. Place 12-inch cardboard circle on top of tray; press down so frosting holds circle in place. Spread a little frosting in center of cardboard circle. Place 1 (12-inch) layer, bottom-side up, on cardboard. Spread 1-1/2 cups frosting over top of layer. Top with second 12-inch layer, bottom-side up. Spread 1 cup frosting over layer. Center 8-inch cardboard circle on top of 12-inch layers. Spread a little frosting on cardboard. Place 1 (9-inch) layer, bottom-side up, on cardboard. Spread 1 cup frosting over top of layer. Top with second 9-inch layer, bottom-side up; spread with 3/4 cup frosting. Center 5-inch cardboard circle on top of 9-inch layers. Spread a little frosting on cardboard. Place 1 (6-inch) layer, bottom-side up, on cardboard. Spread 1/2 cup frosting over top of layer. Top with remaining 6-inch layer, bottom-side up. Spread 1/2 cup frosting over top of layer. Spread a thin layer of frosting around all sides of cake layers to seal. Let stand until frosting sets. Reserve 2-1/2 to 3 cups frosting for decoration. Spread remaining frosting over entire cake, covering completely. Smooth frosting with a long flat icing spatula. Spoon 1/2 of reserved frosting into a pastry

Clockwise from center: Wedding Cake; Chocolate-Hazelnut Gâteau, page 42; Petits Fours, pages 200-201.

bag fitted with a medium plain writing tip. Pipe row of dots around bottom edge of cake and between each layer. Spoon remaining frosting into a pastry bag fitted with a small plain writing tip. Pipe decorative rows of dots around outside edge of each cake layer. Decorate cake with candy roses and marzipan leaves. Makes 1 wedding cake or 50 to 60 servings.

Note: Colorless vanilla and glycerine are available in speciality shops and gourmet stores. If regular vanilla is used, icing will not be as white. Do not use butter or margarine in frosting because they add a yellow tinge to frosting. Meringue powder, diluted with water, can be substituted for egg whites.

Amaretto-Chocolate Gâteau

Photo on pages 198-199.

Crisp Cake Layers:
2 cups all-purpose flour
1 cup finely ground toasted almonds
3/4 cup sugar
2 tablespoons unsweetened cocoa powder
2 teaspoons baking powder
1/2 teaspoon salt
1 cup butter or margarine, chilled
4 egg yolks, slightly beaten
2 oz. semisweet chocolate
2 teaspoons vegetable shortening

amaretto and melted chocolate; beat until blended. Add powdered sugar; beat until stiff peaks form.

To complete, spoon 1/2 of filling into a large pastry bag fitted with a star tip. Place 1 cake layer on a flat surface. On top, pipe 14 spokes of filling, starting at center and piping to outside edge. Arrange chocolate wedges at an angle between each spoke; set aside. On remaining 2 cake layers, pipe remaining filling in spirals, starting from center and covering each base. Stack layers with decorated layer on top. Refrigerate until ready to serve. Makes 1 cake.

Groom's Fruitcake

1 cup vegetable shortening
2-1/4 cups sugar
3 eggs, slightly beaten
2 cups mashed bananas
6 cups all-purpose flour
3/4 teaspoon baking soda
3/4 teaspoon salt
1/4 teaspoon pepper
1 tablespoon ground cinnamon
1 tablespoon ground mace
1-1/2 teaspoons ground cloves
3/4 teaspoon ground allspice
1 cup milk
2-1/2 cups walnut or pecan halves
1 cup dark raisins
1 cup golden raisins
1 cup red candied cherries, quartered
1 cup green candied cherries, quartered
3/4 cup chopped dried apricots
1/3 cup diced candied citron

Preheat oven to 325F (165C). Grease and flour 2 (15" x 10") jelly-roll pans; set aside. In a large bowl, beat shortening and sugar until creamy. Stir in eggs and bananas. Blend 5-1/2 cups flour, baking soda, salt, pepper, cinnamon, mace, cloves and allspice. Stir into banana mixture alternately with milk. If batter is too dry, add 1 to 2 tablespoons milk. In another large bowl, toss together nuts, raisins, cherries, apricots, citron and remaining 1/2 cup flour. Fold fruit-and-nut mixture into batter. Pour 1/4 of batter evenly into each prepared pan; smooth surfaces. Reserve remaining batter. Bake 45 to 50 minutes or until a wooden pick inserted in center comes out clean. Let stand in pan 15 minutes. Invert onto wire racks to cool. Repeat with remaining batter, cleaning pans and preparing as before. Cut cooled cake into 2-inch squares. Wrap and tie with ribbons. These are the groom's gift to wedding guests. Makes about 160 servings.

Variation

Pour batter into 5 to 6 greased, floured 7" x 3", 8" x 4", or 9" x 5" loaf pans. Bake about 1 hour in a 325F (165C) oven or until a wooden pick inserted in center comes out clean. Remove from pans; cool on wire racks. Slice cooled cakes; wrap slices for gifts.

Amaretto Filling:
1 (1/4-oz.) envelope unflavored gelatin powder
3 tablespoons warm water
3 cups whipping cream (1-1/2 pints)
2 to 3 tablespoons amaretto
8 oz. semisweet chocolate, melted
1/2 cup powdered sugar, sifted
Finely grated semisweet chocolate

To make cake layers, preheat oven to 375F (190C). Grease bottom of a 10-inch springform pan; set aside. In a medium bowl, combine flour, almonds, sugar, cocoa powder, baking powder and salt. Use a pastry blender or 2 knives to cut in butter or margarine until mixture resembles coarse crumbs. Add egg yolks; toss with a fork until mixture binds together. Gather dough into a ball; divide into 4 equal pieces. Press 1 piece of dough evenly into bottom of greased pan. Lightly prick with a fork. Bake 12 to 15 minutes or until edge is lightly browned. Cool in pan on a wire rack 5 minutes. Carefully remove from pan; cool on wire rack. Repeat with remaining dough, making 3 more cake layers. Immediately cut last layer into 14 equal wedges. *Do not cool before cutting.* In a small heavy saucepan, melt chocolate and shortening over low heat. Stir until smooth; set aside to cool. Spread chocolate mixture over top of each wedge. Place wedges, chocolate-side up, on a wire rack; let stand until set.

To make filling, in a small saucepan, combine gelatin and water; let stand 3 minutes. Stir over low heat until gelatin dissolves; set aside to cool. In a large bowl, whip cream until soft peaks form. Add cooled gelatin mixture,

Cherry Valentine

Cherry Valentine

2 to 2-1/4 lbs. dark sweet cherries, halved, pitted
1/3 to 1/2 cup sugar
1 (16-oz.) pkg. white yeast-bread mix
1 egg yolk beaten with 1 tablespoon milk for glaze
1/2 cup apple jelly or red-currant jelly
2 tablespoons orange-flavored liqueur, if desired

Place cherries in a medium bowl; sprinkle with sugar. Toss lightly; let stand at room temperature. Prepare bread mix according to package directions. Cover with mixing bowl; let stand 5 minutes. Grease a large baking sheet; set aside. Pinch off 1/4 of dough; set aside. On a lightly floured surface, roll out large piece of dough to a 14'' x 10'' rectangle. Trim edges to make a large heart.

Fold heart over rolling pin; carefully lift and place on greased baking sheet. Adjust shape of heart, if necessary. Brush outside edge of heart with glaze. Gather dough scraps; knead into reserved dough until smooth. Cut dough into 8 equal pieces. Shape each piece into a 12-inch rope. Twist 2 ropes together; place on top of outside edge of heart. Repeat with remaining ropes, making a border all around heart. Arrange cherries inside border, cut-side down, filling heart completely. Brush border with egg-yolk glaze. Bake 25 to 30 minutes or until golden brown. Carefully remove heart from baking sheet; place on a wire rack to cool. In a small saucepan, melt jelly over low heat. Cool slightly; stir in liqueur. Brush over cherries. Let stand until glaze sets. Makes 1 filled heart.

Sweetheart Cake

1 (18-1/4-oz.) pkg. yellow-cake mix

Chocolate Glaze:
4 oz. semisweet chocolate
1 tablespoon vegetable shortening

Whipped-Cream Filling:
1-1/2 cups whipping cream
3 tablespoons powdered sugar
1-1/2 teaspoons vanilla extract or 1 teaspoon almond extract
Coarsely grated semisweet chocolate
Sugar flowers

Preheat oven to 350F (175C). Grease and flour 2 (9-inch) heart-shaped cake pans. Prepare and bake cake mix as directed. Remove cakes from pans; cool on wire racks.

To make glaze, melt chocolate and shortening in a small heavy saucepan over low heat; stir until smooth. Set aside to cool. Place 1 cooled cake layer, bottom-side up, on rack. Spread Chocolate Glaze over top and side of layer; let stand until glaze sets.

To make filling, in a medium bowl whip cream until soft peaks form. Add powdered sugar and vanilla or almond extract; beat until stiff peaks form. Refrigerate until ready to use.

To complete, place remaining cake layer on a platter or cake plate. Spoon 3/4 cup Whipped-Cream Filling into a pastry bag fitted with a small star tip; set aside. Spread remaining Whipped-Cream Filling over top and side of layer. Carefully place chocolate-covered layer on top. Lightly press grated chocolate around side of cake. Pipe small whipped-cream rosettes around top edge of cake. Pipe another row of rosettes inside first row, retaining heart shape. Decorate center rosettes with sugar flowers. Fill center of heart with grated chocolate. Refrigerate until ready to serve. Makes 1 cake.

Sweetheart Cake

George Washington Tarts

George Washington Tarts

1 (17-1/4-oz.) pkg. frozen puff pastry (2 sheets), thawed,
    or 1 recipe Puff Pastry, page 232
1 (21-oz.) can cherry-pie filling
1 tablespoon lemon juice
1 egg yolk blended with 1 tablespoon water for glaze

Preheat oven to 400F (205C). On a lightly floured surface, unfold pastry; roll out each sheet to a 16-inch square. Cut each pastry sheet in half lengthwise, then crosswise into 4 (8'' x 4'') rectangles. Cut to round corners, if desired. Spoon about 1/4 cup cherry filling off center on each rectangle. Moisten edges of pastry with water; fold pastry over filling, bringing short ends together. Pinch seams to seal. Place tarts, 1/2 inch apart, on an ungreased baking sheet. Brush with egg-yolk glaze. Bake 20 to 25 minutes or until pastry is puffed and golden brown. Remove from baking sheet; arrange on serving dishes. Makes 8 servings.

Easter-Egg Nests

Easter-Egg Nests

2 (3-oz.) pkgs. cream cheese, room temperature
6 tablespoons butter or margarine, room temperature
1/2 cup sugar
6 tablespoons milk
2-1/4 cups all-purpose flour
2 teaspoons baking powder
1/2 teaspoon salt
1 egg yolk blended with 1 tablespoon milk for glaze
12 hard-cooked eggs, dyed

In a large bowl, beat cream cheese, butter or margarine, sugar and milk until blended. Blend flour, baking powder and salt; stir into cream-cheese mixture. Stir with a wooden spoon until dough begins to bind together. Knead dough in bowl 10 strokes or until smooth. Shape dough into a flat ball. Wrap in plastic wrap or waxed paper; refrigerate 1 hour. Preheat oven to 375F (190C). Grease baking sheets; set aside. Divide dough into 24 equal pieces. Shape each piece into a thin 8-inch rope. Tightly twist 2 ropes together. Shape into a circle; pinch ends together. Repeat with remaining dough. Place on greased baking sheets; brush nests with egg-yolk glaze. Bake 15 to 18 minutes or until golden brown. Remove from baking sheets; press a dyed egg into center of each nest while baked dough is still warm. Cool on wire racks. Makes 12 nests.

Easter Hen & Nests

1 (1/4-oz.) pkg. active dry yeast (1 tablespoon)
1 teaspoon sugar
1/4 cup warm water (110F, 45C)
1 cup hot milk
5 tablespoons butter or margarine
1/3 cup sugar
1 teaspoon salt
1 egg (reserve egg shell)
About 4-1/4 cups all-purpose flour
1 egg yolk blended with 1 tablespoon milk for glaze
**   (reserve egg shell)**
1 raisin, hazelnut or almond
4 hard-cooked eggs, dyed

In a large bowl, combine yeast and 1 teaspoon sugar. Stir in warm water; let stand until foamy, 5 to 10 minutes. Pour milk into a medium bowl. Stir in butter or margarine, 1/3 cup sugar and salt; cool to lukewarm. Stir cooled milk mixture into yeast mixture. Beat in egg and 3 cups flour. Stir in enough remaining flour to make a stiff dough. Turn out dough onto a lightly floured surface. Knead until dough is smooth and elastic, 8 to 10 minutes. Clean and grease bowl. Place dough in greased bowl, turning to coat all sides. Cover; let rise in a warm place, free from drafts, until doubled in bulk.

To make hen, grease a large baking sheet; set aside. Punch down dough. Cut off 1/4 of dough; reserve for nests. Shape remaining dough into a 21-inch log. Cut off 7 inches from log; set aside. Cut remaining portion of log into 10 equal pieces. Shape into slightly flat balls, pinching and tucking sides under. On greased baking sheet, make a hen by using 1 ball for head, 2 balls for neck, and 7 balls for curved body, as shown, with all pieces touching. Shape reserved dough into an 18-inch log. Cut off a 6-inch piece; set aside. Cut remaining dough into 24 equal pieces; shape into tiny balls, pinching and tucking sides under. Arrange balls in a fan shape, making a tail. Cut off a 2-inch piece from reserved dough log. Roll out until 1/4 inch thick. Cut into a wing shape, as shown; place on chicken. Cut remaining 4-inch piece into 6 equal pieces; shape into balls. Attach 3 balls for head crown; 1 ball for beak, by cutting almost in half; and 2 balls for neck lobes. Cover; let rise 30 minutes.

To make nests, grease a small baking sheet. Cut reserved 1/4 of dough into 6 equal pieces. Shape into 6 (11-inch) ropes. Braid 3 ropes together; shape into a circle. Pinch ends to seal. Repeat with remaining 3 ropes. Cover; let rise 30 minutes.

To bake chicken and nests, preheat oven to 400F (205C). Brush chicken and nests with egg-yolk glaze. Press raisin or nut in head of chicken for eye. Grease outside of 4 reserved egg-shell halves; press gently into area between tail and body, as shown by colored eggs. Bake chicken and nests 18 to 22 minutes or until deep golden brown. Carefully remove from baking sheets; cool on wire racks. Discard empty egg shells; replace with dyed hard-cooked eggs. Makes 1 chicken and 2 nests.

Easter Cheese Pie

Single Crust for 9- or 10-inch Pie, page 142

Filling:
2 cups ricotta or small-curd cottage cheese (16 oz.)
4 eggs
1/2 cup honey
2 teaspoons ground cinnamon
1 teaspoon grated lemon peel

Prepare pastry as directed. Preheat oven to 425F (220C). Fit pastry into a 10-inch pie plate. Trim to 1 inch beyond rim of pan. Fold edge under; flute. Prick bottom crust with tines of a fork; line pastry with foil. Cover foil with rice, dry beans or pie weights. Bake in center of oven 8 minutes. Reduce oven temperature to 375F (190C). Remove foil and rice, beans or pie weights; bake 5 to 7 minutes longer. Cool on a wire rack.

To make filling, in a medium bowl, beat cheese, eggs, honey, 1 teaspoon cinnamon and lemon peel until blended. Pour into cooled crust. Bake 30 to 35 minutes or until filling is set. Cool on a wire rack. Sprinkle top of baked pie with remaining 1 teaspoon cinnamon. Serve at room temperature. Makes 1 pie.

Fancy Easter Eggs

Fancy Easter Eggs

Cookie Eggs:
1/2 cup butter or margarine, room temperature
1/2 cup sugar
1 egg
1 teaspoon vanilla extract
1-3/4 cups sifted all-purpose flour

Icing:
1-1/4 cups powdered sugar, sifted
1 egg white
1 teaspoon water

Decoration:
Colored sprinkles
Chocolate sprinkles
Silver dragees
Small colored candies

To make cookies, in a medium bowl, beat butter or margarine, sugar, egg and vanilla until creamy. Stir in flour, making a smooth dough. Shape dough into a flat ball. Wrap in plastic wrap or waxed paper; refrigerate 1 hour. Preheat oven to 375F (190C). On a lightly floured surface, roll out dough until 1/8 inch thick. Cut dough with a 2- to 3-inch oval cookie cutter. Place cut dough, 1 inch apart, on ungreased baking sheets. Using a small straw, make a hole in one end of each cookie. Bake 8 to 10 minutes or until edges are golden. Remove from baking sheets; cool on wire racks.

To make icing, in a small bowl, beat powdered sugar, egg white and water until smooth. Spread icing on cookies; decorate as desired. Thread small piece of string or ribbon through hole in cookie. Attach cookies to an Easter tree, if desired. Makes 42 to 48 cookies.

Easter Hen & Nests

Hot Cross Buns

Buns:
1 (1/4-oz.) pkg. active dry yeast (1 tablespoon)
1 teaspoon sugar
1/4 cup warm water (110F, 45C)
1/2 cup milk, scalded
1/4 cup butter or margarine, room temperature
1/4 cup sugar
1/2 teaspoon salt
1 egg
About 2-3/4 cups all-purpose or bread flour
1 teaspoon ground cinnamon
1/2 cup currants or chopped raisins
2 tablespoons finely chopped candied orange peel
2 tablespoons finely chopped candied lemon peel
1 egg yolk blended with 1 tablespoon milk for glaze

Icing:
1 cup powdered sugar, sifted
1/2 teaspoon vanilla extract
2 tablespoons milk

To make buns, in a large bowl, combine yeast and 1 teaspoon sugar. Stir in warm water; let stand until foamy, 5 to 10 minutes. Pour hot milk into a medium bowl. Stir in butter or margarine, 1/4 cup sugar, and salt; cool to lukewarm. Stir cooled milk mixture into yeast mixture. Beat in egg and 2 cups flour. Stir in cinnamon, currants or raisins, orange peel, lemon peel and enough remaining flour to make a stiff dough. Turn out dough onto a lightly floured surface. Knead until dough is smooth and elastic, 8 to 10 minutes. Clean and grease bowl. Place dough in greased bowl, turning to coat all sides. Cover; let rise in a warm place, free from drafts, until doubled in bulk. Punch down dough; let rest 10 minutes. Grease a 9-inch-square baking pan; set aside.

To shape dough, divide dough into 12 equal pieces. Shape each piece into a ball, pinching and tucking sides under. Arrange balls in prepared pan. Cover; let rise until doubled. Preheat oven to 375F (190C). Brush tops of raised buns with egg-yolk glaze. Bake 25 to 30 minutes or until tops are golden brown. Remove from pan; cool on a wire rack.

To make icing, in a small bowl, combine powdered sugar, vanilla and milk; beat until smooth. Spoon icing over cooled buns or drizzle icing in a cross on top of each bun. Let stand until icing sets. Makes 12 buns.

Easter Bell Cake

Easter Bell Cake

1 (18-1/4-oz.) pkg. yellow- or white-cake mix
1 recipe Vanilla Butter Cream, page 71, or
   Cream-Cheese Frosting, page 48
Coarsely grated semisweet chocolate
Chocolate sprinkles
Finely chopped toasted almonds
Small sugar candies

Preheat oven to 350F (175C). Grease and flour a 10-inch bell mold or deep 10-inch cake pan; set aside. Prepare and bake cake mix in prepared pan as directed. Remove from pan; cool on a wire rack. In place of a bell mold, make a cardboard pattern of a bell. Place pattern on top of cake; cut around pattern, making a bell-shaped cake. Cover a 12- to 14-inch-square piece of cardboard with foil. Place cake on foil-covered cardboard. Prepare Vanilla Butter Cream or Cream-Cheese Frosting as directed. Spoon 1 cup butter cream or frosting into a pastry bag fitted with a small star tip; set aside. Spread remaining butter cream or frosting over top and side of cake. Lightly press grated chocolate around side of cake. Pipe small butter-cream or frosting stars around top edge of cake. Pipe rosettes across cake near bottom to outline bottom of bell. Pipe 2 double rows of rosettes from top of bell to rosettes outlining bottom of bell. Pipe rosettes to make bell clapper. Except for clapper, fill bottom of bell with chocolate sprinkles. Decorate rosettes with almonds and small colored candies, as shown. Makes 1 cake.

Anniversary Bread

Anniversary Bread

1 (1-lb.) loaf frozen white-bread dough, thawed
1 egg yolk blended with 1 tablespoon milk for glaze
Coarse sugar or crushed sugar cubes

Grease a medium bowl; place dough in greased bowl, turning to coat all sides. Cover with a clean towel. Let rise in a warm place, free from drafts, until doubled in bulk. Grease a large baking sheet; set aside. Punch down dough. Divide dough in half; shape each into a 22-inch rope. On greased baking sheet, shape ropes into desired numbers. Cover; let rise 15 minutes. Preheat oven to 375F (190C). Brush bread with egg-yolk glaze; sprinkle with sugar. Bake 20 to 25 minutes or until bread is golden brown and sounds hollow when tapped on bottom. Remove baked numbers from baking sheet; cool on a wire rack. Makes 2 bread numbers.

Chocolate Kisses

2 egg whites
1/2 cup superfine sugar
1 tablespoon unsweetened cocoa powder, sifted
2 oz. semisweet chocolate, grated

Preheat oven to 250F (120C). Line baking sheets with foil. In a medium bowl, beat egg whites until stiff but not dry. Gradually add sugar, beating until stiff peaks form. Fold cocoa powder and grated chocolate into egg-white mixture. Drop by rounded teaspoons, 1-1/2 inches apart, on prepared baking sheets. Bake 30 to 35 minutes. Cool on baking sheets on wire racks. Remove from foil; store in airtight containers. Makes 14 to 16 cookies.

Cran-Apple Pie

Double Crust for 9- or 10-inch Pie, page 142

Filling:
2 cups fresh or frozen cranberries, thawed, if frozen
3 cups diced, peeled, tart apples (about 1 lb.)
1-1/4 cups sugar
3 tablespoons cornstarch
1 teaspoon ground cinnamon
1/2 teaspoon ground nutmeg
2 to 3 tablespoons grated orange peel
Milk
Sugar

Prepare pastry as directed. Roll out larger piece of pastry; use to line a 9-inch pie plate. Do not trim pastry edge.
To make filling, wash cranberries; place in a large bowl. Add apples; toss to distribute. Blend sugar, cornstarch, cinnamon, nutmeg and orange peel. Sprinkle over fruit; gently toss to coat. Spoon into pastry-lined pie plate. Preheat oven to 375F (190C).
To complete, roll out smaller piece of pastry; place over filling. Trim pastry to 1 inch beyond rim of pie plate. Fold edge under; flute. Cut vents in top crust; brush with milk; sprinkle with sugar. Cover pastry edge with foil. Place on a baking sheet. Bake 35 to 40 minutes or until crust is golden and juices are bubbly. Remove foil during final 20 minutes of baking. Cool pie on a wire rack. Serve warm or cold. Makes 1 pie.

Chocolate Kisses

Cinnamon-Almond Stars

3 egg whites
2 cups powdered sugar, sifted
1 teaspoon almond extract
1 tablespoon ground cinnamon
3-1/2 cups ground almonds
Powdered sugar
1 teaspoon cold water

In a large bowl, beat egg whites until slightly stiff. Gradually add 2 cups powdered sugar, beating until stiff peaks form. Beat in almond extract. Reserve 1/4 cup egg-white mixture; set aside. Stir cinnamon and almonds into remaining egg-white mixture. Generously sprinkle a flat surface with powdered sugar. Turn out dough onto sugar-covered surface; knead dough until no longer sticky. Add more powdered sugar to surface, if necessary. Shape dough into a flat ball. Wrap in plastic wrap or waxed paper; refrigerate 30 minutes. Preheat oven to 250F (120C). Line baking sheets with foil; grease foil. On sugar-covered surface, roll out dough until 1/4 inch thick. Dip a 2-1/2-inch star-shaped cookie cutter into powdered sugar; use to cut dough. Place stars, 1 inch apart, on prepared baking sheets. Stir 1 teaspoon water into reserved egg-white mixture; spread mixture over tops of cookies. Bake 50 to 55 minutes or until firm. Cool on baking sheets on wire racks. Store in airtight containers. Makes about 54 cookies.

Holiday Fruit Wafers

Photo on page 221.

3/4 cup light corn syrup
1/3 cup packed dark-brown sugar
1 teaspoon lemon extract
1-2/3 cups all-purpose flour
1 teaspoon baking powder
2 teaspoons ground cinnamon
1/4 teaspoon ground cloves
2 tablespoons finely chopped almonds, walnuts or pecans
2 tablespoons finely chopped candied lemon peel
2 tablespoons finely chopped candied orange peel

In a small saucepan, heat corn syrup and brown sugar, stirring, until sugar dissolves. Pour into a large bowl; set aside to cool. Stir in lemon extract. Blend flour, baking powder, cinnamon and cloves; stir into syrup mixture. Stir in nuts, lemon peel and orange peel. Dough will be sticky. Cover bowl; refrigerate 1 hour. Preheat oven to 375F (190C). Grease baking sheets; set aside. On a generously floured surface, roll out dough until 1/8 inch thick. Flour an assortment of 2-1/2- to 3-inch Christmas cookie cutters; use to cut dough. Place cut dough, 1 inch apart, on greased baking sheets. Bake 8 to 10 minutes or until edges are golden brown. Remove from baking sheets; cool on wire racks. Makes about 60 cookies.

Cinnamon-Almond Stars

Coconut Top Hats

Cookies:
1/2 cup butter or margarine, room temperature
1/2 cup sugar
1 egg
1 egg yolk
1 teaspoon vanilla extract
1-3/4 cups all-purpose flour
1 teaspoon baking powder

Coconut Meringue:
3 egg whites
1/2 cup sugar
1/2 teaspoon almond extract
1-1/2 cups flaked or shredded coconut
1 egg yolk blended with 1 tablespoon milk for glaze

To make cookies, in a medium bowl, beat butter or margarine and sugar until creamy. Add egg, egg yolk and vanilla; beat until blended. Blend flour and baking

Vanilla-Almond Crescents

Cookies:
3/4 cup butter or margarine, room temperature
3/4 cup sugar
3 egg yolks
1 teaspoon vanilla extract
1-3/4 cups all-purpose flour
1 cup ground almonds
1/2 teaspoon baking powder

Topping:
1/2 cup powdered sugar, sifted
1/4 cup finely ground toasted almonds
1/2 teaspoon ground cinnamon

To make cookies, in a medium bowl, beat butter or margarine and sugar until creamy. Add egg yolks and vanilla; beat until blended. Blend flour, ground almonds and baking powder; gradually stir into sugar mixture. Dough will be soft. Cover bowl; refrigerate 1 hour. Preheat oven to 350F (175C). Using a rounded teaspoon of dough, shape into a 2-1/2- to 3-inch log, narrow and pointed at ends. Place on ungreased baking sheets, curving ends slightly to make a crescent shape. Repeat with remaining dough. Bake 12 to 15 minutes or until golden. Remove from baking sheets; cool slightly on wire racks.
To make topping, in a small bowl, blend powdered sugar, toasted almonds and cinnamon. Roll or dip warm cookies in topping. Cool on wire racks. Makes about 60 cookies.

Vanilla-Almond Crescents

powder; stir into sugar mixture. Wrap dough in plastic wrap or waxed paper; refrigerate 1 hour. Preheat oven to 350F (175C). Grease baking sheets; set aside. On a lightly floured surface, roll out dough until 1/8 inch thick. Flour a round 2-inch cookie cutter and a round 3/4- to 1-inch cookie cutter; cut out 36 circles with each cutter. Gather leftover dough pieces; cut into circles.
To make meringue, in a medium bowl, beat egg whites until stiff but not dry. Gradually beat in sugar; continue beating until stiff peaks form. Fold in almond extract and coconut.
To complete, place large cookies on prepared baking sheets. Spoon 1 teaspoon Coconut Meringue on each cookie. Brush top of small cookies with egg-yolk glaze. Place small cookies, glazed-side up and at an angle, on top of coconut-covered cookies. Bake 10 to 12 minutes or until edges are golden. Remove from baking sheets; cool on wire racks. Makes 36 to 42 cookies.

Coconut Top Hats

Mincemeat Pie

Double Crust for 9- or 10-inch Pie, page 142

Filling:
3 cups prepared mincemeat
1 cup diced, peeled pears or apples
1/2 cup raisins
1/3 cup chopped walnuts
1/4 cup orange juice
2 tablespoons brandy or apple juice
1 teaspoon grated orange peel
Milk
Sugar
Flavored whipped cream or hard sauce

Prepare pastry as directed. Roll out larger piece of pastry; use to line a 9-inch pie plate. Do not trim pastry edge.

To make filling, in a large bowl, combine mincemeat, pears or apples, raisins, walnuts, orange juice, brandy or apple juice and orange peel; toss to distribute. Spoon into pastry-lined pie plate. Preheat oven to 425F (220C).

To complete, on a lightly floured surface, roll out smaller piece of pastry to a 12-inch circle. Using center of circle, cut into 12 (1/2-inch-wide) strips. Arrange 6 strips over mincemeat filling, spacing about 1 inch apart. Numbering from one side, fold back strips 1, 3 and 5. Place 1 reserved pastry strip across center of pie at right angle to first 6 strips. Bring strips 1, 3 and 5 back into place. Fold back strips 2, 4 and 6. Place another reserved pastry strip 1 inch from center strip. Bring strips 2, 4 and 6 back into place. Repeat with remaining strips, unfolding and folding first 6 strips to weave a lattice pattern. Press ends of strips to edge of bottom crust. Trim edge to 1 inch beyond rim of pie plate. Fold bottom crust over strips to seal and build up edge; flute edge. Brush strips with milk; sprinkle with sugar. Cover pastry edge with foil. Place pie plate on a baking sheet. Bake 40 to 45 minutes or until crust is golden brown. Remove foil during final 20 minutes of baking. Cool pie on a wire rack. Serve warm or cold with whipped cream or hard sauce. Makes 1 pie.

Sweet-Potato Pie

Single Crust for a 9- or 10-inch Pie, page 142

Sweet-Potato Filling:
1-1/2 cups mashed, cooked sweet potatoes or yams
3/4 cup packed light-brown sugar
1 teaspoon ground cinnamon
1/2 teaspoon ground nutmeg
1/2 teaspoon ground allspice
3 eggs
1-3/4 cups half and half
1 tablespoon butter or margarine, melted

Prepare pastry as directed; do not bake. Preheat oven to 400F (205C). Fit pastry into a 9-inch pie plate. Trim pastry to 1 inch beyond rim of pie plate. Fold edge under; flute edge.

To make filling, in a medium bowl, combine sweet potatoes, brown sugar, cinnamon, nutmeg and allspice. In another medium bowl, beat eggs; stir in half and half and butter or margarine until blended. Stir into sweet-potato mixture. Pour filling into pastry-lined pie plate. Bake 45 minutes or until filling is set. Cool on a wire rack. Serve warm or cold. Makes 1 pie.

Pumpkin-Chiffon Pie

Single Crust for 9- or 10-inch Pie, page 142

Filling:
1 (1/4-oz.) envelope unflavored gelatin powder
3/4 cup packed light-brown sugar
1 teaspoon pumpkin-pie spice
1/2 teaspoon salt
1/4 cup water
1/2 cup milk
3 eggs, separated
1-1/4 cups cooked or canned pumpkin
1 cup whipping cream (1/2 pint)
2 tablespoons powdered sugar

Prepare pastry as directed. Preheat oven to 425F (220C). Fit pastry into a 9-inch pie plate. Trim pastry to 1 inch beyond rim of pie plate. Fold edge under; flute edge. Prick bottom with tines of a fork; line pastry with foil. Cover foil with rice, dry beans or pie weights. Bake in center of oven 8 minutes. Reduce oven temperature to 375F (190C). Remove foil and rice, beans or pie weights; bake 5 to 7 minutes longer. Cool on a wire rack.

To make filling, in a small saucepan, combine gelatin, brown sugar, pumpkin-pie spice and salt. Add water, milk and egg yolks; stir until blended. Stir constantly over low heat until gelatin and sugar dissolve. Stir in pumpkin. Stirring occasionally, cook 5 minutes or until thickened. Pour into a large bowl; refrigerate until mixture mounds when dropped from a spoon, about 1 hour. In a medium bowl, beat egg whites until stiff but not dry; fold into partially set pumpkin mixture. Spoon into cooled crust; smooth top. Refrigerate until set. In another medium bowl, whip cream until soft peaks form. Add powdered sugar; beat until stiff peaks form. Spread whipped-cream mixture over top of pie. Use back of a spoon to make peaks in topping. Refrigerate until ready to serve. Makes 1 pie.

Halloween Cupcakes

Cupcakes:
1 cup butter or margarine, room temperature
1 cup sugar
2 teaspoons vanilla extract
4 eggs
2 cups all-purpose flour
1 tablespoon baking powder
1/2 teaspoon salt
1/2 cup milk

Orange Icing:
3 cups powdered sugar, sifted
4 teaspoons orange juice
3 to 4 tablespoons warm water
Red and yellow food coloring, if desired

Decorations:
Small sugar-coated chocolate candies
Gumdrops
Black-licorice shoelaces
Nuts
Chocolate sprinkles
Flaked or shredded coconut

To make cupcakes, preheat oven to 375F (190C). Line 2 (12-cup) muffin pans with paper baking cups. In a large bowl, beat butter or margarine, sugar and vanilla until creamy. Add eggs, 1 at a time, beating well after each addition. Blend flour, baking powder and salt. Stir into sugar mixture alternately with milk. Spoon batter into lined muffin cups, filling 2/3 full; smooth tops. Bake 18 to 20 minutes or until centers spring back when pressed lightly. Cool in pans on wire racks 5 minutes. Remove from pans; cool on wire racks.

To make icing, in a medium bowl, blend powdered sugar, orange juice and water until smooth and icing is of good spreading consistency. If desired, tint with a few drops of red and yellow food coloring to make orange icing. Spread icing over tops of cupcakes. Use candy, licorice, nuts, sprinkles or coconut to make Halloween faces on cupcakes. Makes 24 cupcakes.

Pumpkin-Raisin Bread

1-1/2 cups raisins
1/2 cup chopped walnuts, pecans or almonds, if desired
1/2 cup unsweetened apple juice
3-1/2 cups all-purpose flour
2 teaspoons baking soda
1/2 teaspoon baking powder
1 teaspoon salt
2 teaspoons ground cinnamon
1 teaspoon ground nutmeg
1 teaspoon ground allspice
1/2 teaspoon ground cloves
4 eggs
2 cups granulated sugar
1 cup packed light-brown sugar
1 cup vegetable oil
1 (16-oz.) can pumpkin (about 2 cups)

Preheat oven to 350F (175C). Grease 2 (9" x 5") loaf pans. In a small bowl, combine raisins and nuts, if desired. Stir in apple juice; set aside to soak. In a sifter, combine flour, baking soda, baking powder, salt, cinnamon, nutmeg, allspice and cloves. Sift into a large bowl. In a medium bowl, beat eggs; stir in sugars, oil and pumpkin. Add to dry ingredients; stir in until dry ingredients are moistened. Stir in raisin mixture. Spoon batter into prepared pans; smooth tops. Bake 60 to 70 minutes or until a wooden pick inserted in center comes out clean. Cool in pans on wire racks 10 minutes. Remove from pans; cool on wire racks. Makes 2 loaves.

Speculaas

1 cup butter or margarine, room temperature
1-1/2 cups sugar
2 eggs
1 teaspoon vanilla extract
3-1/4 cups all-purpose flour
2 teaspoons baking powder
2 teaspoons ground cinnamon
1 teaspoon ground cardamom
1/2 teaspoon ground cloves

In a large bowl, beat butter or margarine and sugar until creamy. Add eggs and vanilla; beat until blended. Blend flour, baking powder, cinnamon, cardamom and cloves; gradually stir into sugar mixture. Wrap in plastic wrap or

Speculaas

waxed paper; refrigerate 1 hour. Preheat oven to 350F (175C). Grease baking sheets; set aside. Flour a 6-inch wooden speculaas cookie mold; gently tap out excess flour. Using about 3 tablespoons of dough for each cookie, press dough into floured mold. Use a taut piece of clean fishing line, unwaxed dental floss or thin wire to remove excess dough from top of mold. Use excess dough to make next cookie. Pick up filled mold and slam it upside down onto a flat surface so cookie falls out of mold. If cookie does not fall out, mold has not been properly floured. Use a wide metal spatula to lift cookies onto prepared baking sheets. Cookie molds should be floured again for every third cookie. Repeat with remaining dough. Bake 15 to 18 minutes or until golden. Cool on baking sheets on wire racks 2 minutes. Remove from baking sheets; cool on wire racks. Store cookies in airtight containers 1 week before serving. Makes about 34 (6-inch) cookies.

Christmas Stollen

2 (1/4-oz.) pkgs. active dry yeast (2 tablespoons)
1 teaspoon granulated sugar
1/2 cup warm water (110F, 45C)
3/4 cup milk, scalded
1 cup butter or margarine, room temperature
3/4 cup granulated sugar
1 teaspoon salt
2 eggs, slightly beaten
1 teaspoon ground cinnamon
1 teaspoon ground cardamom
1/4 teaspoon ground mace
About 4-3/4 cups all-purpose flour
1 cup golden raisins
1/2 cup dark raisins
1 cup finely chopped almonds, walnuts or pecans
1/2 cup diced candied lemon peel or candied orange peel
3 tablespoons butter or margarine, melted
Powdered sugar

In a large bowl, combine yeast and 1 teaspoon granulated sugar. Stir in warm water; let stand until foamy, 5 to 10 minutes. Pour milk into a medium bowl. Stir in 1 cup butter or margarine, 3/4 cup granulated sugar and salt; cool to room temperature. Stir cooled milk mixture into yeast mixture. Stir in eggs, cinnamon, cardamom, mace and 3 cups flour; beat until blended. Stir in raisins, nuts and lemon peel or orange peel. Stir in enough remaining flour to make a stiff dough. Turn out dough onto a lightly floured surface. Knead until dough is smooth and elastic, 8 to 10 minutes. Clean and grease bowl. Place dough in greased bowl, turning to coat all sides. Cover; let rise in a warm place, free from drafts, until doubled in bulk.
To complete, punch down dough; divide into 2 equal pieces. Grease a large baking sheet. Roll out 1 piece of dough to a 12'' x 8'' oval. Brush with melted butter or margarine. Fold oval lengthwise, almost in half, letting about 1-1/2 inches of bottom dough extend. Gently press fold; press top edge to bottom edge to seal. Place on prepared baking sheet; repeat with remaining dough. Cover; let rise until almost doubled. Preheat oven to 375F (190C). Brush tops of loaves with melted butter or margarine. Bake 25 to 30 minutes or until loaves sound hollow when tapped on bottom. Remove from baking sheet; cool on a wire rack. Dust tops with powdered sugar. Makes 2 loaves.

Christmas Stollen

Gugelhupf

1 (1/4-oz.) pkg. active dry yeast (1 tablespoon)
1 teaspoon granulated sugar
1/4 cup warm water (110F, 45C)
3/4 cup milk, scalded, cooled
1/2 cup butter or margarine
1/2 cup granulated sugar
1 teaspoon salt
4 eggs
4 cups all-purpose or bread flour
1 tablespoon grated lemon peel
1 cup golden raisins
1/2 cup slivered almonds
3 tablespoons fine dry breadcrumbs
Powdered sugar

In a large bowl, combine yeast and 1 teaspoon granulated sugar. Stir in warm water; let stand until foamy, 5 to 10

Panettone

1 (1/4-oz.) pkg. active dry yeast (1 tablespoon)
1 teaspoon sugar
1/4 cup warm water (110F, 45C)
1/2 cup milk, scalded
1/4 cup butter or margarine, room temperature
1/4 cup sugar
1/2 teaspoon salt
2 eggs, slightly beaten
2-3/4 to 3 cups all-purpose flour
1 cup golden raisins
1/2 cup candied fruit
1/3 cup slivered almonds
1 tablespoon crushed aniseed
1 egg yolk blended with 1 tablespoon milk for glaze

In a large bowl, combine yeast, 1 teaspoon sugar and water. Let stand until foamy, 5 to 10 minutes. Pour hot milk into a small bowl; stir in butter or margarine, 1/4 cup sugar and salt. Cool to room temperature. Stir milk mixture into yeast mixture. Add eggs and 2 cups flour; beat until smooth. Stir in raisins, candied fruit, almonds, aniseed and enough remaining flour to make a stiff dough. Turn out dough onto a lightly floured surface; knead until dough is smooth and elastic, 8 to 10 minutes. Clean and grease bowl; place dough in greased bowl, turning to coat all sides. Cover; let rise in a warm place, free from drafts, until doubled in bulk. Punch down dough; let rest 10 minutes. Grease a large baking sheet. Shape dough into a round loaf; place on greased baking sheet. With a razor blade, cut a cross, 1/2 inch deep, in top of loaf. Cover; let rise until doubled in bulk, about 45 minutes. Preheat oven to 375F (190C). Brush loaf with egg-yolk glaze. Bake 30 to 35 minutes or until loaf sounds hollow when tapped on bottom. Remove from baking sheet; cool on a wire rack. Makes 1 loaf.

Cranberry-Nut Bread

2 cups all-purpose flour
1 cup packed light-brown sugar
1-1/2 teaspoons baking powder
1 teaspoon baking soda
1/2 teaspoon salt
2 cups coarsely chopped fresh or frozen cranberries
1/2 cup coarsely chopped walnuts or pecans
2 tablespoons grated orange peel
1 egg
3 tablespoons vegetable oil
1 cup orange juice

Preheat oven to 350F (175C). Grease a 9'' x 5'' loaf pan; set aside. In a large bowl, blend flour, brown sugar, baking powder, baking soda and salt. Stir in cranberries, nuts and orange peel. In a small bowl, beat egg; stir in oil and orange juice. Add to dry ingredients; stir only until dry ingredients are moistened. Pour batter into greased pan. Bake 60 minutes or until a wooden pick inserted in center comes out clean. Cool in pan on a wire rack 10 minutes. Remove from pan; cool on rack. Makes 1 loaf.

minutes. Stir in milk. In a large bowl, beat butter or margarine, 1/2 cup granulated sugar and salt until creamy. Beat in eggs, 1 at a time, beating well after each addition. Add yeast mixture; beat until blended. Beat in 2 cups flour. Stir in lemon peel, raisins, 1/4 cup almonds and remaining 2 cups flour, making a soft dough. Cover bowl; let rise in a warm place, free from drafts, until doubled in bulk. Stir down batter. Generously grease a 10-cup turk's-head mold or large gugelhupf pan. In a small bowl, combine remaining 1/4 cup almonds and breadcrumbs. Sprinkle into greased pan, covering inside. Spoon batter into prepared pan. Cover; let rise until almost doubled. Preheat oven to 375F (190C). Bake 45 to 50 minutes or until top is golden brown. Remove from pan; cool on a wire rack. Place on a platter or cake plate; dust top with powdered sugar. Makes 1 cake.

Holiday Almond Cake

Holiday Almond Cake

5 eggs, separated
1/4 cup orange juice
1 teaspoon orange extract
2/3 cup sugar
3/4 cup cake flour
1 teaspoon baking powder
2 cups ground toasted almonds
2 tablespoons grated orange peel
Vanilla Butter Cream, page 71, or
   Cream-Cheese Frosting, page 48
1/2 cup finely chopped toasted almonds
   or prepared nut topping
About 3/4 cup halved blanched almonds, toasted

Preheat oven to 350F (175C). Grease and flour a 10-inch springform pan or deep cake pan. In a large bowl, beat egg yolks and orange juice until foamy. Add orange extract and sugar; beat until thick and pale. In another large bowl, beat egg whites until stiff but not dry; fold into egg-yolk mixture. In a sifter, combine cake flour and baking powder. Gradually sift over egg mixture, folding in while sifting. Fold in ground almonds and orange peel. Pour batter into prepared pan; smooth top. Bake 30 to 35 minutes or until a wooden pick inserted in center comes out clean. Cool in pan on a wire rack 10 minutes. Remove from pan; cool on wire rack. Cut into 2 horizontal layers. Prepare butter cream or frosting as directed.

To complete, place 1 cooled cake layer, cut-side down, on a platter or cake plate; spread with 1/3 of butter cream or frosting. Add remaining layer, cut-side down; spread remaining butter cream or frosting over side and top of cake. Lightly press chopped almonds around side of cake. Use almond halves to make a decorative star on top. Refrigerate until ready to serve. Makes 1 cake.

foamy. Gradually add granulated sugar, beating until thick and pale. Dissolve coffee powder in hot water; stir into egg-yolk mixture. In a sifter, combine cake flour, baking powder and salt. Gradually sift over egg-yolk mixture, folding in while sifting. In a large bowl, beat egg whites until stiff but not dry; fold into egg-yolk mixture. Spread batter in prepared pan. Bake 15 minutes or until top springs back when pressed lightly. Place a clean towel on a flat surface; sprinkle with powdered sugar. Immediately invert cake onto sugar-coated towel. Peel off paper; trim edges of cake. Starting at a short end, roll up cake with towel. Cool on a wire rack. Unroll cooled cake; sprinkle with liqueur. Let stand about 15 minutes.

To make butter cream, in a medium bowl, beat egg yolks until smooth; set aside. In a medium saucepan, combine sugar and water. Stirring constantly, bring to a boil over medium heat. Boil gently until syrup reaches 240F (115C) on a candy thermometer, about 5 minutes. Beating constantly, pour syrup into beaten egg yolks in a thin, steady stream. Beat until mixture is pale yellow and cool; set aside. In another medium bowl, beat butter until creamy and very fluffy. Beat fluffy butter into egg-yolk mixture, a little at a time. Sprinkle cocoa powder over butter mixture; beat until blended. Add liqueur; continue beating until mixture is very fluffy and of spreading consistency. Refrigerate until ready to use.

To complete, spread 1/2 of butter cream over cake. Reroll cake without towel; place, seam-side down, on a platter. Spread remaining butter cream over top and side of cake. Do not frost ends. Draw lines through frosting with tines of a fork to give the effect of tree bark. Refrigerate until ready to serve. Decorate with imitation holly or other Christmas greens. *Do not use real holly because berries are poisonous.* Makes 1 cake.

Buche de Nöel

Cake:
5 eggs, separated
1 cup granulated sugar
1 tablespoon instant-coffee powder
2 tablespoons hot water
1 cup sifted cake flour
1/2 teaspoon baking powder
1/4 teaspoon salt
Powdered sugar
1/4 cup coffee-flavored liqueur

Mocha Butter Cream:
6 egg yolks
3/4 cup sugar
1/2 cup water
1-1/2 cups butter
1/4 cup unsweetened cocoa powder, sifted
2 tablespoons coffee-flavored liqueur

To make cake, preheat oven to 375F (190C). Grease a 15'' x 10'' jelly-roll pan. Line pan with waxed paper; grease paper. In a medium bowl, beat egg yolks until

English Gingerbread

1/2 cup butter or margarine
1/2 cup dark corn syrup
1/2 cup light molasses
1/4 cup packed dark-brown sugar
2 cups all-purpose flour
1 teaspoon baking soda
1/2 teaspoon salt
1 tablespoon ground ginger
1 teaspoon ground cinnamon
2 eggs, beaten
3/4 cup milk
1/4 cup slivered almonds
Sweetened whipped cream or applesauce

Preheat oven to 325F (165C). Grease an 8-inch-square baking pan; set aside. In a small saucepan, combine butter or margarine, corn syrup, molasses and brown sugar. Stirring constantly, cook over low heat until brown sugar melts. Cool slightly. In a large bowl, blend flour, baking soda, salt, ginger and cinnamon. Stir in molasses mixture, eggs and milk. Fold in almonds. Pour into greased pan. Bake 50 to 55 minutes or until a wooden pick inserted in center comes out clean. Cool in pan on a wire rack 10 minutes. Remove from pan; cool on wire rack. Serve warm with whipped cream or applesauce. Makes 1 cake.

Honey Ring Cake

Honey Ring Cake

Honey Cake:
3/4 cup honey
2/3 cup butter or margarine
1/4 cup apricot jam or preserves
2 eggs, slightly beaten
2 teaspoons rum extract
2-1/4 cups all-purpose flour
2 tablespoons unsweetened cocoa powder
1 tablespoon baking powder
1/2 teaspoon baking soda
2 teaspoons ground cinnamon
1/2 teaspoon ground cardamom
1/2 teaspoon ground nutmeg
1/4 teaspoon ground cloves
1 cup raisins
1/2 cup chopped almonds, walnuts or pecans

Icing:
1 cup powdered sugar, sifted
1/2 teaspoon lemon extract
1 to 2 tablespoons milk
Raisins
Whole almonds

To make cake, preheat oven to 350F (175C). Grease and flour an 11-cup ring mold or 12-cup Bundt pan. In a medium saucepan, combine honey, butter or margarine, and jam or preserves. Stir over low heat until butter or margarine melts. Pour into a large bowl; let stand until cool. Stir in eggs and rum extract. Blend flour, cocoa powder, baking powder, baking soda, cinnamon, cardamom, nutmeg and cloves; stir into honey mixture. Stir in 1 cup raisins and nuts. Pour into prepared pan. Bake 35 to 40 minutes or until a wooden pick inserted in center comes out clean. Cool in pan on a wire rack 10 minutes. Remove from pan; cool on wire rack.

To make icing, in a small bowl, blend powdered sugar, lemon extract and enough milk to make a smooth drizzling icing. Place cooled cake on a platter or cake plate; spoon icing over cake. Decorate with raisins and whole almonds. Makes 1 cake.

Christmas Fruitcake

1 cup butter or margarine, room temperature
1 cup packed dark-brown sugar
1 teaspoon vanilla extract
4 eggs
3 tablespoons honey
2/3 cup apple juice or brandy
2-1/4 cups all-purpose flour
1 teaspoon baking powder
1 teaspoon ground cinnamon
1/2 teaspoon ground nutmeg
1 cup dark raisins
1/2 cup golden raisins
1/2 cup chopped red candied cherries
1/4 cup chopped green candied cherries
1/2 cup chopped candied lemon peel
1/2 cup chopped candied orange peel
1/4 cup chopped candied citron
1/2 cup coarsely chopped almonds
Brandy
1/2 cup red-currant jelly, melted
Candied cherries
Pecan or walnut halves

Preheat oven to 325F (165C). Grease a 9-inch springform pan. Line with a double thickness of foil, extending foil 2 inches above rim of pan. Grease foil. In a large bowl, beat butter or margarine, brown sugar and vanilla until creamy. Add eggs, 1 at a time, beating well after each addition. Stir in honey and apple juice or brandy. In a sifter, combine 2 cups flour, baking powder, cinnamon and nutmeg. Gradually sift over egg mixture, folding in while sifting. In a medium bowl, combine raisins, cherries, lemon peel, orange peel, citron and almonds. Sprinkle with remaining 1/4 cup flour; toss to coat. Stir fruit-and-nut mixture into batter. Spoon batter into prepared pan; smooth top. Bake 2 hours and 15 minutes or until a wooden pick inserted in center comes out clean. Cool in pan on a wire rack. Remove cooled cake from pan; discard foil. Cut a double thickness of cheesecloth large enough to wrap around cake twice. Thoroughly moisten cheesecloth with brandy; use to wrap cake. Wrap airtight in foil; set cake aside in a cool place for several weeks. Remoisten cheesecloth with brandy once a week. When ready to serve, brush melted jelly over top of cake; decorate cake with cherries and nut halves. To serve, cut in thin slices. Rewrap leftover fruitcake in cheesecloth. Makes 1 cake.

Spicy Christmas Shortcake

Dundee Cake

1/2 cup butter or margarine, room temperature
1 cup packed light-brown sugar
4 eggs
2-1/2 cups all-purpose flour
3 tablespoons grated orange peel
1-1/2 teaspoons allspice
1/4 cup orange juice
1-1/2 cups golden raisins
1-1/2 cups dark raisins
1 cup currants or chopped dark raisins
1/2 cup chopped red or green candied cherries
1/4 cup chopped mixed candied fruit
Blanched whole almonds

Preheat oven to 325F (165C). Grease an 8-inch springform pan; set aside. In a large bowl, beat butter or margarine and brown sugar until creamy. Add eggs, 1 at a time, beating well after each addition. Blend 2 cups flour, orange peel and allspice. Stir into egg mixture alternately with orange juice. In a medium bowl, combine raisins, currants or chopped raisins, cherries and fruit. Sprinkle remaining 1/2 cup flour over fruit; toss to coat. Fold into batter. Spoon batter into greased pan; smooth top. Decorate with almonds. Bake 1 hour. Reduce oven temperature to 300F (150C). Bake 1-1/2 hours longer or until a wooden pick inserted in center comes out clean. Cool in pan on a wire rack 10 minutes. Remove from pan; cool on wire rack. Makes 1 cake.

Spicy Christmas Shortcake

2/3 cup butter or margarine, room temperature
1/2 cup granulated sugar
1 egg, slightly beaten
1 teaspoon lemon extract
2 cups all-purpose flour
1/2 teaspoon salt
1 teaspoon ground cinnamon
1/2 teaspoon ground nutmeg
2 tablespoons half and half
1 egg yolk blended with 1 tablespoon milk for glaze
Crystal sugar

In a large bowl, beat butter or margarine and granulated sugar until creamy. Stir in egg and lemon extract. Blend flour, salt, cinnamon and nutmeg; stir into sugar mixture alternately with half and half. Shape dough into a flat ball. Wrap in plastic wrap or waxed paper; refrigerate 1 hour. Preheat oven to 350F (175C). On a lightly floured surface, roll out dough until 1/4 inch thick. Flour an assortment of 2-inch Christmas cookie cutters; use to cut dough. Place cut dough, 1 inch apart, on ungreased baking sheets. Brush with egg-yolk glaze; sprinkle with crystal sugar. Bake 12 to 15 minutes or until edges are golden. Remove from baking sheets; cool on wire racks. Makes about 48 cookies.

Honey Couples

Honey Couples

Cookie Boy & Girl:
3/4 cup honey
1/2 cup packed light-brown sugar
1 egg
1 teaspoon lemon extract
3 cups all-purpose flour
2 teaspoons baking powder
1/2 teaspoon baking soda
2 teaspoons ground cinnamon
1/4 teaspoon ground cloves
1/4 teaspoon ground nutmeg

Glaze:
1 egg white
1 teaspoon water
1 teaspoon powdered sugar

Decorations:
Ground toasted hazelnuts
Finely chopped almonds
Candied cherries
Currants
Colored sprinkles

Chocolate sprinkles
Finely chopped chocolate
Candied orange peel
Brown sugar

To make cookies, in a large bowl, beat honey, brown sugar, egg and lemon extract until creamy. Blend flour, baking powder, baking soda, cinnamon, cloves and nutmeg. Gradually stir into honey mixture; knead until smooth. Shape into 2 flat balls. Wrap separately in plastic wrap or waxed paper; refrigerate 1 hour. Preheat oven to 350F (175C). Grease baking sheets; set aside. Remove 1 ball of dough from refrigerator. On a lightly floured surface, roll out until 1/4 inch thick. Cut dough with floured 5-inch gingerbread-boy and gingerbread-girl cookie cutters. Repeat with remaining dough. Place on greased baking sheets. Bake 15 minutes. Remove from baking sheets; cool on wire racks.

To make glaze, in a small bowl, beat egg white, water and powdered sugar until foamy. Brush glaze over cookies; decorate as desired. Let stand until decorations are set. Makes about 22 cookies.

Holiday Fruit Wafers, page 210; German Marzipan Cookies

Almond Stars

German Marzipan Cookies

1/2 (7-oz.) pkg. marzipan or 1/2 recipe Marzipan, page 232
1/4 cup powdered sugar, sifted
2 oz. semisweet chocolate, grated
2 teaspoons vegetable shortening
1/2 cup butter or margarine, room temperature
2/3 cup granulated sugar
2 tablespoons milk or half and half
1 teaspoon vanilla extract
1-3/4 cups sifted all-purpose flour
1/4 teaspoon salt
1 recipe Decorator's Icing, page 57
Red-currant jelly

Crumble marzipan into a medium bowl. Knead in powdered sugar, making a firm paste. Roll out marzipan mixture between 2 sheets of waxed paper. Remove from waxed paper; place on a flat surface. In a small, heavy saucepan, melt chocolate and shortening over low heat; stir until smooth. Set aside to cool. Spread cooled chocolate mixture over marzipan; let stand until chocolate sets. Cut out tiny shapes with assorted small cookie cutters or hors d'oeuvres cutters; set aside. In a medium bowl, beat butter or margarine, granulated sugar, milk or half and half and vanilla until creamy. Blend flour and salt; stir into sugar mixture. Preheat oven to 350F (175C). On a lightly floured surface, roll out dough until 1/8 inch thick. Flour a 2-inch cookie cutter; use to cut dough. Place cut dough, 1 inch apart, on ungreased baking sheets. Bake 8 to 10 minutes or until golden. Cool on baking sheets 2 minutes. Remove from baking sheets; cool on wire racks. Prepare Decorator's Icing as directed. Spread jelly over bottom side of 1/2 of cookies. Sandwich with remaining cookies, bottoms together. Spread icing over tops of cookies. Place a chocolate-covered-marzipan cutout in center of each iced cookie. Let stand until icing sets. Makes about 24 cookies.

Almond Stars

2 cups all-purpose flour
3/4 cup sugar
1 teaspoon baking powder
2 tablespoons unsweetened cocoa powder
1 cup butter or margarine, chilled
3 tablespoons milk
1 teaspoon almond extract
Milk
Sugar
Chopped or slivered almonds

In a medium bowl, blend flour, sugar, baking powder and cocoa powder. Use a pastry blender or 2 knives to cut in butter or margarine until mixture resembles coarse crumbs. Blend 3 tablespoons milk and almond extract; sprinkle over flour. Stir in; knead to make a smooth dough. Shape dough into a flat ball. Wrap in plastic wrap or waxed paper; refrigerate 30 minutes. Preheat oven to 350F (175C). Grease baking sheets. On a lightly floured surface, roll out dough until 1/4 inch thick. Flour a 2-1/2-inch star-shaped cookie cutter; use to cut dough. Place stars, 1 inch apart, on greased baking sheets. Brush stars with milk; sprinkle with sugar and almonds. Bake 10 to 12 minutes or until edges are firm. Remove from baking sheets; cool on wire racks. Makes about 60 cookies.

Holiday Hearts

Cookies:
2 egg whites
1 cup packed light-brown sugar
1/2 teaspoon salt
2 tablespoons butter or margarine, melted
1/2 teaspoon rum extract
1/2 cup plus 2 tablespoons all-purpose flour
1 teaspoon baking powder
2 tablespoons unsweetened cocoa powder
2 teaspoons ground cinnamon
1/2 teaspoon ground cloves
1-3/4 cups ground almonds

Icing:
1 cup powdered sugar, sifted
1 to 2 teaspoons warm water

To make cookies, in a medium bowl, beat egg whites until stiff but not dry. Add brown sugar and salt; beat until stiff peaks form. Fold in butter or margarine and rum extract. In a sifter, combine flour, baking powder, cocoa powder, cinnamon and cloves. Gradually sift over egg-white mixture, folding in while sifting. Fold in almonds. Cover bowl; refrigerate 30 minutes. Preheat oven to 325F (165C). Grease baking sheets; set aside. On a lightly floured surface, roll out dough until 1/4 inch thick. Flour a 2-1/2-inch heart-shaped cookie cutter; use to cut dough. Place hearts, 1 inch apart, on greased baking sheets. Bake 12 to 15 minutes or until edges are firm. Remove from baking sheets; cool on wire racks.

To make icing, in a small bowl, blend powdered sugar and water until smooth. Spread icing on cooled cookies. Let stand until icing sets. Makes 36 cookies.

Holiday Hearts

Marzipan Holiday Cookies

1 (7-oz.) pkg. marzipan or Marzipan, page 232, crumbled
3/4 cup butter or margarine, room temperature
1 cup sugar
1 egg
1/2 teaspoon lemon extract
2-3/4 cups all-purpose flour
1 teaspoon baking powder
Milk
1 teaspoon ground cinnamon

In a large bowl, beat marzipan and butter or margarine until creamy. Add 1/2 cup sugar, egg and lemon extract; beat until blended. Blend flour and baking powder; add to marzipan mixture. Using a wooden spoon, stir until smooth. Shape dough into a flat ball. Wrap in plastic wrap or waxed paper; refrigerate 2 hours. Preheat oven to 375F (190C). Grease baking sheets; set aside. On a lightly floured surface, roll out dough until 1/4 inch thick. Flour an assortment of 2-1/2- to 3-inch Christmas cookie cutters; use to cut dough. Place cut dough, 1 inch apart, on greased baking sheets. Brush dough with milk. In a small bowl, blend remaining 1/2 cup sugar and cinnamon; sprinkle over cookies. Bake 8 to 10 minutes or until edges are golden. Remove from baking sheets; cool on wire racks. Makes about 60 cookies.

Marzipan Holiday Cookies

Gingerbread Stars

Cookies:
2/3 cup butter or margarine, room temperature
2/3 cup sugar
1/2 cup light molasses
1/4 cup milk
1 egg
3-1/4 cups all-purpose flour
1-1/2 teaspoons baking powder
1/2 teaspoon baking soda
1 teaspoon ground cinnamon
1 teaspoon ground ginger
1 teaspoon ground cloves

Icing:
2 cups powdered sugar, sifted
1 egg white
1 teaspoon lemon juice
1 to 2 teaspoons water
Food coloring, if desired

To make cookies, in a large bowl, beat butter or margarine, sugar, molasses, milk and egg until creamy. Blend flour, baking powder, baking soda, cinnamon, ginger and cloves; stir into sugar mixture. Shape dough into a flat ball. Wrap in plastic wrap or waxed paper; refrigerate 1 hour. Preheat oven to 350F (175C). Grease baking sheets; set aside. On a lightly floured surface, roll out 1/2 of dough until 1/8 inch thick. Flour a 2-1/2-inch star-shaped cookie cutter; use to cut dough. Repeat with remaining dough. Place cookies, 1 inch apart, on greased baking sheets. Use a small straw to make a hole in 1 point of each star. Bake 8 minutes or until browned. Cool on baking sheets on wire racks 1 minute. Remove from baking sheets; cool on wire racks.

To make icing, in a medium bowl, beat powdered sugar, egg white and lemon juice until smooth. Beat in water, 1 teaspoon at a time, until of piping consistency. Tint with food coloring, if desired.

To complete, spoon icing into a pastry bag fitted with a small plain writing tip. Pipe icing decoratively on cookies. Let stand until icing sets. Thread a small piece of string or ribbon through hole in each cookie. Attach cookies to a Christmas tree. Makes about 125 cookies.

Gingerbread Stars

Chocolate-Tipped Stars

Cookies:
1/2 cup butter or margarine, room temperature
1/2 cup sugar
1 egg
1-3/4 cups all-purpose flour
1/2 teaspoon baking powder
1/4 teaspoon salt
1/2 teaspoon ground cinnamon
1/2 teaspoon ground cardamom
1/2 teaspoon ground nutmeg
1/4 teaspoon ground cloves

Topping:
4 oz. semisweet chocolate, melted
Colored sprinkles

To make cookies, in a medium bowl, beat butter or margarine and sugar until creamy. Add egg; beat until blended. Blend flour, baking powder, salt, cinnamon, cardamom, nutmeg and cloves; stir into sugar mixture.

Wrap dough in plastic wrap or waxed paper; refrigerate 1 hour. Preheat oven to 350F (175C). Grease baking sheets; set aside. On a lightly floured surface, roll out 1/2 of dough until 1/8 inch thick. Flour a 3-inch star-shaped cookie cutter; use to cut out 30 stars. Using a small straw, make a small hole in 1 point of each star. Place cookies, 1 inch apart, on prepared baking sheets. Using a 2-1/2-inch star-shaped cookie cutter, repeat with remaining dough. Do not make holes. Bake 8 to 10 minutes or until golden. Remove from baking sheets; cool on wire racks.

To complete, spread tops of larger cookies with melted chocolate, being careful not to cover holes. Place 1 small cookie on top of each chocolate-coated cookie, offsetting points. Sprinkle chocolate-coated points of bottom cookies with colored sprinkles. Let cookies stand until chocolate sets. Thread a small piece of string or ribbon through hole in each cookie. Use to attach cookies to a Christmas tree. Makes 30 cookies.

Christmas Angels

Christmas Angels

Cookies:
1/2 cup butter or margarine, room temperature
1/2 cup sugar
1 egg
1 teaspoon vanilla extract
1-3/4 cups all-purpose flour
1 teaspoon baking powder
1 teaspoon ground cinnamon
1 teaspoon ground cardamom

Icing:
1-1/2 cups powdered sugar, sifted
1 egg white
1 to 2 teaspoons water
Food coloring, if desired

To make cookies, in a medium bowl, beat butter or margarine, sugar, egg and vanilla until creamy. Blend flour, baking powder, cinnamon and cardamom; gradually stir into sugar mixture. Knead in bowl to make a smooth dough. Shape dough into a flat ball. Wrap in plastic wrap or waxed paper; refrigerate 1 hour. Preheat oven to 350F (175C). Grease baking sheets; set aside. On a lightly floured surface, roll out dough until 1/8 inch thick. Use a floured 5-inch angel-shaped cookie cutter to cut dough. Place angel-shaped dough, 1 inch apart, on greased baking sheets. Bake 10 minutes or until lightly browned. Cool on baking sheets on wire racks 2 minutes. Remove from baking sheets; cool on wire racks.
To make icing, in a small bowl, combine powdered sugar and egg white; mixture will be thick. Stir in water, 1 teaspoon at a time, until of spreading consistency; beat until smooth. Tint with food coloring, if desired. Spread or pipe icing on cookies. Let stand until icing sets. Makes 18 cookies.

Pfeffernüsse

1/4 cup butter or margarine, room temperature
1 cup packed light-brown sugar
3 eggs
2 teaspoons grated lemon peel
1/2 teaspoon aniseed
3 cups all-purpose flour
1 teaspoon baking soda
1/4 teaspoon salt
1/4 teaspoon pepper
1 teaspoon ground cinnamon
1/2 teaspoon ground nutmeg
1/2 teaspoon ground allspice
Powdered sugar

In a large bowl, beat butter or margarine and brown sugar until creamy. Add eggs; beat until blended. Stir in lemon peel and aniseed. Blend flour, baking soda, salt, pepper, cinnamon, nutmeg and allspice; stir into egg mixture. Cover bowl; refrigerate 12 hours or overnight. Preheat oven to 375F (190C). Grease baking sheets. Shape dough into 1-inch balls; place balls, 1 inch apart, on greased baking sheets. Bake 10 to 12 minutes or until lightly browned. Remove from baking sheets; cool on wire racks. To serve, roll in powdered sugar. Makes about 48 cookies.

Nürnberg Lebkuchen

Honey Cookies:
1 cup honey
2 eggs
1/2 cup packed light-brown sugar
1 cup finely ground almonds
1/2 cup finely chopped almonds
1 tablespoon lemon juice
1/2 cup finely chopped candied lemon peel
1-3/4 cups all-purpose flour
1/2 teaspoon baking powder
1 teaspoon ground cinnamon
1/2 teaspoon ground nutmeg
1/2 teaspoon ground cloves

Glaze:
1-1/4 cups powdered sugar, sifted
2 teaspoons lemon juice
1 to 2 teaspoons warm water
Colored sprinkles

To make cookies, in a large bowl, beat honey, eggs and brown sugar until blended. Stir in almonds, lemon juice and lemon peel. Blend flour, baking powder, cinnamon, nutmeg and cloves. Add to honey mixture; stir until blended. Cover bowl; refrigerate 12 hours or overnight. Preheat oven to 375F (190C). Line baking sheets with foil; grease foil. Drop dough by heaping teaspoons, 2 inches apart, on prepared baking sheets. Dip a table knife in hot water; flatten dough mounds with flat side of blade. Bake 12 to 15 minutes or until firm. Remove from baking sheets; cool slightly on wire racks.
To make glaze, in a small bowl, beat powdered sugar, lemon juice and 1 teaspoon water until smooth. Add more water if necessary. Spoon glaze over warm cookies. Sprinkle colored sprinkles over glaze; let stand until glaze sets. Store in airtight containers 4 to 6 weeks before serving. Makes 36 to 42 cookies.

Lebkuchen

Lebkuchen

Cookies:
1/2 cup honey
1/4 cup packed light-brown sugar
2 tablespoons vegetable oil
1 egg yolk, slightly beaten
1 tablespoon lemon juice
2 teaspoons grated lemon peel
2 cups all-purpose flour
2 teaspoons baking powder
1 teaspoon ground cinnamon
1/2 teaspoon ground cloves
1/2 cup finely chopped almonds or hazelnuts
2 tablespoons finely chopped candied lemon peel
1/3 cup finely chopped raisins, if desired

Icing:
1 cup powdered sugar, sifted
1 egg white
1/2 to 1 teaspoon water
Colored sprinkles

To make cookies, in a small saucepan, combine honey, brown sugar and oil. Stir over low heat until sugar melts. Do not overcook. Pour honey mixture into a large bowl; set aside to cool. Stir in egg yolk, lemon juice and grated lemon peel. Blend flour, baking powder, cinnamon and cloves. Gradually stir into honey mixture. Fold in nuts, chopped lemon peel and raisins. Cover; refrigerate 1 to 2 hours. Preheat oven to 350F (175C). Generously grease baking sheets. Using 1 teaspoon dough, shape into a ball; repeat with remaining dough. Place balls, 2-1/2 inches apart, on greased baking sheets. Dip bottom of a juice glass in sugar; use to flatten balls until 1/4 inch thick. Bake 12 to 15 minutes or until golden brown. Remove from baking sheets; cool on wire racks.

To make icing, in a small bowl, blend powdered sugar, egg white and water until smooth. If icing is too thick to spread, add a few drops of water. Spread icing over tops of cooled cookies; top with colored sprinkles. Let stand until icing sets. Makes 40 cookies.

Snow-Scene Cookies

Snow Caps

3 egg whites
2 cups powdered sugar, sifted
3/4 cup ground almonds
3/4 cup ground toasted hazelnuts
1 teaspoon water

In a large bowl, beat egg whites until stiff but not dry. Gradually add powdered sugar, beating until stiff peaks form. Reserve 1/4 cup egg-white mixture; set aside. Fold ground nuts into remaining egg-white mixture. Cover bowl; refrigerate 30 minutes. Preheat oven to 250F (120C). Line baking sheets with foil; grease foil. Drop dough by rounded teaspoons, 1 inch apart, on prepared baking sheets. Using the back of a spoon, flatten each cookie slightly. Stir 1 teaspoon water into reserved egg-white mixture; spread over top of cookies. Bake 30 to 40 minutes or until firm. Cool on baking sheets on wire racks. Store in airtight containers. Makes about 48 cookies.

Snow-Scene Cookies

Cookies:
1/3 cup light molasses
1/4 cup sugar
2 tablespoons butter or margarine
1/2 teaspoon salt
1 egg, slightly beaten
1 teaspoon vanilla extract
1-3/4 cups all-purpose flour
2 tablespoons unsweetened cocoa powder
2 teaspoons baking powder
1/2 teaspoon baking soda
1 teaspoon ground ginger

Snow Icing:
2 cups powdered sugar, sifted
1 egg white
1 to 2 teaspoons water

Decoration for Snowmen:
Colored sprinkles
Small red and pink candies
Red candied cherries, slivered

In a small saucepan, combine molasses, sugar, butter or margarine and salt. Stir over low heat until butter or margarine melts and sugar dissolves. Pour into a large bowl; set aside to cool. Stir in egg and vanilla. Blend flour, cocoa powder, baking powder, baking soda and ginger. Stir into molasses mixture. Wrap dough in plastic wrap or waxed paper; refrigerate 1 hour. Preheat oven to 350F (175C). Grease baking sheets; set aside. On a lightly floured surface, roll out dough until 1/4 inch thick. Using diagram, opposite, as a pattern, cut out 4 large snowmen and 4 small snowmen. Using a wide spatula, place snowmen, 1 inch apart, on greased baking sheets. Using a 6-piece star cookie-cutter set, cut out 2 stars in each size. Gather dough scraps; reroll. Using a nickel as a guide, cut out 10 small circles. Place cut dough on greased baking sheets. Bake 10 to 13 minutes or until cookies are firm to the touch. Remove from baking sheets; cool on wire racks.

To make icing, in a small bowl, blend powdered sugar and egg white. Mixture will be very stiff. Add 1 teaspoon water; stir until mixture is smooth and spreadable. Add more water, if necessary.

To complete, spread icing over snowmen; decorate as desired. Build fir trees by placing largest star cookies side by side on a flat surface. Place a dab of icing in center of each cookie; cover icing with small round cookies. Place a dab of icing on small cookies. Cover each with next largest star cookies; press down lightly. Continue with remaining stars and round cookies, ending with smallest star cookies. Drizzle icing over trees, letting icing drip down sides. To make a winter snow scene, arrange snowmen and trees on a foil-covered cardboard. Add small candies and a miniature sled, if desired. Makes 4 large snowmen, 4 small snowmen and 2 fir trees.

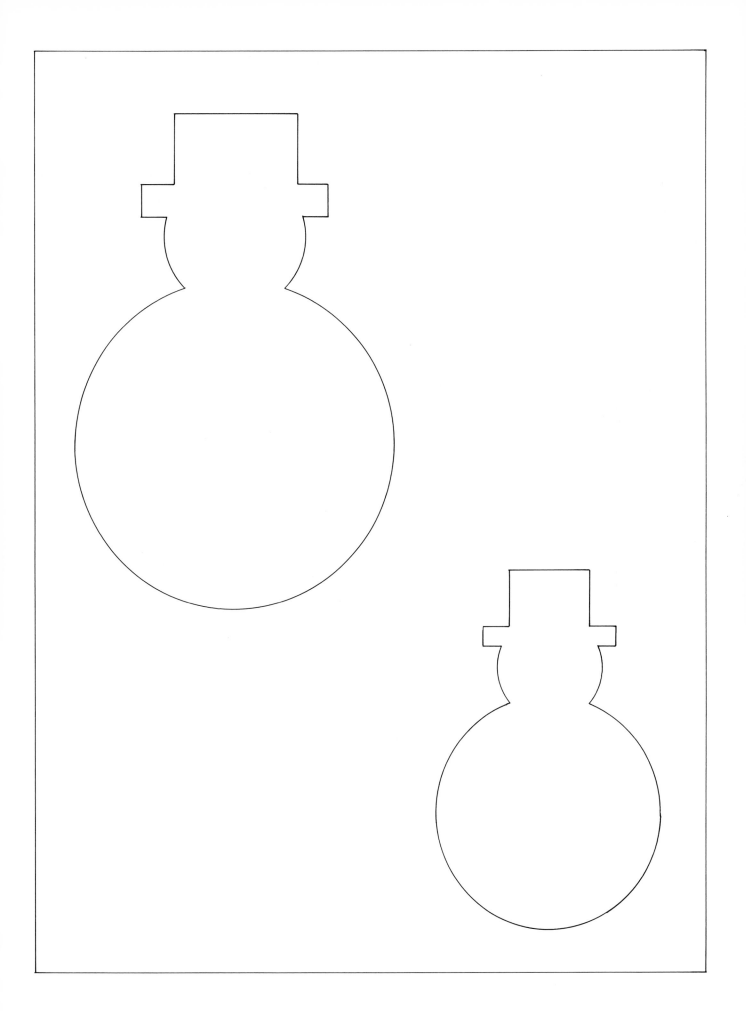

Gingerbread House

Gingerbread House

Gingerbread Dough:
1 cup honey
1-1/4 cups packed light-brown sugar
1 cup butter or margarine
2 eggs, slightly beaten
6 cups all-purpose flour
2 teaspoons baking powder
1 teaspoon baking soda
1 teaspoon salt
2 teaspoons ground ginger
2 teaspoons ground cinnamon
1/2 teaspoon ground cloves
1/2 teaspoon ground nutmeg

Builder's Icing:
3 egg whites
6 cups powdered sugar, sifted
3 to 4 teaspoons water

Decoration:
Small foil-covered box, cotton, assorted Christmas candies,
    small candy-coated chocolate candies, small round candies,
    assorted candy sticks

To make dough, in a small saucepan, combine honey, brown sugar and butter or margarine. Stir over low heat until butter or margarine melts and brown sugar dissolves. Pour into a large bowl; let stand until cool. Stir in eggs. Blend flour, baking powder, baking soda, salt, ginger, cinnamon, cloves and nutmeg; stir into honey mixture. Gather dough together; cut off 2/3 of dough. Shape each piece into a flat ball. Wrap separately in plastic wrap or waxed paper; refrigerate 1 hour. Using measurements opposite, make a pattern of house from cardboard. Preheat oven to 350F (175C).

To make base, line a large baking sheet with foil; grease foil. On foil-lined baking sheet, roll out small piece of dough to a 12'' x 9'' rectangle. Bake 12 to 15 minutes or until firm when touched. Immediately cut into an 11'' x 8'' rectangle; remove excess dough. Remove rectangle from baking sheet; cool on a wire rack. Let stand overnight to harden.

To make house, line an 18'' x 12'' baking pan with foil; grease foil. In prepared pan, roll and press out large piece of dough to an even thickness, filling pan completely. Place house pattern over dough; cut around edges of pattern with a sharp knife. *Do not cut along dotted lines.* Remove pattern. Bake cut dough 15 minutes or until firm when touched. Immediately cut along dotted lines and re-cut house pieces. Using baked pieces between house pieces, quickly cut into small rectangles for wood pile. Cool in pan on a wire rack. When cool, carefully remove from pan; let stand overnight to harden.

To make icing, in a large bowl, beat egg whites until foamy. Gradually beat in powdered sugar, beating until stiff. Add water, 1 teaspoon at a time, as necessary, beating until very stiff. Keep icing covered with a damp towel to prevent drying out. *Recipe can be cut in half if house is not assembled all at once.*

To assemble house, spoon icing into a pastry bag fitted with a 3/8-inch plain writing tip. Stand 1 side of house upright on a flat surface. Pipe icing up edge of wall where it will be joined to front. Place house front in position, at right angle to side. Hold pieces firmly together 3 to 4 minutes or until icing sets. Pipe icing up opposite edge of side; place back wall in place. Hold until set. Place small jars or drinking glasses with straight sides against front, back and side to hold house upright. Let stand until icing is completely dry. Pipe icing up 2 edges of remaining side piece; position between front and back walls. Let stand until icing is completely dry. Pipe icing along edges of

front and back where roof will be attached. Pipe icing on upper edges of house. Set roof in place; pipe icing along seam where pieces of roof join. Fill spaces in seams with icing. Let stand until icing is completely dry. Spread icing over base, covering completely. Place house on base, on a diagonal, in far right corner. Pipe a thin strip of icing around bottom edge of entire house where it touches base. Let stand until icing sets and house is firmly attached to base.

To complete, spread icing over roof. Place a small foil-covered box on top of roof for chimney. Partially press cotton into box to simulate smoke. Pipe small dabs of icing on back of assorted candies; press to roof. Decorate house with more assorted candies. Arrange 3 rows of small candy-covered chocolates to make a path to front door of house. Secure candies to base with icing. Make a wood pile at side of house with small rectangle cookies. Pipe icing between cookies; stack in an alternating pattern. Build a fence around house, alternating small round candies and candy sticks. Use icing to hold fence together. Let stand until all decorations are dry. Pipe icing around edges of roof and along top of fence. Lightly dust house and base with powdered sugar. Sprinkle cinnamon over base and wood pile, if desired. Makes 1 gingerbread house.

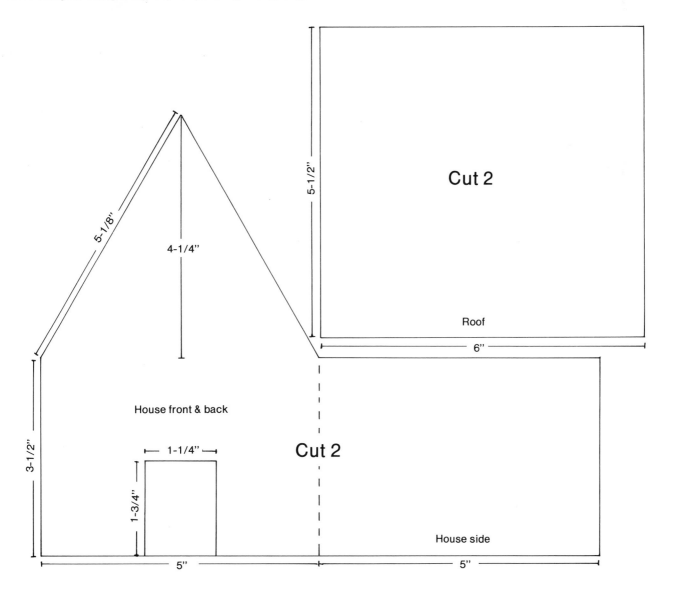

Basic
Information

Puff Pastry

2/3 cup unsalted butter, chilled
1-1/3 cups all-purpose flour
2/3 cup cake flour
1 teaspoon salt
1 teaspoon lemon juice
1/2 to 2/3 cup ice water

Melt 1 tablespoon butter; refrigerate remaining butter. Sift flours onto a cool marble slab or board. Make a large well in center. Place salt, lemon juice, 1/2 cup water and 1 tablespoon melted butter in center of well. Blend ingredients in well, using your fingertips. Using fingertips of both your hands, gradually work in flour to form coarse crumbs. If crumbs are dry, add more water, a few drops at a time. Cut dough several times with a metal spatula to be sure ingredients are blended. Do not knead. Press dough into a ball. Dough will be soft. Wrap in waxed paper or plastic wrap; refrigerate 15 minutes.

To continue, lightly flour remaining chilled butter. Place floured butter between 2 sheets of waxed paper; flatten with a rolling pin. Remove top sheet of waxed paper. Fold butter in half; replace between waxed paper. Continue flattening and folding until butter is pliable but not sticky. Butter should have same consistency as dough. Shape butter into a 6-inch square; lightly sprinkle with flour.

To complete, on a cool surface, roll out dough to a 12-inch square slightly thicker in center than at sides. Set butter in center of dough. Fold corners of dough toward center of butter, then fold sides of dough over butter, like an envelope. Place dough, seam-side down, on a floured surface. Press down on top with a rolling pin to flatten dough slightly. Roll out dough to a rectangle 7 to 8 inches wide and 18 to 20 inches long. Fold in thirds like a business letter. Gently press seams with rolling pin to seal. Turn dough to bring seam-side to your left so dough opens like a book. This is called a *turn*. Again roll dough to a large rectangle and fold in thirds. This is the second *turn*. Wrap dough in waxed paper; refrigerate 15 minutes. Repeat rolling process, giving dough a total of 6 turns. Refrigerate at least 1 hour after last turn. Makes 1 pound.

Deep-Frying

Deep-fried foods are baked by being completely submerged in hot oil. Use a mild-flavored oil that will not affect the flavor of the cooked food. Use a deep-fat or candy thermometer to cook foods at the right temperature.

If you do not have a deep-fat or candy thermometer, use the bread-cube method to determine temperatures. When deep-frying, a 1-inch cube of bread will turn golden brown in:

65 seconds at	345-355F (175-177C)
60 seconds at	356-365F (180-185C)
50 seconds at	366-375F (186-190C)
40 seconds at	376-385F (191-195C)
20 seconds at	386-395F (196-200C)

Tips for Using Puff Pastry

• Let frozen puff-pastry dough thaw at room temperature.
• Roll out puff-pastry dough on a lightly floured surface. Roll dough in two directions, from top to bottom and from left to right. If rolled in only one direction, it will not rise evenly during baking.
• Cut puff-pastry dough with a very sharp knife to prevent edges from sticking together. If using a pastry cutter, dip it in cold water before cutting out dough.
• Do not brush cut edges of puff-pastry dough with egg yolk or pastry will not rise evenly during baking.
• Stack dough trimmings. Press firmly together and rolled out again. Use small pieces and strips for decoration.
• Always place puff-pastry dough on a baking sheet or in a pan that has been sprinkled lightly with cold water. Steam from the water helps the pastry to rise.
• Refrigerate puff-pastry dough 15 minutes before baking.

Marzipan

1 cup plus 2 tablespoons granulated sugar
1/3 cup water
Pinch of cream of tartar
1-1/2 cups finely ground, blanched almonds
1 egg white, beaten stiff but not dry
1/4 to 1/2 cup powdered sugar

Lightly oil a marble slab or baking sheet; set aside. In a small saucepan, combine granulated sugar and water. Stir over medium heat until sugar dissolves. Stir in cream of tartar until dissolved. Bring to a boil; boil until mixture reaches soft-ball stage (238F, 115C) on a candy thermometer or until a teaspoon of mixture dropped in very cold water forms a soft ball. Soft ball will flatten slightly when removed from water. Remove from heat. Stir in almonds and beaten egg white. Stir over medium heat 2 to 3 minutes. Turn out onto oiled marble or baking sheet. Work paste with a wide dough cutter or a spatula 5 to 10 minutes, bringing edges to center. When cool enough to work by hand, knead until smooth. If necessary, add powdered sugar to surface to keep paste from sticking. Wrap airtight; store in a cool place. Use within 3 months.

For marzipan cutouts, roll marzipan to 1/4 inch thickness. Cut in desired shapes. Makes 7 to 8 ounces.

Clarified Butter

Melt 1 cup butter in a small saucepan. Simmer until butter separates; do not brown. Let butter cool slightly. Strain separated butter through a muslin cloth or several layers of cheesecloth. Discard milky solids. Store in refrigerator. Makes about 3/4 cup.

Testing for Doneness

Due to variance in oven temperature, it is always wise to test baked goods for doneness.

Quick breads and breads containing nuts or fruit are tested by inserting a wooden pick in or near center of the loaf. If it comes out clean and dry, the bread is done. If bottom of the bread is not as browned as you desire, place the loaf directly on the oven rack. Bake 5 minutes or to desired brownness.

Yeast breads are tested by tapping the top with your fingertips. If it sounds hollow, the bread is done. Or, remove the bread from pan or baking sheet and tap the bottom with your fingertips. It should sound hollow.

Cakes are baked the minimum time specified before testing. To test most cakes, insert a wooden pick near the center. If the pick comes out clean and dry, the cake is done. If the cake layer is thin, or is baked in a jelly-roll pan, press the top with your fingertips. If the surface springs back, the cake is done. At any time, if the cake does not test done, bake for another 5 to 10 minutes. When done, the cake should pull away from the side of the pan.

Cookies are baked the time specified unless their appearance tells you the cookies are done early. Use baking sheets with low edges or no raised edges. Baking pans with high sides prevent cookies from browning evenly. Bake cookies in center of the oven. If two baking sheets are used at the same time, leave space between them for air circulation. Cut cookies the same size to ensure even baking.

Sugar Syrups & Confections

Test	Description	Temperature
Veil	Sugar is dissolved. Syrup drops in a sheet.	200-215F (95-100C)
Thread	Syrup spins a 2-inch thread.	230-234F (110-112C)
Soft ball Fondant Fudge Penuche	In very cold water, forms a soft ball; flattens slightly when removed. Becomes soft and pliable when kneaded.	234-240F (112-116C)
Firm ball	In very cold water, syrup forms a firm ball that does not flatten.	244-248F (118-120C)
Hard ball Divinity	In very cold water, syrup forms a hard ball.	250-266F (121-130C)
Soft crack Butter-scotch Taffy	In very cold water, syrup separates into a hard but not brittle thread.	270-290F (132-143C)
Hard crack Brittle	In very cold water, syrup separates into a hard, brittle thread.	300-310F (149-154C)
Caramel-ized sugar	Syrup turns dark golden, but will turn black at 350F (175C).	310-338F (155-170C)

Leavening Agents

Three types of leavening agents are used in this book:

Yeast, when combined with flour, moisture and warmth, begins to ferment and converts flour into alcohol and carbon dioxide. These gas bubbles are what leavens bread. Oven heat kills the yeast and causes the gas to expand, causing the bread to rise in a final *oven spring.*

Active dry yeast comes in 1/4-ounce envelopes or in larger bulk packages. *Compressed fresh yeast* comes in .60-ounce cakes. One envelope of dry yeast equals 1 scant tablespoon dry yeast or 1 cake compressed fresh yeast.

Store dry yeast in a cool, dry place—not in the refrigerator or freezer. Use by the expiration date. Or, *proof yeast* by combining 1 envelope active dry yeast, 1 teaspoon sugar and 1/4 cup warm water. If the yeast begins to bubble and swell, it is active. If not, discard the yeast and begin with another package.

Compressed fresh yeast must be refrigerated and used within 1 to 2 weeks or by the expiration date on the package. It should always be proofed.

Baking soda or *bicarbonate of soda* gives off carbon dioxide when moistened. It is especially volatile when combined with an acid liquid, such as buttermilk.

Baking powder is a combination of baking soda and cream of tartar. *Single-acting* baking powder immediately releases its gas into the wet batter. *Double-acting* baking powder releases some gas when it is moistened and again when the batter is heated.

Blend baking soda or baking powder with other dry ingredients before adding liquid, then bake as soon as possible. Too much baking soda or baking powder gives a dry, crumbly texture and a bitter taste. It also causes the product to overrise and fall. Too little baking soda or baking powder makes a heavy, gummy product.

Cake Baking at High Altitudes

Batters and doughs rise faster at high altitude than they do at sea level. Because of this, oven temperatures should be raised. Yeast breads will take less time to rise.

Most cake recipes need no adjustments up to 2500 feet. Above that altitude, use the following chart for adjusting recipes:

Adjustment	3,000 Feet	5,000 Feet	7,000 Feet
Reduce baking powder For each teaspoon	1/8 tsp	1/8 to 1/4 tsp	1/4 tsp
Reduce sugar For each cup	0 to 1 Tbsp	0 to 2 Tbsp	1 to 3 Tbsp
Increase liquid For each cup	1 to 2 Tbsp	2 to 4 Tbsp	3 to 4 Tbsp

Equivalency Chart

Food Item	Market Unit	Household Measurement
Apple	1 medium	1 cup chopped
Bacon	1 lb.	24 slices
crisply fried, crumbled	1 lb.	3 cups
	8 slices	1 cup
Butter or margarine	1 lb.	2 cups
	1/4 lb.	1/2 cup
Cereal, cold flaked	15 oz.	about 11 cups
Cheese		
Cheddar-type, shredded	1 lb.	4 cups
cottage cheese	1 lb.	2 cups
cream cheese	3 oz.	6 tablespoons
	8 oz.	1 cup
Chocolate		
pieces (chips)	6 oz.	about 1 cup
unsweetened baking	8 oz.	8 squares
	1 oz.	1 wrapped square
Cocoa powder, unsweetened	8 oz.	2 cups
Coconut, shredded or flaked	4 oz.	1-1/3 cups
Corn syrup	16 oz.	2 cups
Cream		
sour	1 lb.	2 cups
whipping cream	1/2 pint	1 cup
whipped	1/2 pint	2 cups
Egg whites	12 eggs	1-1/4 cups
	1 egg	5 tablespoons
Egg yolks	12 eggs	3/4 cup
	1 egg	about 4 teaspoons
Flour		
all-purpose	5 lbs.	about 20 cups
	1 lb.	3-1/2 to 4 cups
instant	13.5 oz.	about 3 cups
whole-wheat	5 lbs.	about 18-1/3 cups
Gelatin		
unflavored	1 oz.	1/4 cup
flavored	3 oz.	7 tablespoons
Graham crackers	1 lb.	about 4 cups crumbs
Lemon juice	1 lemon	3 to 4 tablespoons
Lemon peel, grated	1 lemon	about 2 teaspoons
Milk, instant nonfat powder	1 lb.	about 6 cups
Nuts, shelled		
almonds	1 lb.	3 cups
peanuts	1 lb.	3 cups
pecans		
halves	1 lb.	4 cups
chopped	1 lb.	3-1/2 to 4 cups
pistachios	1 lb.	3-1/4 to 4 cups
walnuts		
halves	1 lb.	3-1/2 cups
chopped	1 lb.	3-1/2 cups
Oats, rolled	18 oz.	about 6 cups
Onion	1 whole	3/4 to 1 cup chopped
chopped fresh	1/4 cup	1 tablespoon dried
Orange juice	1 orange	6 to 8 tablespoons
Orange peel	1 orange	3 to 4 teaspoons
Shortening	1 lb.	2 cups
Sugar		
brown, packed	1 lb.	2-1/4 cups
granulated	5 lbs.	about 15 cups
	1 lb.	3 cups
powdered, unsifted	1 lb.	3 to 4 cups
sifted	1 lb.	about 4-1/2 cups
Yeast		
active dry	1/4 oz.	scant 1 tablespoon
compressed	0.60 oz.	4 teaspoons

Metric Chart

Comparison to Metric Measure

When You Know	Symbol	Multiply By	To Find	Symbol
teaspoons	tsp	5.0	milliliters	ml
tablespoons	tbsp	15.0	milliliters	ml
fluid ounces	fl. oz.	30.0	milliliters	ml
cups	c	0.24	liters	l
pints	pt.	0.47	liters	l
quarts	qt.	0.95	liters	l
ounces	oz.	28.0	grams	g
pounds	lb.	0.45	kilograms	kg
Fahrenheit	F	5/9 (after subtracting 32)	Celsius	C

Fahrenheit to Celsius

F	C
200—205	95
220—225	105
245—250	120
275	135
300—305	150
325—330	165
345—350	175
370—375	190
400—405	205
425—430	220
445—450	230
470—475	245
500	260

Liquid Measure to Milliliters

1/4 teaspoon	=	1.25 milliliters
1/2 teaspoon	=	2.5 milliliters
3/4 teaspoon	=	3.75 milliliters
1 teaspoon	=	5.0 milliliters
1-1/4 teaspoons	=	6.25 milliliters
1-1/2 teaspoons	=	7.5 milliliters
1-3/4 teaspoons	=	8.75 milliliters
2 teaspoons	=	10.0 milliliters
1 tablespoon	=	15.0 milliliters
2 tablespoons	=	30.0 milliliters

Liquid Measure to Liters

1/4 cup	=	0.06 liters
1/2 cup	=	0.12 liters
3/4 cup	=	0.18 liters
1 cup	=	0.24 liters
1-1/4 cups	=	0.3 liters
1-1/2 cups	=	0.36 liters
2 cups	=	0.48 liters
2-1/2 cups	=	0.6 liters
3 cups	=	0.72 liters
3-1/2 cups	=	0.84 liters
4 cups	=	0.96 liters
4-1/2 cups	=	1.08 liters
5 cups	=	1.2 liters
5-1/2 cups	=	1.32 liters

Index

8.2386503810